Schooling for Social Change

D1523408

Schooling for Social Change:

The Rise and Impact of Human Rights Education in India

Monisha Bajaj

B L O O M S B U R Y

NEW YORK · LONDON · NEW DELHI · SYDNEY

Bloomsbury Academic
An imprint of Bloomsbury Publishing Plc

175 Fifth Avenue	50 Bedford Square
New York	London
NY 10010	WC1B 3DP
USA	UK

www.bloomsbury.com

First published 2012

© Monisha Bajaj, 2012

First published in hardback 2012
This paperback edition published 2012

Earlier and modified versions of certain chapters appeared in the following publications:
Bajaj, Monisha. "Human Rights Education: Ideology, Location, and Approaches." Human Rights Quarterly 33 (2011): 481–508.

Bajaj, Monisha. "Teaching to Transform, Transforming to Teach: Exploring the Role of Teachers in Human Rights Education in India." Educational Research. 53, no. 2 (2011): 207–21.

Bajaj, Monisha. "From "Time Pass" to Transformative Force: School-Based Human Rights Education in Tamil Nadu." International Journal of Educational Development (2010). doi:10.1016/j.ijedudev.2010.10.001.

Library of Congress Cataloging-in-Publication Data
Bajaj, Monisha.
Schooling for social change: the rise and impact of human rights education in India / Monisha Bajaj.
p. cm.
Includes bibliographical references and index.
ISBN-13: 978-1-4411-7674-5 (hardcover: alk. paper)
ISBN-10: 1-4411-7674-8 (hardcover: alk. paper) 1. Human rights – Study and teaching – India. I. Title.
JC573.2.I4B35 2011
370.11'50954–dc23
2011024095

ISBN: HB: 978-1-4411-7674-5
PB: 978-1-4411-7305-8

Typeset by Newgen Imaging Systems Pvt Ltd, Chennai, India
Printed and bound in the United States of America

Contents

Map of India

List of Figures

Acknowledgments

I am deeply indebted to many individuals and institutions for their contributions to this project. The seeds of this project were sown in 2002 when I met Henri Tiphagne, Executive Director of People's Watch, through Smita Narula, whose generous advice and willingness to help were greatly appreciated. The Institute of Human Rights Education and People's Watch's leaders and staff members were consistently helpful and supportive; special thanks to Henri, Cynthia, Anita, and Alina Tiphagne; Vasanthi Devi, I. Devasahayam, M. Louis, Anna Durai, Saji Thomas, Veena Shankar, Maria Soosai, R. Thirunavukkarasu, Pradipta Nayak, L. Bernat, Uma Maheshwari, P. Chellapandi, J. Sharmila, Ananth Ramakrishnan, R. Chokku, J. Shiyam Sundar, M. A. Booma, John Kennedy, Rajshree Mohanty, Edward Thma, Manimaran, and Anitha Princy.

Other individuals and organizations involved in human rights and education in India were extremely helpful in developing this research as well. I offer my gratitude to: Ashok Mathews Philip and Margaret Sampath (South Indian Cell for Human Rights Education and Monitoring, Bengaluru); Teesta Setalvad and Noorjahan Shaikh (KHOJ, Mumbai); Sister Cyril Mooney and Christine Gupta (Loreto Sealdah School, Kolkata); Nupur, Gagan Sethi, and Dipika (Janvikas and Centre for Social Justice, Ahmedabad); and Martin Macwan and Manjula Pradeep (Navsarjan Trust, Ahmedabad).

Conversations with several individuals in India, Europe, and the United States shed light on new dimensions and ideas for this project. I am thankful for the generous insights of the following individuals: Upendra Baxi, Paul Divakar, Akhil Gupta, Amita Gupta, Elena Ippoliti, Christophe Jaffrelot, Sangeeta Kamat, Nancy Kendall, P. S. Krishnan, Joel Lee, Ruth Manorama, Annie Namala, D. P. Pattnayak, N. Ram, Nidhi Sadana, Shanta Sinha, Felisa Tibbitts, Sukhdeo Thorat, and Christine Min Wotipka. I extend special thanks to the Office of the UN High Commissioner for Human Rights.

Mentors from different stages of my professional life offered wisdom, advice, and direction throughout the process: the late Lila Jacobs, Kathleen Morrison, Lesley Bartlett, Frances Vavrus, and Ofelia Garcia. These women exemplify the definition of what mentors are: "wise and trusted counselors, teachers," and friends.

The scholarly environment at Teachers College, Columbia University has been a highly productive place to develop my ideas, projects, and research. I thank my colleagues Susan Fuhrman, Tom James, Janice Robinson, George Bond, Henry Levin, Andrew Shiotani, Regina Cortina, and Gita Steiner-Khamsi for their collegiality and assistance. Friends and colleagues within and outside Teachers College also offered important support and feedback at different stages of this project: Chitra Aiyar, Carrie Bettinger-Lopez, Maria Hantzopoulos, Brooke Harris, Patricia Krueger-Henney, Ameena Ghaffar-Kucher, Monika Kalra Varma, Tatyana Kleyn, Jennie Luna, Mary Mendenhall, Kate Menken, Kiruba Murugaiah, Varsha Puri, Karuna Ramachandran, Santhosh Ramdoss, Aly Remtulla, Mathangi Subramanian, Aleesha Taylor, Laura Valdiviezo, Nisha Varia, Wendy Ward-Hoffer, and Zeena Zakharia.

Several current and former students generously contributed their time and energy to assist in various tasks related to the development of this project and the production of this book, namely: Heidi Batchelder, Stephanie Bengtsson, Radhika Iyengar, Staci Johnson, and Annie Smiley. A special thank you to Huma Kidwai for drawing the map of India that appears in this book.

This project could only come to fruition because of the financial support provided by the National Academy of Education/Spencer post-doctoral fellowship and the Office of the Provost of Teachers College, Columbia University. The mentorship, feedback, and camaraderie provided through the NAEd/Spencer meetings were essential and I am particularly thankful to John Meyer, Luis Moll, Brett Gadsden, Janelle Scott, Wade Cole, and Jennifer Tinch. David Barker of Continuum Publishing provided important guidance and enthusiasm in getting this book from proposal to print.

Friends and family also offered considerable assistance and encouragement. In India, I am indebted to the Bajaj, George, Kuruvila, Makrandi, and Matthew families; Arati Kumari, Nilen Jha, and Aiyana Kashyap; Sara Poehlman; Anit Mukherjee; and Surabhi Chopra and Simon Cox. In particular, I am sincerely grateful to Asha, Dinesh, Rajeev, Carolyn, and Dylan Bajaj as well as Ishwari and (the late) Anand Sachdev, and Sosanna Kuruvila. Bikku Kuruvila has been an integral part of this project in its conception and actualization; I offer my deepest appreciation for his immense support and assistance at every step of the way.

Personally, this project has been guided and sustained by the illuminating work of Paulo Freire that I first read over 15 years ago and has imbued a desire to explore how individuals seek to expand horizons of possibility through education in distinct corners of the globe. As Freire (1970) noted, "For apart from inquiry, apart from the praxis, individuals cannot be truly human. Knowledge emerges only through invention and re-invention, through the restless, impatient, continuing, hopeful inquiry human beings pursue in the world, with the world, and with each other" (72).

Abbreviations

ADW	Adi Dravidar Welfare Department
BJP	Bharatiya Janata Party
DIET	District Institute for Education and Training
HRE	Human Rights Education
HREA	Human Rights Education Associates
IHRE	Institute of Human Rights Education
KWIRC	Karnataka Women's Information and Resource Center
NAC	National Advisory Committee
NCERT	National Council of Educational Research and Training
NCF	National Curriculum Framework
NCPCR	National Commission for Protection of Child Rights
NCTE	National Council for Teacher Education
NGO	Non-Governmental Organization
NHRC	National Human Rights Commission
NPE	National Policy on Education
NREGA	National Rural Employment Guarantee Act
NSS	National Service Scheme
OHCHR	Office of the United Nations High Commissioner for Human Rights
PW	People's Watch
RTE	Right to Education
RTI	Right to Information
SAC	State Advisory Committee
SC	Scheduled Caste
SICHREM	South India Cell for Human Rights Education and Monitoring
SSA	*Sarva Shiksha Abhiyan* (India's Domestic Education for All Program)
ST	Scheduled Tribe
UDHR	Universal Declaration of Human Rights

UGC	University Grants Commission
UN	United Nations
UNDP	United Nations Development Programme
UNESCO	United Nations Educational, Scientific, and Cultural Organization
UNICEF	United Nations Children's Fund
UNRWA	United Nations Relief and Works Agency

Chapter One

Introduction

I started learning about human rights in class six. I first thought they are giving us more of a burden with yet another subject and more books. But the teachers were so different after they started teaching human rights: human rights teachers talk nicely to us, they don't scold and beat us. They encouraged us to try new things and cultivate different talents like dance, poetry, drama, singing, and everything. Other subject teachers would just teach their subjects and they beat us also. They put the pressure of other people on us. But the human rights teachers release us from that. So I thank God for the introduction of human rights. Through this course, I started writing poems about women's rights and children's issues and my human rights teacher encouraged me to send it to the newspaper when I was in class eight. They liked it and even published it! I had never ever thought something like that would happen. My grandmother can't read, but I showed it to her in the newspaper and she was so happy. I kept writing poems and made a collection of 125 of them. My teacher encouraged me to put them together in a book and she raised money from teachers and got the publisher to give us a discounted rate. They are putting all the proceeds of the book sales in a bank account under my name so that I can go to college. I can't imagine what my life would be if this human rights class would not have been there. I thank God for it and for my teachers and this Institute also for introducing it in our school. When I grow up, I would like to do a lot more in the field of human rights.

(Interview with Fatima, Class 12 student, May 2009)

I first met Fatima in February 2009 when she shared how human rights education (HRE) had transformed her educational experiences since she began participating in the programs of the non-governmental organization (NGO), People's Watch and its Institute of Human Rights Education (IHRE) in India. In subsequent visits, I learned that Fatima was the first child born in a family whose custom was, if the child was a girl, to kill it in the practice of infanticide that still lingers in certain parts of India. Fatima's maternal grandmother intervened, and was then given the child to raise on her meager salary as the sweeper at a local school. IHRE staff, teachers, and peers all noted Fatima's increased confidence, aspirations for higher education, and community involvement as a result of participation in HRE.

At the outset of this project, I thought that such examples of impact were isolated, circumstantial, and anecdotal. Yet, in school after school over a period of more than 13 months, I found an abundance of students and teachers reporting individual, household, and community-level changes they had undergone or influenced as a result of specific instruction about human rights. Some of these changes, such as increased knowledge about human rights that participants then shared with others, were expected; some, however, were entirely unanticipated, such as middle-school age students confronting abusers and otherwise finding ways to intervene in or reporting abuses. Often, students sacrificed their own relative privileges to stand in solidarity with those less fortunate.

This book explores the variety of meanings attached to human rights education in a single nation-state, India, by tracing the rise and impact of the reform over the past three decades. By charting how human rights education came into Fatima's under-resourced government school in rural Tamil Nadu (as well as thousands of other schools), we can better understand the genealogy, spread, and subsequent impact of the reform, including its limits and possibilities. India's sheer size, its recent economic growth, and geopolitical strategic significance have drawn media and scholarly attention, though, unfortunately, there has been little critical focus on the relationship between education and political development in what is termed "the world's largest democracy." While scholars have interrogated the scope, nature, and dimensions of political integration (Appadurai 2001; Chatterjee 2004), the interplay between rights-based educational initiatives and their corresponding reformulations of notions of agency and citizenship offer many lessons for scholars interested in India and beyond.

This book explores and argues three premises rooted in evidence from India. First, I hold that there are many different manifestations of human rights education. The ideology, content emphasis, and outcomes of HRE initiatives are differentially constructed depending on context, implementing agency, teacher mediation of information, and (presumed) audience. Data from India shed light on the diversity of understandings that surround human rights education in one nation-state as well as internationally.

Second, strategy is as important as content and pedagogy in securing support for expanding human rights education. The Institute of Human Rights Education's strategy of "persuasive pragmatism" identified and constructively engaged with a variety of interests and stakeholders to advance HRE nationwide. Securing broader acceptance of human rights involved going beyond merely enlisting those individuals and agencies already committed to rights promotion. In this process, the global diffusion of human rights terms and concepts informs local debates and how students, teachers, parents, and officials react to the implementation of HRE in distinct ways.

Third, the impact of human rights instruction differs depending on the social location of students and teachers and their ability to influence change. For marginalized students, strategic agency, such as engaging in collective action or seeking support from teachers and textbooks, may be required to enact the human rights learning received in the classroom. Even for more privileged students, the issue of social status is important to consider and is often absent from discussions of human rights education. An in-depth exploration of human rights education in India provides the opportunity to explore its varied nature through elaborating the multiple ideological orientations, strategies, impact, and relationships of power contained in a singular educational project.

THE RISE OF HUMAN RIGHTS EDUCATION

Globally, human rights education, generally defined as the incorporation of content and pedagogy with the aim of inculcating knowledge of international human rights norms in diverse educational settings, has grown in popularity in educational policy discourse, particularly at the United Nations and among transnational human rights organizations.[1] Though popular or community education aimed at raising awareness of human rights issues has been a strategy utilized by non-governmental organizations since the 1950s in building social movements (Kapoor 2004), the advancement of national initiatives on HRE by more than 100 countries of the world to date suggests the diversification of its role and scope in international educational policy discourse in the past three decades (OHCHR 2009).

Perhaps not unsurprisingly, along with the expansion and diffusion of HRE as a fashionable reform through international policy networks (Halligan 1996; Ramirez, Suarez, and Meyer 2007; Strang and Lee 2006), there are many versions of "human rights education." Indeed, significant variation exists in beliefs about what HRE *is*, *does*, and *means*. While governments across the globe adopt HRE for perhaps different motivations, its practice can also be characterized by considerable "decoupling," which refers to the nominal adoption of a reform for legitimacy concerns, but the subsequent non-implementation or significant adaptation of the reform for efficiency or other reasons (Meyer and Rowan 1978). Scholars have explained the rise of HRE and the ways in which global pressures have led to greater policy adoption even amidst decoupling (Ramirez, Suarez, and Meyer 2007; Meyer, Bromley-Martin, and Ramirez 2010).

Legal scholars have noted variation in what the term "human rights" means to various groups (Baxi 2006; Dembour 2010). These different approaches to and understandings of human rights education mirror what noted Indian scholar, Upendra Baxi, terms the different "languages and logics of human rights," that vary from the discourse of international covenants, to the use of rights language as a part of corporate social responsibility and the use of human rights to frame the struggles of historically disadvantaged groups (Baxi 2006, 119). The diffusion and popularization of human rights as the range of actors operating within this field has expanded creates a certain amount of conceptual ambiguity that may hide the concrete achievements, problems, and differences in HRE practice globally.

Scholars in the field of International and Comparative Education have developed a substantial literature exploring civic education and political socialization, specifically the role and purpose of schooling as part and parcel of nation-building in diverse regions (Boli, Ramirez, and Meyer 1985; Fagerlind and Saha 1989; Fuller and Rubinson 1992; Torney-Purta, Schwille, and Amadeo 1999). In contrast, HRE implies that students will develop allegiance to a supranational system of norms developed through international human rights law and that they will, in effect, claim global in addition to national citizenship (Soysal 1994; Suarez and Ramirez 2004). The stated willingness of governments to implement HRE, in addition to the actual implementation (by them and by other actors) that occurs on the ground, is considered here through the example of India. Situated within the growing exploration of multilevel (or vertical) case studies of single nation-states in the field of International and Comparative Education (e.g., Vavrus and Bartlett 2009), this book is driven by the premise that it is impossible to think about HRE (and relatedly, the nation-state) apart from the multiple pressures—from above and below—guiding and shaping the adoption, adaptation, and implementation of such reforms. As such, this book contributes a vertical case study of how external and internal forces have come together to produce localized and varied versions of Indian human rights education.

The following chapters chart the rise of HRE to determine how differentiated motivations for, conceptualizations of, and initiatives toward HRE operate at the levels of policy, curriculum and pedagogy, and practice in India. What factors account for the rise of HRE in India over the past three decades? What are the differing understandings of the rationale, goals, and meanings of HRE expressed by international organizations, different Indian government agencies, and local NGOs? What impact has HRE had on Indian teachers and youth from diverse backgrounds who have participated in one NGO program? I explore these questions through a multilevel examination of human rights education across several states in India.

India offers a complex case study. The country's tremendous diversity (1.21 billion residents in 28 states) and uneven socioeconomic development across regions, social groups, and gender complicate the ways that educational efforts figure into larger goals of economic and political development. Despite India's record economic growth in recent years (around 7 percent per annum in recent years according to the World Bank 2010), income inequality has *increased* in the last two decades (OECD 2010). An estimated 42 percent of Indians (nearly 500 million people) survive on less than US $1.25 per day, though down from 60 percent in the 1980s (World Bank 2008). International organizations have also found that 75.6 percent of all Indians live on less than US $2 per day (UNDP 2009).

India recently guaranteed a right to education as a matter of law, yet questions of universal educational access continue to plague the country. Ensuring access is not necessarily a linear process; once enrolled, many factors, such as discriminatory practices, inadequate facilities, and poor instructional quality, push children out of school (UNICEF 2010). As will be discussed subsequently, school dropout rates are particularly high in India for marginalized groups, namely those from Dalit (formerly called "untouchable") and Adivasi ("tribal" or rural indigenous) communities. Reforms focusing on ensuring quality and equity in education, such as HRE, have had a complex reception by both marginalized and privileged students. This book explores these paradoxes and offers an in-depth examination of understandings of HRE by students and teachers of distinct socioeconomic backgrounds in their homes, schools, and communities.[2]

In the 1990s, in line with the United Nations (UN) Decade for Human Rights Education (1995–2004) and subsequent international efforts, the government of India began to develop a plan of action to integrate HRE into schools nationwide, with the support of high-level officials such as the then-President, K. R. Narayan, and, in more recent years, several national-level entities and authorities. While HRE is not an officially mandated or required subject of the Indian education system at any level, the chapters that follow detail national efforts in teacher training, textbook development, and informal education, as well as significant initiatives run by non-governmental organizations.

The NGO most active in this area has been the Institute of Human Rights Education (IHRE), part of the larger human rights organization People's Watch, that has offered HRE to over 300,000 students in nearly 4,000 government schools across 18 Indian states since 1997 (see Appendix A). This book focuses primarily on IHRE and affiliated partner organizations in examining their approaches to human rights education and corresponding impact. IHRE's work is significant for two primary reasons. First, IHRE's programs constitute the largest NGO effort advancing curriculum development, teacher training, and instruction on any non-mandatory subject in Indian schools. Second, for scholars of HRE globally, the scale of instruction is unprecedented vis-à-vis other initiatives seeking to impart human rights instruction in government-run schools. This study is not an evaluation of the Institute of Human Rights Education's operations, but rather an exploration of how the organization has secured support and been effective in advancing human rights through instruction. At the national level, engaging with India's unique experiences in HRE offers scholars and practitioners a rich case study of the conditions of possibility, emergence, impact, and range of human rights education in a single nation-state.

RESEARCH DESIGN

Scholars in the field of International and Comparative Education have increasingly argued for multilevel analyses (Bray and Thomas 1995; Bartlett and Vavrus 2009). In developing their framework of "vertical case studies," Frances Vavrus and Lesley Bartlett advocate for research methods that "strive to situate local action and interpretation within a broader cultural, historical, and political investigation" (2006, par. 4). Research that examines policy and practice across multiple levels recognizes the significant pressures brought to bear by global development institutions and the declining relevance of the nation-state as the sole unit of analysis in cross-national comparative educational research. In her work, Vavrus (2005) discusses the blurred line between international and national reforms given the influence of intergovernmental organizations in advocating, funding, and sometimes even writing policies for nations in the global South. She terms this inability to decipher the origins of a particular reform, and the space in which national governments navigate the mandates of international donors, the "inter/national" level. Multilevel studies also balance and link national-level studies with investigation at regional and local levels. Taken together, multilevel approaches can provide important insights into the multiple dimensions of schooling (here, educational reform) in highly stratified societies for various stakeholders.

While the inter/national level of human rights education discourse makes up one dimension of this vertical case study, the strategies and approaches of the Institute of Human Rights Education and localized understandings and experiences with HRE across several states in India make up the other components (see Figure 1.1).

Data Sources and Data Collection Procedures

The data presented in this book emerge from 13 months of fieldwork in India (over the period of August 2008 to August 2010), which examined the multiple conceptualizations of and experiences with human rights education. The primary methods utilized for the research were semi-structured interviews, focus groups, observations of teacher training workshops and human rights summer camps, school visits, and participant observation. Semi-structured interview and focus group questions generally included information on the individual's engagement with human rights education broadly and IHRE specifically and, for teachers and students, what human rights meant to them. Follow-up questions included how human rights had affected them. These few questions generally resulted in considerable responses.

Respondents included 118 human rights education teachers, 625 students, 80 staff and policymakers of human rights education, and 8 parents.

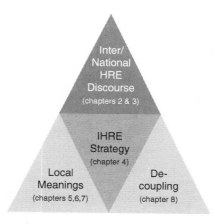

Figure 1.1 Vertical Case Study Design of Human Rights Education in Indian Schools

I visited more than 60 schools and 9 different NGOs operating in 6 states; I also selected key events organized by the focal NGO, the Institute of Human Rights Education, for observation, such as teacher trainings in multiple states, a week-long summer camp for HRE students in Tamil Nadu, a national HRE conference in Orissa, and a National Advisory Committee meeting in New Delhi, among others. Observations and interviews in everyday settings where HRE was practiced as well as special events provided an understanding of the scope of HRE activities and the diversity of participants' experiences.

The programs selected represent a range of human rights, socioeconomic, and geographic realities in different states. In addition, I focused on states where human rights education initiatives had been in operation through IHRE and its partner organizations for at least three years (one full cycle of HRE as per their model). Students, teachers, parents, and alumni of HRE were selected utilizing maximum variation sampling to include a variety of schools in distinct parts of the states visited (urban and rural), and a diversity of respondents based on caste, age, length of time learning/teaching HRE, gender, and educational background. Interviews and focus groups generally lasted between 45 and 60 minutes, with some lasting as long as two hours. State visits varied in duration from ten days to two months, depending on issues of sampling and the scope of the program(s) in operation. I sought to spend enough time in each site to understand the challenges facing HRE programs as well as the successes they may have achieved.

I primarily utilized qualitative research methods in this study. Research questions sought to understand different approaches to HRE at multiple levels, distinct organizational strategies, and participants' varied experiences. An inductive data analysis and interpretation strategy rooted in grounded theory was utilized (Strauss and Corbin 1990). I regularly reviewed the interviews, observations, and documents in order to discern themes emerging from the data and began to identify categories for open coding. I maintained thorough field notes and periodically reviewed all the data collected in order to draw preliminary conclusions, which I submitted to tests of validity such a member-checking (consulting with participants regarding emerging analyses) and triangulation (Lincoln and Guba 2000; Stake 1995).

This book draws primarily on qualitative data about human rights education; however, questionnaire surveys were collected from approximately 10,000 students (HRE and non-HRE) across several Indian states. The quantitative survey data was used to compare student responses from schools that had the HRE intervention with students who did not have the HRE course. A six-page questionnaire was prepared after considerable consultation with Indian educators and human rights experts. I trained individuals and prepared a short manual to administer the surveys in different states. Research assistants identified the same number of students who had and who had not taken HRE to complete the survey on a voluntary basis. Questions included situations of abuse that students had to identify, agree/disagree statements associated with local examples of human rights, and definitions of human rights and related concepts. Simple descriptive statistics generated the means, which were compared for both types of students (HRE and non-HRE). Tests also indicated if the difference between the means was statistically significant. A subset of the quantitative data is presented and discussed in Chapter Five.

I carried out all interviews and focus groups as the primary researcher, although assistance was sought with administering surveys and transcription. Where necessary, translators were utilized for interviews and focus groups. After meeting the executive director of the NGO People's Watch initially in 2002 to discuss possibilities for research, conversations were resumed in 2007 to collaboratively design a research study that analyzed the active role of their Institute of Human Rights Education within a broader policy framework. Pilot data was collected in 2008, and fieldwork ensued across the various states in 2009 and 2010.

Researcher's Perspective

My methods and approach to this study were shaped considerably by "critical approaches" to International and Comparative Education, as well as the tenets of critical research in education. My broader research examines participants' experiences in educational innovations, differences between official policy and actual practice, and the nature of political spaces in democratic states in the global South for such innovation to exist in dialogue with partners in the broader international community (e.g., Bajaj 2009, 2010). In utilizing multiple research traditions and diverse disciplinary approaches, I follow in what Klees (2008) terms "critical comparative education," in which "critical/transformative research takes an explicit position to work in the interests of the marginalized" (323). This process, as scholars of critical research in education have similarly noted, operates "in solidarity with a justice-oriented community" and with an eye toward how "greater degrees of autonomy and human agency can be achieved" (Denzin and Lincoln 2000, 282). Schooling, as a process which can either reproduce or transform social inequalities, becomes an opportune site in which to explore attempts that seek to destabilize exclusionary social practices, be they rooted in class, caste, gender, or otherwise.

Human rights education offers one example of how educators and activists have sought to transform social relations through an alternative educational program. India offered a productive locale in which to study HRE both because of the active engagement of this educational reform by policymakers and practitioners, and also because of my personal familiarity with the country as a result of living and traveling between India and the United States throughout my life. Having worked in the field of human rights and then human rights education for many years, knowledge of the varied issues, actors, and debates in India certainly facilitated the project. This research highlights HRE efforts in India, offering critical analysis of the strengths and shortcomings of distinct models and providing those interested in advancing HRE empirical data and contextualized perspectives on how such initiatives might be improved and expanded.

SUMMARY OF CHAPTERS

In line with the three premises set forth at the beginning of this chapter—that there is no one HRE, that strategy and deep engagement matter, as does social location—the following chapters offer scholars and practitioners a vertical case study of human rights education in India. Chapter Two provides a history of human rights education globally and the various models that have guided its practice. The chapter first discusses the emergence of human rights education as a field of advocacy and scholarship, tracing its increasing presence in international educational policy discussions, national textbook reforms, and post-conflict educational strategies. Debates in human rights education are also highlighted as these educational reforms have grown in popularity over the past three decades, especially through the declaration of 1995–2004 as the UN Decade for Human Rights Education and the subsequent establishment of a World Programme for Human Rights Education housed at the UN. The chapter then reviews existing definitions and models of HRE, and argues that ideology as much as location or other factors offers a means of categorizing varying approaches to human rights education. The different approaches to HRE are presented as inherently linked to the context and participants involved. I also present a new model for examining HRE organized differentially around principles of global citizenship, coexistence, and transformative action, which I then use to situate an analysis of HRE initiatives in India.

Chapter Three provides information on the context and the current landscape of HRE in India. I first examine socioeconomic characteristics of the states and populations involved in this study, and second, chart the rise of human rights education in India over the past three decades in policy discussions and in NGO models. At the national level, government bodies like the National Council of Educational Research and Training (NCERT), the

National Council for Teacher Education (NCTE), the University Grants Commission (UGC), and the National Human Rights Commission (NHRC) have all taken steps toward incorporating human rights education into their work. Chapter Three also examines national policy documents, such as National Curriculum Frameworks that influence and guide educational planning and practice as well as teacher formation nationwide. These national efforts generally follow the HRE for Global Citizenship model outlined in Chapter Two.

Chapter Four introduces the non-governmental organization People's Watch and its Institute of Human Rights Education. The chapter presents the history and key events that have led to the growth and expansion of the Institute's programs to 18 states across India, focusing specifically on the six states in which data were collected. As a non-governmental institute charged with developing curriculum, training teachers, and implementing human rights education, the structure, activities, and strategies of the organization are outlined, discussed, and analyzed. The unique role that IHRE plays in advancing human rights education in government schools is directly related to what I term its "strategy of persuasive pragmatism," a relational model of deep engagement with stakeholders, who range from classroom teachers and headmasters to state and national level policymakers, to secure permission and support for HRE. While the organization does not use this terminology, I define "persuasive pragmatism" as a strategy that has three components: first, a relational and contextual approach that endorses the legitimacy of the bearer of human rights information; second, an approach that considers and addresses the multiple reasons why stakeholders may be interested in advancing or participating in HRE; and third, the creation and provision of an extensive network of supporters of IHRE that can enhance the status of and provide incentives to participants, whether teachers or students. At the levels of adoption, implementation, and curricular impact, IHRE's strategy of persuasive pragmatism is consistent in that the Institute works to convince individuals that knowledge about human rights (and support for human rights education initiatives) is in their interest, as varied as those interests may be. Also fundamental to such a strategy is the organization's ability to think seriously about power and social location, factors that are largely absent in previous analyses of human rights education.

Chapter Five focuses directly on the impact of human rights education on marginalized students in IHRE's program. This chapter explores gender violence, caste discrimination, and child labor, as well as how human rights education has provided victims of abuses a framework for understanding the dynamics of social exclusion and violence. The term "time pass" is often used in Indian education for anything that distracts from preparation for high-stakes examinations. At the inception of the program, and as a non-examinable subject, human rights education was perceived by many students as a "time pass." However, after engaging with human rights content and seeing changes among their teachers, students discussed how they used this knowledge to take action against abuses in their communities and to spread the information learned to neighbors, friends, and family members. The chapter also explores the role of status in promoting respect for human rights by students who have been directly affected by abuses in their homes and communities. Using rich examples from interviews and observations, the chapter analyzes the varied responses by students who have gone through the IHRE program and their enhanced efficacy in bringing about change. The chapter shows how IHRE's strategy of persuasive pragmatism has resulted in marginalized students' heightened human rights consciousness, utilization of collective action, and ability to situate their personal experiences within a broader framework of rights.

Chapter Six focuses on students with relative privilege (whom I describe as *coalitional agents*) in schools where human rights education is offered to show how social location mediates learnings and shapes action. This includes boys from marginalized communities (whose privilege often shifts depending on the context) as well as students of higher caste/religious backgrounds and students in private schools where HRE is offered. Coalitional agents are not thought to have an immediate "self-interest" in advancing human rights, as the students discussed in Chapter Five do. However, the chapter uses these relatively privileged students' own words and examples to show how they are inspired to take action and intervene on behalf of siblings, friends, and community members. The curriculum and ideological approach of the Institute of Human Rights Education offers more privileged students a framework and rationale for caring about the rights of others, which most students appear to embrace. Representative examples are provided and analyzed to situate the contextual efficacy of action by those with greater social and economic status on behalf of others. These examples range from solidarity with victims to advocacy on their behalf to charitable actions, depending largely on the social distance from the abuse. Whether the students' responses are oriented toward charity or more urgent attempts to shield victims from abuse, the outcome, I contend, is coalitional agency. As the chapter demonstrates, these stories make important points about the value of human rights training, not to mention human capacity to act beyond narrow self-interest. Coalitional agency often proves effective in creating micro-level changes, leading toward greater social equity.

Chapter Seven examines the role of teacher training and textbook development in the expansion of human rights education in India. While teachers are often discussed as the primary conduit for human rights education globally, the Indian teachers interviewed also repeatedly discussed their *own* transformation as a result of participation in HRE. The chapter highlights teachers' responses to human rights training and situates them within the literature on the role of teachers in human rights education. The teachers interviewed discussed how trainings secured their interest in human rights and/or affiliation with IHRE; implementation of the educational program and intervention in their communities as "legitimating agents" often followed. This is a significant position for teachers given the authority afforded to them, and to the printed word, in semiliterate Indian contexts. In narratives of students' responses to human rights education, teachers often played an important role in assisting in intervention, modeling the outcomes of HRE through their own changed behavior, and convincing parents and community members of the legitimacy of human rights information that countered oppressive local customs or traditions. As an oft-discussed, but little theorized, component of human rights education, this chapter delves deeply into the role of teachers and textbooks in the human rights learning endeavor.

Chapter Eight juxtaposes the success of IHRE in program expansion, implementation, and impact with some forms of "decoupling" or redefinition (Meyer and Rowan 1978), as well as forms of resistance. Various stakeholders within and outside IHRE's program conflated HRE with other social programs or embedded their own interests and agendas into "human rights." Evidence of this decoupling and conflation with other concepts emerged around three themes that are explored in this chapter. First, some purposefully and some unintentionally linked human rights education to lessons on religious morality whether to ensure support or to advance their own beliefs. Second, larger messages toward hygiene and public health were sometimes folded into the understandings of human rights held by some participants, especially those in rural Adivasi communities where such health campaigns were most active. Third, some officials and teachers brought their interests and commitments in left politics to HRE, linking lessons with political forms of social equality. Decoupling from global and national discourses, as well as selective and situational "coupling" for diverse purposes, is explained through data from policymakers, activists, administrators, teachers, and students. This chapter also examines the views of policymakers and staff at NGOs that purposely do not use the term "human rights education" for similar educational programs as part of an analysis of the perceptions and associations that go along with "human rights" in India today. This chapter explores the sometimes unexpected sources of support and opposition to HRE rooted in these diverse forms of decoupling and reinterpretation.

The concluding chapter highlights the lessons learned in previous chapters about India's experience with human rights education at the levels of policy, pedagogy and textbook development, and community-level practice through the work of IHRE. The chapter suggests ways for scholars and practitioners to apply these lessons to promote educational equity and quality in other parts of the globe. The chapter also discusses further directions for HRE in India, including competing visions of different stakeholders with regards to the role of HRE in primary, secondary, and tertiary education. As human rights education becomes an increasingly central part of larger human rights strategies and international educational policy, the chapter ends on a speculative cautionary note about the malleability and multiple interpretations of HRE while resisting the urge to pronounce what constitutes "valid" HRE practice.

Chapter Two

Human Rights Education: Definitions, History, Ideologies

Human rights education (HRE) has become a greater part of international discussions of educational policy (Ramirez, Suarez, and Meyer 2007), national textbook reform (Meyer, Bromley-Martin, and Ramirez 2010), and the work of non-governmental organizations (NGOs) worldwide over the past several decades (Tibbitts 2008). While scholars and practitioners alike have noted the rise in educational strategies as part of larger human rights efforts as well as HRE as an independent field of scholarship and practice (Mihr and Schmitz 2007), there appears to be a diversity of perspectives on what exactly HRE *is, means,* and *does* beyond a basic transmission of knowledge of human rights.

This chapter explores existing definitions and models of human rights education, distinguishing between "top-down" and "bottom-up" approaches to the reform (Claude 2011). As HRE spreads and expands, understandings of the field proliferate in complex ways not always in perfect alignment with the social movements from which human rights activism originally emerged. These processes of adaptation can generate greater variation among HRE programs if pressure from above depoliticizes it and pressure from below attempts to maintain an integral link of HRE to social justice struggles. The second half of this chapter offers a new framework in which to analyze HRE efforts globally. This schema is then utilized to discuss the variation among human rights education advanced independently by Indian government agencies, schools, and non-governmental organizations in subsequent chapters.

STRUCTURE OF HRE

While there are many versions of HRE, there is broad consensus about certain core components of human rights education. First, most scholars and practitioners agree that HRE must include both *content* and *process* related to human rights (Flowers 2003; Meintjes 1997; Reardon 2010; Tarrow 1992; Tibbitts 2002). Indeed, Tibbitts (2005) finds that "nearly all formal literature associated with HRE will mention the importance of using participatory methods" for effectively teaching about human rights (107). Second, most literature discusses the need for HRE to include goals related to cognitive (content), attitudinal or emotive (values/skills), and action-oriented components. Amnesty International's Human Rights Friendly Schools framework (2009) weaves together the processes of HRE and their intended outcomes by highlighting three prepositions linking education and human rights in a comprehensive manner: education *about* human rights (cognitive), education *through* human rights (participatory methods that create skills for active citizenship), and education *for* human rights (fostering learners' ability to speak out and act in the face of injustices). Within these broad parameters, different definitions and models developed over the past six decades reflect varied practices grounded in different histories as well as the socioeconomic locations and ideological frameworks of practitioners.

Normative Definitions of HRE

Definitions of HRE reflect their emergence in distinct moments. Article 26 of the 1948 Universal Declaration of Human Rights (UDHR) identifies, first, the right to education and, second, to an education directed toward "the full development of the human personality and to the strengthening of respect for human rights and fundamental freedoms." Building upon the universal ideals advanced in the UDHR, HRE figured more prominently in intergovernmental discussions, notably the World Conference on Human Rights held in Vienna in 1993 where raising public awareness (in large part, through education) about human rights was a main theme of discussion. Subsequently, the United Nations declared 1995–2004 the International Decade for Human Rights Education. Work within the UN around this topic then grew into the ongoing UN World Programme for Human Rights Education, housed within the Office of the United Nations High Commissioner for Human Rights (OHCHR). The UN General Assembly also more recently declared 2009 the International Year of Human Rights Learning.[1]

UN definitions shape much of the HRE work carried out by its affiliated agencies active in this area, such as UNICEF, UNESCO, and the OHCHR. As suggested by the UN:

> Human rights education can be defined as education, training and information aimed at building a universal culture of human rights through the sharing of knowledge, imparting of skills and moulding of attitudes directed to:
>
> (a)   The strengthening of respect for human rights and fundamental freedoms;
>
> (b)   The full development of the human personality and the sense of its dignity;
>
> (c)   The promotion of understanding, tolerance, gender equality and friendship among all nations, indigenous peoples and racial, national, ethnic, religious and linguistic groups;
>
> (d)   The enabling of all persons to participate effectively in a free and democratic society governed by the rule of law;
>
> (e)   The building and maintenance of peace;
>
> (f)   The promotion of people-centred sustainable development and social justice. (UN 2006)

Emphasized in the UN's definition of HRE is knowledge about human rights and tolerance/acceptance of others based on such knowledge. NGOs, also active in making the case for the decade and the international year, pushed for the addition of sub-points "e" and "f" in 2005 to acknowledge a more active role for individuals and social movements as a result of HRE. However, by and large, the UN definition largely reflects the role of international norms for ensuring social cohesion and peace, and is largely directed at national policymakers; as such, it provides a "top-down" statement of what HRE is and should be (Flowers et al., 2000). UN initiatives are largely targeted toward member states and attempt to foster adoption of national plans of action toward integrating HRE in their educational systems.

UN agencies take a very favorable view of national governments adopting comprehensive human rights content and pedagogy of their own will. However, scholars such as Cardenas (2005) have a more skeptical perspective on the role of the state in advancing HRE since it may work against their own interests:

> While in principle virtually everyone takes for granted the benefits of HRE, such endeavors can be potentially costly from the perspective of a state. Human rights education is inherently revolutionary: If implemented effectively, it has the

potential to generate social opposition, alongside rising demands for justice and accountability. (Cardenas 2005, 364)

Cardenas sees the state as resistant to incorporating HRE because of increased demands related to guarantees and entitlements vocalized by those educated about human rights. Other scholars in education, however, have suggested that the form of HRE, or any global education reform, that gets incorporated into national textbooks is related to trends in practice in the world society where reforms that are fashionable are adopted for a variety of reasons beyond mere interest (Meyer et al., 1997). Corresponding implementation and local practice may differ greatly from the version of HRE originally conceptualized since reforms often go through a process of decoupling or adaptation (Meyer and Rowan 1978). By the time human rights content gets incorporated into textbooks, HRE may lose its activist-oriented edge as human rights are presented in isolation from the struggles that secured them (J. Meyer, personal communication, October 2009).

Bottom-Up Models

NGOs and social movements have long been active in human rights education and tend to utilize human rights discourse as a strategy to frame the demands of diverse and typically marginalized social groups. At the grassroots level, HRE has often taken the form of popular education or community education to mobilize constituencies for expanding social movements (Kapoor 2004). In Latin America, for example, many efforts involving human rights education blossomed immediately after the end of dictatorships when NGOs that had fought for human rights turned their attention to education as a tool for reconciliation and the prevention of a return to authoritarian rule (Magendzo 1997). In these contexts, human rights education efforts are seen as both a political and pedagogical strategy to facilitate democratization and active citizenship.

Drawing on the promise of grassroots efforts to promote human rights, Amnesty International defines HRE as the following:

> Human rights education is a deliberate, participatory practice aimed at empowering individuals, groups, and communities through fostering knowledge, skills, and attitudes consistent with internationally recognized human rights principles. . . . Its goal is to build a culture of respect for and action in the defence and promotion of human rights for all. (AI 2010)

The Amnesty International definition places greater responsibility on human rights learners becoming activists for human rights through the process of

HRE by sharing information with others and actively working to defend human rights. The goals of promoting action by learners and encouraging social change outcomes are central to this definition.

While the UN's endorsement of HRE has resulted in greater coordination, funding, and legitimacy for NGOs working in this area, the collaborative process with national governments has posed potential dilemmas for activists. HRE has often grown out of human rights legal, advocacy, and activist work of NGOs that place their members in direct confrontation with state forces; this conflictive relationship with the state may sometimes prove difficult to transcend when the same organizations attempt to introduce HRE in government schools, as many NGOs have sought to do. Additionally, while much HRE, such as community education programs or education for professionals like judges, police, lawyers, armed forces, and health-workers, falls outside the purview of formal schooling, these actors are still, no doubt, integrally involved professionally with the state, as are teachers in government schools. As such, the expanding role of human rights movements and organizations in educational efforts requires attention to the ways in which the nation-state and international community structure, limit, and enable their activities.

Global HRE Community

Over the past two decades, various models have been advanced for understanding the diverse programmatic approaches to HRE. These models provide productive schemas for theorizing the emergence, conceptualization, and implementation of HRE across the globe. One vital forum is the online list-serve and "epistemic community" coordinated by the US-based Human Rights Education Associates (HREA) (Suarez 2007). This sphere allows its more than 8,000 members from 190 countries to, as Suarez notes, "practice, negotiate, refine, and mold HRE" through "discourse and active reflection" (66). Populated by many officials of member UN agencies, the discursive engagement on various issues of HRE through the online community has played a considerable role in facilitating international discussions on the topic. Arguably, since many messages and postings are from practitioners seeking advice, materials, or input, the online community also influences practice as well.

Scholars have catalogued the types of HRE by the content of the programs as well as participants' level of engagement. HREA Executive Director Felisa Tibbitts (2002) has proposed a model of differentiated content and constituencies for HRE distinguishing among general "values and awareness," the "accountability" model for adult professionals directly involved with human rights victims, and the more comprehensive "transformational" model which includes students and community members (Tibbitts 2002). Nancy Flowers (1998) elaborates a schema that distinguishes the age of learners with appropriate concepts, goals, and content (as cited in Tibbitts 2008). For example, Flowers advocates an emphasis on concepts of community and responsibility in childhood 'progressing to more complex issues, such as freedom, equality, fairness, and moral exclusion, later in adolescence and adulthood.

LOCATION

While these models generally offer universal visions for HRE across contexts, other scholars have distinguished HRE by location. For example, scholars have noted the types of societies to explain differences between HRE approaches (Flowers 2004; Tarrow 1992). Tarrow (1992) highlighted how HRE content may be different in "first," "second/socialist," and "third" world contexts based on emphases on individual versus collective rights. Flowers et al. (2000) similarly noted that different types of rights are emphasized based on context and institution. These perspectives range from "survival" or economic/social rights to civil and political rights, activist-oriented education, and moral education, which sees human rights as part of "natural law." Tibbitts (2008) contends that HRE is affiliated with different constituencies in different nations:

> HRE in post-conflict or post-colonial countries tends to be associated with the rule of law and authorities trying to establish their legitimacy. Among groups that experience a high amount of discrimination, and within countries that are highly repressive and undemocratic, HRE tends to be focused on popular empowerment and resistance in relation to these issues. HRE in countries that are democratic but struggling with development can be oriented towards the infusion of human rights principles within sustainable development. In countries that enjoy strong democratic and economic development, HRE is often focused on issues of discrimination, for example in relation to migrants, minorities, or women. (101–2)

HRE content and constituencies sometimes differ across nation-states and are linked to ongoing national debates in education. In the United Kingdom, for example, HRE correlates to the evolution and conceptualization of citizenship education. The 1998 Crick Report identified three dimensions of citizenship education—political literacy, social and moral responsibility, and community involvement—and was influential in its becoming a statuary subject within the 2002 National Curriculum (QCA 1998). Scholars Audrey Osler and Hugh Starkey (2006), however, note the absence of antiracist education in the citizenship education project, and instead advocate for "education for cosmopolitan citizenship [which] needs to address peace, human rights, democracy, and development, equipping young people to make a difference at all levels, from the local to the global" (244). The authors further argue that utilizing a human rights framework for citizenship education challenges nationalistic narratives that exclude certain groups from claiming membership, as has been seen across Europe (Osler and Starkey 2010).

HRE can also reflect a broader regional commitment, drawing support from distinct sectors in various nations. The Council of Europe's Education for Democratic Citizenship and Human Rights initiative explores the relationships between citizenship and HRE to promote tolerance and pluralism in an increasingly multicultural Europe. Established in 1997 after the second summit of Council of Europe heads of state, the project develops materials and resources and conducts trainings (Council of Europe 2010). The Council assumes that certain overarching values are shared across all contexts and programs, offering in its *Compasito* manual a useful diagram (see Figure 2.1). The Council's model draws on the generations of human rights—a concept that has been critiqued by human rights scholars as inadequate (Tomaševski 2005), but that is still widely utilized—to distinguish between different HRE programs.

Conceptualizing HRE by generations offers distinct ways of comparing these practices among countries with different income levels and political structures. Figure 2.1 provides a composite picture of HRE efforts. While, arguably, such a holistic perspective is rarely incorporated into a singular program or reform in a particular nation-state, the Council of Europe's model suggests how would-be educators and planners in distinct locations might emphasize different aspects of human rights in order to address the contextual issues with which learners are confronted.

IDEOLOGICAL ORIENTATIONS AND OUTCOMES OF HRE

The differences in understandings of HRE can be viewed through the lens of ideology as much as location. In particular, the varied ideological content of these programs bear some relation to where such programs locate themselves in relation to local, national, and international sites of power, not geography or nationhood understood in any simple, homogenous sense. An elite private school and a school serving a marginalized indigenous community in the same area may both offer human rights education, though their approaches may vary widely based on the material realities of each group, the manner in which HRE is introduced, and the anticipated outcome. Certainly, relationship to power is not an absolute determinant of ideology though the correlation between social location and approach, in practice, is often significant.

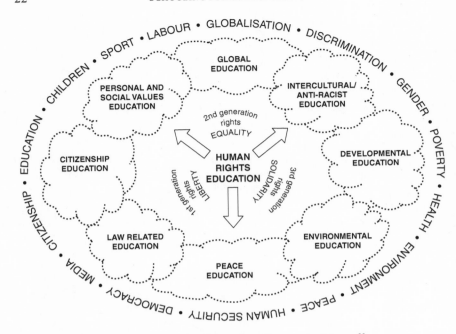

Figure 2.1 Types of Human Rights Education, Compasito Manual[2]

The model presented in Table 2.1 distinguishes between three distinct types of human rights education with distinct approaches to content, pedagogy, and action. None of these forms of human rights education is mutually exclusive of the others, but rather each offers a way to conceptualize the vision and methodology of different versions of HRE. These forms generally respond to some perceived need in a particular educational system, program, or school. While the goals and objectives of HRE can embody aspects of any of the three approaches, I argue that the ideological orientations of most HRE initiatives are generally rooted in one of the following three categories: (1) Human Rights Education for Global Citizenship; (2) Human Rights Education for Coexistence; or (3) Human Rights Education for Transformative Action.

Human Rights Education for Global Citizenship seeks to provide learners with membership to an international community through fostering knowledge and skills related to universal values and standards. *Human Rights Education for Coexistence* focuses on the interpersonal and intergroup aspects of rights and is usually a strategy for tolerance utilized where conflict emerges not from absolute deprivation, but from ethnic or civil strife. The third approach, *Human Rights Education for Transformative Action*, usually

Table 2.1 Differentiated Ideological Orientations of HRE

Model	Content	Level of Affiliation	Underlying Ideology	Desired Outcome
HRE for Global Citizenship	* Information on International Covenants Norms/Standards * Human Rights (HR) as diplomacy and international relations * Emphasis on Civil and Political Rights	* Nation-States * Inter-governmental Agencies * Learners may have relatively privileged social position	HR as new global political order	International Awareness + Interdependence → Membership in International Community
HRE for Coexistence	* Information on Pluralism and Diversity * Conflict Resolution Techniques * HR as "learning to live together" * Emphasis on Right to Equality and Freedom from Discrimination	*Group * Multi-Ethnic Nation-State * Post-conflict settings * Learners may possess unequal social positions/privilege	HRE as healing and reconciliation	Inter-group Contact + Mutual Understanding → Social Cohesion
HRE for Transformative Action	* Historic and ongoing violations discussed * People's movements as part of HR struggles * Emphasis on instances of social inequality & discrimination * Economic and Social Rights * HRE as a critique of power & unequal power relations (local, national, global)	* Learners who may face exclusion/ rights abuses/ extreme poverty * Critical consciousness and agency for marginalized learners * For more privileged learners, solidarity with marginalized peoples across the globe	HRE as radical politics of inclusion and social justice	Activism + Participation → Social Change

involves learners who are marginalized from economic and political power and for whom HRE includes a significant process of understanding their own realities. This approach is most akin to Paulo Freire's (1970) process of developing a critical consciousness and what Meintjes (1997) terms a "critical human rights consciousness" (78).

In HRE scholarship, many programs appear to espouse all three outcomes and involve transformative action. Yet, as funding agencies promote—and national authorities adopt—human rights education, various definitions of HRE appear that are less critical of the state, dominant social structures, and relationships to power. No doubt, global citizenship, coexistence, and transformation are valuable goals in their own right. Still, distinguishing the forms of HRE can draw attention to the ways in which human rights education practices are inflected by local settings, funding availability, and ideology.

Human Rights Education for Global Citizenship

The first model, HRE for Global Citizenship, presents international standards as the ideal, repositioning learners as members of a global community instead of simply as national citizens. Content may include treaties and conventions, the words and practices of national and international leaders and movements, and a history of human rights. Values and skills that are imparted in such an approach include empathy and compassion. Resultant actions may include letter-writing, fundraising for services addressing basic needs of those less fortunate, and a "model UN" or other simulations that prepare learners for potential participation in such international arenas in the future.

This form of HRE seeks to cultivate vibrant global citizenship, a goal seen as beneficial on its own terms. There are many conceptualizations of education for global citizenship (e.g., Davies 2008; Noddings 2005; Oxfam 1997); most share an emphasis on interdependence, global knowledge, and a commitment to counter injustice wherever in the world it may take place. These principles are rooted in a cosmopolitan ethic that is often linked to universal notions of human rights, but also discussed vis-à-vis the interplay between global and local forces. For example, philosopher Kwame Anthony Appiah's (1997) notion of "rooted cosmopolitanism" acknowledges interdependence beyond one's own kin as well as the possibilities for mutual learning that diversity presents. Global citizenship, and arguably HRE initiatives that have this vision as their desired outcome, are aligned with cosmopolitanism and the increasingly de-territorialized perception of universal rights.

Scholars have also noted the worldwide increase in human rights content in textbooks around the globe in line with the rise in rights discourse in international fora. Ramirez, Suarez, and Meyer (2007) attribute this rise to globalization and changing conceptions of citizenship:

> The rise of human rights education is linked closely to processes of globalization over the period since the Second World War, and particularly in the most recent decades. A global society has been constructed and imagined during this period. This is a society in which individual persons are both entitled members and pro-active agents. Human rights education . . . reflects both this developing emphasis on world citizenship and the strong assumption of personal commitment required for global citizenship. (36)

The authors note that the rise in human rights education has matched an increasing emphasis on individual rights and personal agency in the global community. As such, HRE for Global Citizenship's emphasis on individual rights as part of an international community may or may not be perceived as a direct challenge to the state. Through the rise in cosmopolitanism and global citizenship in textbooks (Bromley 2009)—even if disconnected from contemporary local examples of rights issues—students interested in human rights will be introduced to a framework that can spur further investigation into concepts, movements, and local struggles.

Human Rights Education for Coexistence

HRE for Coexistence, instead, presents information related to "other-ed" or excluded groups, often in post-conflict settings, that may have been silenced in previous historical narratives in an effort to reexamine and come to terms with histories of violence. This approach emphasizes the role of minority rights and pluralism as part of a larger human rights framework (Fritzsche 2006). Information on each group is taught as a way of creating greater empathy and understanding. In some cases, educators may search for evidence of collaboration and cooperation rather than competition in the past to reframe historical understandings of intergroup conflict, recognizing the role that the teaching of history has played in inter-ethnic violence in various locales (Freedman et al., 2008; Setalvad 2010). Values and skills may be related to conflict transformation, respect for difference, mutual understanding, and dialogue. Action may include learning about other groups, intergroup events and interactions (such as inter-ethnic/religious encounter camps like Seeds of Peace), and exchanges for greater understanding across groups (van Woerkom 2004).

Initiatives promoting coexistence, whether labeled peace education or human rights education, generally draw upon the contact hypothesis, a theory developed by Gordon Allport (1954) in the field of social psychology. He argued that intergroup contact, operating within certain parameters, can play an important role in reducing prejudice and stereotypes. Allport noted that contact alone would not be enough to achieve positive changes, but that intergroup interactions could bring about desired effects when the two parties (a) held equal status, (b) cooperated toward common goals, and (c) participated in an institutional climate that valued integration. Scholars have built on Allport's theory over the past six decades suggesting various modifications, such as the need to prioritize individual rather than group characteristics so as not to reify difference (Hantzopoulos 2010; Miller and Brewer 1984); nonetheless, his ideas remain influential in guiding the philosophy of encounter camps, dialogue groups, integrated education, and post-conflict initiatives across the globe (e.g., Ohanyan and Lewis 2005; van Woerkom 2004; Vandeyar and Esakov 2007).

Human Rights Education for Transformative Action

HRE for Transformative Action reflects a politically radical approach to the analysis of historical and present conditions and the need for action to rectify the often-wide gap between current realities and human rights guarantees. HRE for Transformative Action is implicitly and explicitly concerned with relationships of power. As Indian legal scholar Upendra Baxi has noted, human rights (and human rights education) have long been characterized by the "continuing confrontation between emergent cultures of rights and entrenched cultures of power" (1997, 142). This concern with power and resultant asymmetries in relations translates into an analysis of how human rights norms and standards are often selectively respected based on communities' varied access to resources, representation, and influence.

Human Rights Education for Transformative Action is rooted in the concepts of agency and solidarity. For learners who may be victims of or witnesses to frequent abuses, this type of human rights education can foster a sense of transformative or strategic agency defined by educational scholars as a larger critique of one's social realities and a willingness to act upon them (Apple 1982; Aronowitz and Giroux 1993; Freire 1970; Giroux 1988; Noguera 2003). For those who may not be directly affected by abuses, or who may witness abuses but hold some relative privilege in a given situation (e.g., boys versus girls from a marginalized group), HRE for Transformative Action may foster a sense of coalitional agency, defined by scholars Karma Chavez and Cindy Griffin (in regards to cross-cultural feminist solidarity) as a relational process in which social change happens collectively and "necessitates seeing people, history, and culture as inextricably bound to one another" (Chavez and Griffin 2009, 8). This might also be referred to as solidarity with victims and willingness to act on their behalf guided by the belief that injustice faced by any target group represents a threat to the society as whole, as Chapter Six will explore.

HRE for Transformative Action is primarily concerned with understanding how power relationships are structured, and the possibilities for greater collaboration across groups that might effectively result in greater respect for human rights. Meintjes (1997) notes, "Human rights are inherently about relationships; and whatever their nature, whether they concern the power relations between individuals, groups, society, and/or the state, they are inevitably always dynamic and relative" (74). As such, for the two different constituencies of marginalized and privileged learners (that are not static and may change from situation to situation), this type of HRE prioritizes an analysis of power and how one might act in the face of injustice. Thus, content might include examples of social injustice that learners collect from their own homes or communities; values and skills might include solidarity with victims, equality, and justice; and actions might include collective protest, intervening in situations of abuse, and joining NGOs or social movements to advance greater participation and inclusion.

CONCLUSION

Ideology, constituency, and objectives offer rich ways of schematizing the varied forms of HRE. Global citizenship, coexistence, and transformative action are all noble goals, but the different values and ends reflect important differences in location and relationships to power that are worth foregrounding. Given increasing socioeconomic and political inequalities, multiple forms of HRE may likely operate within a single nation-state. Since the 1990s, international mandates have combined with pressure from local non-governmental organizations and activists in India engaged in HRE to advocate for greater policy action on human rights. Certainly in India, a variety of national-level and local initiatives, reflecting the different ideological approaches to HRE discussed above, coexist, as the next chapter explores.

Chapter Three

Education and Human Rights in India: Policy, Pedagogy, and Practice

Human rights education (HRE) in India unfolds in the context of larger educational structures, not to mention the country's uneven development. This chapter first explores India's strategies to ensure access, quality, and equity in primary and secondary schooling since its independence from colonial rule in 1947. The chapter also explores unequal levels of social and economic development across the states from which data were collected and among social groups (low-income women, Dalits, Adivasis) that have significantly lower levels of educational attainment. The second half of this chapter charts the landscape of HRE in India and the different institutions and actors involved in its rise in educational policy and practice. The data presented on policy documents and positions toward HRE come from interviews with national-level officials, observations, and extensive document review during the research period (2008–2010).

INDIAN EDUCATION: FROM HUMAN CAPITAL TO HUMAN RIGHTS

Education has figured prominently in discussions of growth, progress, and national development since independence, influenced by Mahatma Gandhi's vision for schooling in a sovereign India.[1] The first Prime Minister, Jawaharlal Nehru, was faced with a largely illiterate populace—only 16.7 percent of all Indians and 7.9 percent of women could read or write basic texts at the time;

as such, he promoted education significantly, to the point that education is enshrined in the first Constitution (1950) as a "directive principle," guiding the central and state governments in formulating policy (Premi 2002). The prioritization of education resulted in massive school construction, village enrollment drives, free basic education for children, and the development of vocational education and literacy campaigns for adults. Nehru's vision for creating world-class higher educational institutions also resulted in the expansion of tertiary education, most notably the Indian Institutes of Technology, predicated on the belief that "scientists and technologists of the highest calibre . . . would engage in research, design and development to help build the nation . . ." (as cited in Murali 2003). Inspired by the belief that an educated citizenry would drive economic growth, national cohesion, and self-reliance, the emphasis on primary, secondary, tertiary, and adult education was a fundamental part of Nehru's brand of socialism and resonated with global discourses of schooling as an integral factor in human capital development (Becker 1964).

Under subsequent governments after Nehru's tenure (1947–1964), enrollment rates grew throughout the 1970s and 1980s. Schooling was a state responsibility in the years following independence, but in 1976, a constitutional amendment made education a "concurrent" responsibility of states and the central or national government. In 1986, the National Policy on Education (NPE) was adopted, which resulted in various initiatives that sought to utilize technology and equip all schools with the basic classroom materials needed for teaching (e.g., Operation Blackboard) (NPE 1986). The National Literacy Mission was also launched to combat adult illiteracy, particularly of women, nationwide. Some states in India had been providing "mid-day meals" to children at schools since the 1960s, though nation-wide adoption of the program commenced only after a landmark 2001 Supreme Court decision provided a legal entitlement to the right to food in primary schools (Asia-Pacific Human Rights Network 2002).

Globally, the right to education was referenced in UN documents as early as 1948 and began to be discussed as a basic human right in international meetings and conferences in the 1990s and 2000s. Drawing on international agreement around accomplishing universal primary enrollment, notably the consensus achieved in the Millennium Development Goals and Education for All Conferences (1990 and 2000), India's domestic *Sarva Shiksha Abhiyan* (SSA) program, first announced in 2000, has sought to eradicate all obstacles to primary school access (Iyengar 2010). Significant activities under this campaign have included teacher training, district resource centers, free materials and supplies to marginalized children, construction of new classrooms, and in some states, the recruitment of para-professional teachers (UNESCO 2004). In 2010, the Right to Education (RTE) Act came into force, shifting education from a nonbinding "directive principle" to an enforceable "fundamental right" in Indian constitutional law and providing all children aged 6–14 the right to a free and compulsory education in a school within 1 to 3 kilometers of their home.

Despite these advances in educational enrollment and attainment in India, problems related to access to schools, quality of education, and equal opportunity for all children remain. India leads the world in the number of illiterate adults at 270 million and in the number of out-of-school children at 8 million (UNESCO 2010). India's high absentee rate in schools means that on any given day, an average of 20–25 percent of teachers are absent (Kingdon and Banerji 2009; Kremer et al., 2005). Perhaps unsurprisingly, a recent study found that just 66 percent of sixth standard (or grade) students across India could read a standard two-level story (ASER 2009), as Table 3.1 further details.

Nation-wide, literacy rates differ significantly by gender. According to India's most recent census (GOI 2011), the male literacy rate is 82.1 percent, while for women it is 65.5 percent. The high dropout rate of young women, especially as they reach secondary school, may contribute to this sizeable differential between male and female literacy rates. Insufficient or nonexistent latrines, particularly as girls hit puberty, is a significant cause of drop out. In

Table 3.1 Literacy, Poverty, and Dropout Rates for Dalits and Adivasis in India

Education, Poverty, and Social Exclusion			
Group	Literacy	Below National Poverty Line	Drop out before Class 8
All Indians	74.0%	27.5%	48.8%
Male	82.1%		
Female	65.5%		
"Scheduled Castes" or Dalits	54.7%	36.8%	56.2%
Male	66.6%		
Female	41.9%		
"Scheduled Tribes" or Adivasis	47.1%	47.2%	62.7%
Male	59.2%		
Female	34.8%		

Sources: Government of India Census (GOI 2011); Indian Planning Commission 2006; UNDP 2009; UNESCO 2005; and UNICEF 2010

fact, UNICEF reports that just 54 percent of schools across India had a separate girls' toilet that was usable for children in standards one through eight (UNICEF 2010).

Additional school-based human rights issues include the still-common practices of corporal punishment, discrimination based on caste or gender, and corruption in schools (Nambissan 1995; Nambissan and Sedwal 2002; NCPCR 2008). Corporal punishment was outlawed at the national level under the National Policy on Education and the Right to Education Act, but not all states have abided by these laws despite considerable efforts, such as those by the National Commission for Protection of Child Rights, to seek their compliance. Further violating children's rights, students repeatedly mentioned forms of corruption, such as the extraction of money by teachers and headmasters, the siphoning off of government-allotted funds intended for students' mid-day meals and/or uniforms by headmasters and teachers, and sexual abuse in schools without report or sanction.

Additionally, absent significant financial resources for securing fee-based extra lessons ("coaching" or "tuitions"), textbooks and exams often proved difficult and/or irrelevant for low-income, low-caste, and rural students in India. Scholar Prema Clarke (1997) has noted the "significant presence of the 'high culture' of the center and a concomitant absence of the physical and sociocultural world of the periphery within textbooks" (134). Textbooks and exams are often "normed" to middle-class, urban students and fail to consider the realities of students living outside these conditions. Clarke argues that these situations limit the interest of marginalized children in schooling as well as the ability of their parents to appreciate the relevance and benefit of education.

India's examination-driven system also results in fierce competition for scores and resulting admissions to further studies. One student interviewed who was preparing for his twelfth standard exams instructively noted, "I've drank the book, now I'm ready to vomit it" (interview, February 2009). The emphasis on literal and figurative regurgitation of content for high-stakes examinations limits the institutional space for other forms and functions of education, such as human rights learning.

Structure of Education

The structure and organization of schooling in India also colors students' experiences of the process. While education is technically a "concurrent" subject jointly funded and administered by the state and national governments, in practice, 90 percent of schools are operated by each of India's 28 states, which determine their own curricula. The other 10 percent consist of centrally-run schools for government employees, model schools in each district, and private schools affiliated to different national "boards" that administer their exams (Dev et al., 2007).

The Indian educational system categorizes students into classes or standards one through twelve, generally grouping them by age. Class one is open to students at six years of age, though child labor, late enrollment, and other factors often result in over-aged children in schools. Schooling is further divided into four stages: Primary, classes or standards one through five; Upper Primary, classes six through eight; Secondary, classes nine and ten; and Higher or Senior Secondary, eleventh and twelfth standard, though some state variation exists.

Schools are also categorized according to their management: government, government-aided (private, but almost fully funded by the government), and private schools that are not assisted by the government (Dev et al., 2007). Many religious organizations manage government-aided schools that are low-cost, government-subsidized, and that follow the state curriculum. Human rights education programs operate primarily in government and government-aided schools, though a handful of elite private schools have also begun to adopt the reform as will be discussed in subsequent chapters. Given the primacy of states in administering education in India, exploring the regional patterns of educational development in distinct states is important to understanding the integration of HRE into Indian schooling.

UNEVEN DEVELOPMENT

Education is one aspect of uneven development across the diverse socioeconomic, language, caste, religious, and regional groups of India. Human rights education programs of NGOs generally target marginalized youth from low-income backgrounds, Dalits (formerly called "untouchables"), and Adivasi or indigenous communities (referred to in India as "tribal" groups). In Tamil Nadu, a state-wide department (the Adi Dravidar Welfare or "ADW" Department) overseeing educational strategies to increase the enrollment, retention, and attainment among Dalit students adopted the three-year human rights course developed by the Institute of Human Rights Education in the over 1,000 schools it operates.[2] Similarly, the state-wide Ministries overseeing "tribal affairs" in both Tamil Nadu and Orissa implemented IHRE's course to be delivered to all schools under their charge. These efforts correspond with international trends to offer HRE to marginalized groups, whether low-income, minority (Mihr 2006), or refugee (INEE 2006) populations as a strategy of either "rehabilitation" or "empowerment."

Dalits in Schools and Society

Of India's total population, Dalits, or members of "Scheduled Castes," constitute 16 percent (approximately 185 million) and face considerable cultural, political, and social exclusion (HRW 2007a). After independence, members of certain castes considered "untouchables" and historically subject to severe forms of discrimination were placed on a "schedule" for certain compensatory measures, and as such, are considered "Scheduled Castes." The term "Dalits," though literally translated as "broken people," was reclaimed by nineteenth-century social activist Jyotirao Phule (Naik 2003) and others as a form of self-definition and resistance, and is widely used by scholars and human rights activists. The majority of Dalits live on less than one dollar per day (Thornton and Thornton 2006) and still face considerable discrimination in accessing resources and opportunities for social mobility. Human Rights Watch (2007a) finds that,

> Entrenched discrimination violates Dalits' rights to education, health, housing, property, freedom of religion, free choice of employment, and equal treatment before the law. Dalits also suffer routine violations of their right to life and security of person through state-sponsored or -sanctioned acts of violence, including torture. (p. 1)

India's Constitution and subsequent Acts of Parliament, specifically the Prevention of Atrocities Act (1989), have made caste discrimination illegal, though it continues to permeate most aspects of social life in India to varying degrees.

In schools, scholars have found a considerably strong "hidden curriculum of discrimination" that includes teacher involvement in or unwillingness to condemn incidents where Dalit children are forced to sit and/or eat separately (sometimes outside of the classroom), are denied access to school materials, and/or are beaten up by their higher-caste peers (Nambissan and Sedwal 2002, 84). This research found several instances of caste discrimination reported by students related to separation, being singled out for punishment, as well as being forced to clean toilets or other school premises while higher-caste peers were in class learning. In one severe case related during this study, a teacher threw hot tea at a Dalit child because he had touched the cup the teacher was to drink out of, an act believed to cause the higher-caste teacher to become "polluted." Notions of "pollution" and "purity" drive many practices of caste-based discrimination related to maintaining physical distance, relegation of "impure" tasks to Dalits, and residential segregation (HRW 1999). These were especially found in rural areas and in states such as Karnataka, Tamil Nadu, and Gujarat where caste discrimination has been well documented by human rights groups (HRW 2007a; Navsarjan Trust and RFK Center for Justice and Human Rights 2010). Perhaps as a result, the dropout rate for Dalit children before class eight is 55.2 percent as opposed to the national average of 48.8 percent, as seen in Table 3.1 (UNICEF 2010). While the types of discrimination faced by Dalit students in schools largely relate to their treatment by students and teachers of higher castes, Adivasi or tribal students attend remote schools and face distinct challenges to educational and social participation.

Adivasi Communities

"Scheduled Tribes" or Adivasis,[3] translated as "original inhabitants," comprise roughly 8 percent of India's total population. The Government of India recognizes 533 tribes, 62 of them located in the eastern state of Orissa, under this grouping. Adivasi communities "do not strictly fall within the [Hindu] caste hierarchy" since they have distinct practices and customs (Das et al., 2010, 2). In Orissa, however, there has been considerable violence in recent years between Hindu and Christian fundamentalists seeking to "convert" and claim tribal communities under their respective banner (HRW 2007b). Additionally, historic disenfranchisement and a combination of government and corporate takeover of collectively owned lands has been a factor in decisions by Adivasis to join movements, such as the armed Naxalite (Maoist) movement (Roy 2010). Violence by these groups as well as that of state-supported paramilitary forces seeking to eradicate them color the experiences of many Adivasi communities, particularly in the states of Bihar, Jharkhand, Chhattisgarh, Andhra Pradesh, Orissa, and West Bengal.

The national Ministry of Tribal Affairs (constituted in 1999) and several state-level departments, commissions, and ministries coordinate special educational services for Adivasi children, among other activities. These services include residential schools, extra tutoring, scholarships, and the provision of school supplies and bicycles (Ministry of Tribal Affairs 2010). Additional efforts to promote education have been hampered by low literacy rates among Adivasi communities as noted in Table 3.1, and the 62.9 percent dropout rate before completion of eight years of schooling (compared to 48.8 percent nation-wide) (UNICEF 2010). Recent efforts to increase enrollment have begun to bear fruit: in 1983, only 8 percent of Adivasis had any post-primary schooling whereas in recent years, this number has tripled (Das et al., 2010). Given the concentration of Adivasi communities in certain states and the divergent development indicators across India, I now turn to a socioeconomic and demographic review of the states from which data were collected for this study.

Education and Development Across Indian States

As suggested earlier, India is characterized by severely uneven development. According to the United Nations Human Development Index (2010), India ranks 119 out of 169 countries. If states are disaggregated, a state like Kerala would rank seventy-seventh in the world in terms of health, literacy, and social development (Stanford 2010). Yet, according to the UN's recent "Multidimensional Poverty Index," eight Indian states would contain more numbers of the "absolute poor" (421 million) than all of sub-Saharan Africa combined (UN 2010); notably, these eight states also have a substantial number of Adivasis.

While human rights education is offered at the national level through textbook reforms and separately as a course in 18 states, this study focused on those that had been offering instruction for at least three years and reached a cross-section of geographic communities. Table 3.2 offers demographic information on the six states from which the majority of data presented come: Gujarat, Orissa, Karnataka, Kerala, Tamil Nadu, and West Bengal.

Table 3.2 demonstrates the range of human development across states of varying size and composition. The inverse correlation between those living beneath the national poverty line and the literacy rate is quite strong; of the selected states, Kerala has the fewest residents living in poverty and the

Table 3.2 Poverty and Literacy Rates Across States and Social Groups

Demographic Information on Selected States[4]				
State	Population	Dalits/SC	Adivasis/ST	Poverty Rate	Literacy Rate
Gujarat	60.4 million	7.1%	14.8%	16.8%	79.3%
Karnataka	61.1 million	16.2%	6.6%	25.0%	75.6%
Kerala	33.4 million	9.8%	1.1%	15.0%	93.9%
Orissa	41.9 million	16.5%	22.2%	46.4%	73.5%
Tamil Nadu	72.1 million	19.0%	1.1%	22.5%	80.3%
West Bengal	91.3 million	23.0%	5.5%	24.7%	77.1%

Note: Poverty figures represent those living below the respective state's poverty line.

Sources: Government of India Census (GOI 2001, 2011); Ministry of Social Justice (2005); Ministry of Tribal Affairs (2010)

Table 3.3 Indicators of Educational Quality Across Selected States

Educational Quality Data for Selected States			
State	Primary-Upper Primary Transition Rate	Class 6 student could read class 2 text	Teacher Absentee rate
Gujarat	91.6%	59.1%	17.0%
Karnataka	96.1%	54.0%	21.7%
Kerala	95.9%	82.9%	21.2%
Orissa	84.1%	61.7%	23.4%
Tamil Nadu	98.6%	48.8%	21.3%
West Bengal	69.9%	66.5%	24.7%

Sources: DISE 2009; ASER 2009, 2010; Kremer et al., 2005

highest literacy rates, while Orissa offers the converse with 73.5 percent literacy and nearly half the state's population living in extreme poverty. Given the overrepresentation of marginalized populations (Dalits and Adivasis) among the absolute poor, states with a larger proportion of these groups also fare worse.

Tremendous diversity also exists in educational quality. The 2009 Right to Education Act, which took effect in 2010, specifies children's right to a "quality education." Table 3.3 offers data on educational quality, evidenced by common indicators, including rates of transition from the primary to the upper primary level (the site of most HRE) (DISE 2009), the percentage of class six students who could read a class-two level text in the state language (ASER 2009), and average teacher absentee rates in government schools by state (Kremer et al., 2005). As mentioned earlier, the national average for teacher absenteeism is 24.8 percent, ranging from a low of 14.6 percent in Maharashtra to a high of 41.9 percent in Jharkhand.[5] Regular oversight and school inspections have been cited as ways to alleviate absenteeism, though the simple failure of teachers to appear remains a major challenge (Kremer et al., 2005).

Most international and domestic focus has been on access, though, arguably, the quality of instruction poses one of the largest challenges to keeping children in school. Table 3.3 provides useful data on educational quality, detailing what happens after children actually reach school. For example, despite a 96.1 percent transition rate from primary to upper primary in Karnataka, only 54 percent of sixth standard students could read a basic standard two-level text.[6] Human rights education overlays the challenges to access, equity, and quality in schools across the states in which it has been introduced.

THE EMERGENCE AND LANDSCAPE OF HUMAN RIGHTS EDUCATION IN INDIA

Human rights education has evolved significantly over the past three decades in policy discussions and at the level of practice in India, primarily with non-governmental organizations adopting HRE as a strategy for raising awareness and fostering a critical consciousness among marginalized youth. The orientation, scope, and intensity of different initiatives tell interesting stories about goals and impact. Indeed, not all HRE looks the same.

As I detail in the remainder of this chapter, discussions of HRE have permeated virtually all Indian national entities concerned with education and with human rights, such as the University Grants Commission (UGC); the National Council for Teacher Education (NCTE); the National Council of Educational Research and Training (NCERT); and the National Human Rights Commission (NHRC). The role of each of these institutions varies and includes a mix of regulatory powers, policy setting, accreditation, and resource provision. Each government institution responds to different pressures for HRE-related reforms, but all largely follow the HRE for Global Citizenship model (as discussed in Chapter Two), energized by UN and international mandates that prioritize human rights education. These efforts will be contrasted in subsequent chapters with NGO initiatives—usually more limited in scope—to highlight the range of what constitutes HRE in India at present.

Debates on Human Rights Education in India

HRE in India is influenced by several debates and each shapes how agencies and organizations approach the reform.[7]

Human Rights as Western. First, some skeptics contend that human rights are Western concepts; further, some argue that human rights are therefore unsuited to application in India. Indeed, each initiative responds to this debate in some form or another. Nobel laureate Amartya Sen disputes "the claim that 'Asian values' are particularly indifferent to freedom, or that attaching importance to freedom is quintessentially a 'Western' value" (Sen 1999, 244). Sen notes that often those that defend a cultural relativist approach to human rights are the very same people who benefit from power asymmetries and social inequalities. Nonetheless, HRE efforts in India engage a variety of perspectives and approaches to countering the claim that human rights are foreign.

Rights vs. Duties Education. Second, some question whether rights or duties should be the focus of instruction. In line with the Hindu concept of *dharma,* "duties" and/or "values" education is a preferred curricular intervention for many. The definition of these duties and their relationship with human rights differs widely among individuals and institutions. Similarly, some stakeholders argued against teaching human rights as a separate subject because they believed that teaching about discrimination would lead children to *becoming* prejudiced since they would purportedly then see differences they had not before. Proponents of teaching HRE utilizing case studies of violations countered that children were not immune from larger structures of social stratification.

Separate or Integrated Subject. Third, many debate whether HRE should be a separate subject or integrated into existing requirements; a corollary of this debate also explores whether human rights knowledge should be evaluated through examinations or not. Not surprisingly, different entities espouse various positions on the issue. While proponents of integrating human rights content across the curriculum argue that integration is the best way to foster a culture of respect for rights, opponents see the dilution of human rights subject matter if not focused on separately. Many of those advocating for human rights to be included as a separate subject support the integration of rights-friendly content into other subjects across the curriculum as well.

In order to conceptualize the diverse types of HRE policy, pedagogy, and practice-based interventions, Figure 3.1 charts each initiative in terms of its scope and intensity. Scope refers to the reach of the intervention from the school and community to regional and national levels. Intensity is defined by the form that the intervention takes: low intensity is characterized by non-mandatory, self-directed instruction and continues toward high intensity where trained educators offer sustained instruction over at least one year in human rights concepts. While these programs may be self-selecting at some level (either by the individual in the case of higher secondary or university courses, or by the school that has chosen to introduce HRE), once enrolled, instruction is a core component of study and is an integral part of the regular life of the school, college, or university.

Figure 3.1 also groups initiatives into different levels. Scope and intensity are often inversely related: the more people affected by an intervention, the more likely that intensity declines. However, more intense contact, instruction, and engagement are seen primarily in initiatives of limited scope. This study focuses to a large extent on the Institute of Human Rights Education because of the sheer scope and intensity of the organization's programs, with

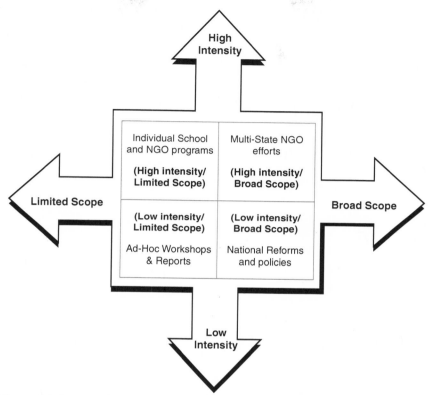

Figure 3.1 Scope and Intensity of HRE Initiatives in India

operations in nearly 4,000 schools in 18 Indian states (see Appendix B for a list of selected other NGO and school-based efforts).

NATIONAL-LEVEL INITIATIVES

Nearly every national body charged with education and human rights in India has engaged the concept of HRE. Moreover, recent legislative victories around education and governance (such as the Right to Education Act and the Right to Information Bill)[8] as well as discussions of curricular reform have all been framed in human rights terms. National initiatives of government institutions are largely rooted in the HRE for Global Citizenship paradigm discussed in Chapter Two and, arguably, are a product of a closer integration of India into the international community (and its normative, political, and discursive emphasis on human rights). The greater incorporation of

human rights into Indian policy discourse is reflected in the work of four
national government bodies: the University Grants Commission (UGC);
the National Council for Teacher Education (NCTE); the National Council
of Educational Research and Training (NCERT); and the National Human
Rights Commission (NHRC).

The University Grants Commission (UGC)

*HRE is acquiring greater importance in the changing national and global
scenario in the wake of globalization. This new context may give rise to [the]
arbitrary exercise of power by organs of the State resulting in legitimacy crisis.
The society should have enough of democratic potential where people, particularly the youth, would play a positive role in facing the new challenges. . . . HRE
can create the necessary moral, intellectual, and democratic resources for this
purpose. . . . Human rights are in themselves ends as well as means. They are
ends in terms of standards to be attained and are means as they enable and
empower the people to use the rights to enjoy the rights. It is both an area of academic enquiry and also a part of every day life experience of humans as members
of a society.*

(UGC 2007b)

The University Grants Commission of India (UGC)—India's national body
charged with oversight of university education—has engaged with the field of
human rights for over three decades.[9] In 1980, the UGC established a committee on human rights education, which, by 1983, prepared a blueprint for the
teaching of human rights in universities and led to changes in legal education.
In 1985, additional guidelines on human rights were prepared that applied to
other subjects and various levels of higher education (Begum 2008). Since then,
various initiatives have been sponsored for university courses in human rights,
special programs, and funding for research that explores rights concepts. In the
late 1990s and in collaboration with the National Human Rights Commission,
the UGC began to develop the infrastructure for the formal teaching of human
rights in universities; this move figured prominently in India's Action Plan
submitted in 1995 to the United Nations as part of the UN Decade for Human
Rights Education (1995–2004). Subsequently, the UGC developed guidelines
and distributed funds for human rights education for the first time in 1997. In
2001, the agency released a model curriculum for colleges and universities on
"Human Rights and Duties Education" (NHRC 2007).

The UGC, as differentiated from other national bodies (such as NCTE,
NCERT, and NHRC), has a mandate for policy-setting and regulation, as well

as a grant-making role for developing new content areas in Indian higher education. The UGC's emphasis on human rights education since the mid-1980s —which has expanded through the interests and priorities of subsequent chairpersons and officials—has resulted in the establishment of various centers and initiatives across the country related to human rights. In 2006–2007, a total of 114 universities and colleges were awarded grants from the UGC under the human rights education program, with funds being used for a range of activities including seminars, centers, undergraduate and graduate courses, research and publication, and full-fledged degree programs in human rights.

Recent developments in HRE at the tertiary level have moved beyond the mere memorization of important treaties and conventions by students in an attempt to develop a greater depth of engagement by the nation's university students. Notably, the XIth Plan guidelines for the UGC's strategic foci heavily emphasized issues of human rights and social exclusion as integral components of human development (UGC 2007b). As highlighted by the XIth Plan Guidelines in the epigraph at the outset of this section, HRE is conceptualized as a way of holding the state accountable and as a form of empowerment for those whose rights have been historically denied (with specific mention of women, Dalits, Adivasi communities, and religious minorities). Linked to UGC's emphasis on HRE is its establishment of Centers for the Study of Social Exclusion and Inclusive Policy (UGC 2002). These centers deal with human rights themes such as caste and religious discrimination, establishing degree programs, course offerings, and research, with added attention to creating links with civil society organizations and providing short-term courses for professionals. To date, the UGC has more than 30 centers focusing on issues of social exclusion. Additionally, there are more than 70 Centers for Women's Studies (with significant rights-based content) supported by the UGC that have been operating since the 1970s. Depending on their orientation and leadership, these centers vary in their programmatic approach from HRE for Global Citizenship to HRE for Transformative Action, as discussed in Chapter Two.

Despite the significant advances toward human rights education at the university level, challenges primarily revolve around the marketability of coursework and degrees in human rights and the limited training of professors in the field. In terms of professional demand for training in human rights, the Dean of one of India's law schools noted, "We have a Human Rights Center here and different faculty are members. We started three years back with a post-graduate diploma in human rights, but it's not very popular with students. . . . We have abandoned it now because students are not getting enough opportunity in the job market with it" (interview, July 2009). The sustainability of UGC's initiative is threatened by limited perceived and actual labor market benefits from a diploma (or degree) in human rights, as may be the case in other parts of the globe as well.[10]

The second challenge to the appeal of HRE and its implementation at the university level is the preparation of educators to effectively teach the subject. In the case where professors are already interested and committed to human rights, there have been exceptional programs and advances. For instance, a professor from St. Joseph's College in Tamil Nadu noted that he used support from the UGC initiative on HRE to hold a symposium on drawing out human rights themes from Tamil literature and subsequently, he published a book on the subject. HRE was less successful in institutions where professors lacked interest or background; indeed, one professor noted, "In my college, the teachers who are teaching human rights have never attended any training program. They are insufficiently trained to offer courses in human rights" (interview, January 2009). Despite these shortcomings, the institutional emphasis on human rights—and national funds available to establish centers, research programs, and new courses—suggest an opening for human rights to establish itself as an integral component of higher education in India.

UGC's initiatives have responded to larger debates about human rights in various ways. In the XIth Plan document, reference is made to three aspects of human rights: moral, legal, and contextual. The moral dimension is linked to the 1948 UN Universal Declaration of Human Rights (UDHR); the legal is rooted in the Indian Constitution and the need to enforce the rule of law uniformly; and the contextual component refers to the need to utilize HRE to overcome discrimination based on gender, caste, Adivasi status, and religion unique to the Indian subcontinent. Hence, a combination of "Asian" and "Western" referents are cited for human rights.

In terms of the debate on duties versus rights, shifts can be seen in the UGC's stance over time. When a model curriculum was prepared in 2001, the UGC initiative was titled "Human Rights and Duties Education." The 2007 XIth Plan Guidelines, however, subsumes duties under "Human Rights Education," but retains its presence; the document identifies three complementary subcomponents of human rights education: human rights and duties, human rights and values, and human rights and human development. The latest UGC document also differs from the stance of other agencies in its proposal for differentiated emphasis on duties and rights for dominant and subordinate social groups respectively.[11] The guidelines state the following:

> In a society which emphasized on duties for centuries [sic], rights education comes as a correction of historical distortions. The violation of rights could be corrected only when the privileged persons are reminded of their duties towards

the marginalized sections, and the marginalized sections are gradually empowered through rights education. HRE at these levels would extend to such areas as gender equity, caste and community relations, majority-minority conflicts, "forward-backward" dilemma and North-South power relations. In short, all power relations have to be humanized and democratized through restructuring of rights and duties. (UGC 2007b)

The XIth Plan's view that HRE, if implemented, could and should lead to a reframing of power relations makes it unlike most other Indian policy documents that tend toward global citizenship rather than radical shifts in societal relationships.

The documents prepared by UGC also address the debate about separate or integrated teaching about rights by offering additional workshops, programs, and coursework on human rights, and suggest a course on human rights for students in all disciplines, which would integrate HRE into other courses of study. While in some nations, teacher education falls under higher education oversight more broadly, in India, teacher training is the purview of the National Council for Teacher Education.

National Council for Teacher Education (NCTE)

The National Council for Teacher Education (NCTE) has been discussing human rights, in some way, since the late 1980s. NCTE was established in 1973 as an advisory body for the national/central and state governments on teacher education, but it expanded to become a statutory body that regulated teacher education institutions nationwide in 1995 (NCTE 2010). While not a curricular development body per se, the NCTE oversees and sets broad frameworks for the pre- and in-service training of India's 6 million teachers (MHRD 2009) and more than 2,500 teacher-training institutions and university departments of education (NCTE 2010; Panda 2001).

NCTE issues a National Curriculum Framework for Teacher Education approximately every decade to emphasize the values, skills, methods, and approaches teachers should be equipped with through their education. In recent decades, human rights, equality, and social action have been highlighted as key priority areas (see Table 3.4).

In the 1970s when India's economic and political landscape was characterized by protectionism and extensive central government regulation of private industry, secular and Gandhian values were emphasized in educational policy. While some values, such as civic responsibility and national unity persisted across the decades, the 1990s and 2000s introduced environmental

Table 3.4 Excerpts from National Curriculum Frameworks for Teacher Education[11] (1978, 1988, 1998, and 2009; *emphasis added*)

1978: "[The purposes of teacher education are] (i) to develop *Gandhian values of education* such as *non-violence, truthfulness, self-discipline, self-reliance, dignity of labor* . . . [and] (ii) to develop an understanding of the objectives of school education in the Indian context and awareness of the role of the school in achieving the goals of *building up a democratic, secular and socialist society*."

1988: "[The objectives of teacher education are] (i) to develop in students qualities of *democratic citizenship, tolerance, concern for others, cooperation, responsibility, commitment to social justice*; (ii) To promote *environmental consciousness, scientific temper*; and (iii) To understand social, cultural and moral values oriented towards the *unity and integration of our people— democracy, secularism,* . . . *civic responsibility*."

1998: "[The objectives of teacher education are] (i) to promote capabilities for inculcating *national values* enshrined in the Constitution of India; (ii) To sensitize teachers towards the promotion of social cohesion, international *understanding and protection of human rights and child rights*; (iii) To sensitize teachers and teacher educators about emerging issues such as *environment, ecology, population, gender equality*, etc."

2009: "[In terms of teacher education], we need to reconceptualise citizenship training in terms of *human rights and approaches of critical pedagogy*; emphasize *environment and its protection, living in harmony with oneself and with the natural and social environment*; promote *peace, democratic way of life, constitutional values of equality, justice, liberty, fraternity, secularism, caring values* . . . *and zeal for social reconstruction*."

awareness, gender equality, and human rights as key objectives of national education. This shift toward greater emphasis on human rights emerged around the time of India's integration into the global economy starting with economic liberalization in 1991. Scholars have noted worldwide the adoption of human rights language in policy and textbooks, particularly after the end of the Cold War when civil and political rights were prioritized in narrating the demise of communist rule in the Soviet Union and Eastern Europe (Ramirez, Suarez, and Meyer 2007; Meyer, Bromley-Martin, and Ramirez 2010).

In line with larger priority areas, NCTE also develops modules for teacher educators periodically. While human rights has never been (and is not slated to be) a mandatory subject for teachers, in 1996—in line with the UN Decade for Human Rights Education's recommendations and growing attention to the issue of teacher training in human rights—NCTE developed a five-unit "self-learning module for teacher educators" entitled "Human Rights Education." Each of the five units (approximately 20 pages each) covered the following topics and asked teacher educators to "check your progress" in sections throughout the module:

Unit 1. Human Rights and Teacher Training
Unit 2. Human Rights Education and the Elementary Level Curriculum
Unit 3. Human Rights Education and the Secondary Level Curriculum
Unit 4. Mechanisms for Enforcement of Human Rights
Unit 5. Rights of the Girl Child

In 1998, four more modules were added for the second volume, and the title of the initiative shifted slightly to "Human Rights and National Values for Teacher Educators," suggesting perhaps an accommodation to larger debates about prioritizing duties over rights. The additional units emphasized the following:

Unit 6. Rights of the Child
Unit 7. Democracy and Education
Unit 8. Egalitarianism and Education: the Indian Experience
Unit 9. Secularism in Education

The chairman's foreword to the nine-part series noted that "the importance of the teacher educator as a carrier of positive social messages cannot be overemphasized" (NCTE 1996, 1). These modules were made available to the 35,000 teacher educators in India's training colleges as were videos and occasional non-mandatory workshops on the topic. In 2003, NCTE partnered with the National Human Rights Commission to publish a handbook titled *Discrimination based on sex, caste, disability and religion* for teacher educators to identify and eradicate discriminatory practices in teaching and learning contexts.

While the NCTE's self-directed modules and handbooks undoubtedly provide important, albeit optional, resources for teacher educators, human rights content in state-level courses is also significant to the extent that the development of teacher and student curriculum is a state-level responsibility. The integration of human rights concepts into the compulsory curriculum of state-level teacher syllabi has not occurred as substantially as projected in the successive National Curriculum Frameworks for Teacher Education highlighted in Table 3.4. Of India's 28 states, only 13 have required content related to human rights under the topics of "human rights," "children's rights," "gender equality," "constitutional rights," "right to education," and "equal opportunity."

NCTE's initiatives on human rights have engaged a variety of debates discussed earlier. First, NCTE's series of modules on HRE emphasizes international as well as domestic constitutional standards for human rights. NCTE's shifting focus to include "national values" as part of human rights in the second volume suggests a correlation and complementarity between the two areas without a priority being placed on either one. Here, NCTE also "indigenizes" human rights—tailoring the concept to the local context—by correlating rights with those values espoused in national documents. Additionally, NCTE's activities suggest that the Council has pursued a supplemental approach to human rights, keeping the subject separate and non-mandatory for teachers, though the Director of NCTE at the time of this research highlighted his commitment to introducing all teachers to human rights and not just those individuals preparing to teach human rights content in civics or history courses (interview, October 2009).

Similarly, the most recent National Curriculum Framework for Teacher Education makes a constructive attempt to challenge the conventional emphasis on memorization of exam-related content. If integrated fully (and much training is needed in this area), children would arguably experience respect for their rights in ways more meaningful than simple content instruction on the history and international standards of human rights. The National Council of Educational Research and Training (NCERT) has also prioritized innovative methods in recent frameworks and guidelines.

The National Council of Educational Research and Training (NCERT)

The greatest national challenge for education is to strengthen our participatory democracy and the values enshrined in the Constitution. Meeting this challenge implies that we make quality and social justice the central theme of curricular reform. Citizenship training has been an important aspect of formal education. Today, it needs to be boldly reconceptualised in terms of the discourse of universal human rights and the approaches associated with critical pedagogy.

(NCERT 2005, 9)

Since its establishment in 1961, NCERT has served in an advisory capacity to states and the national government on educational policy, quality, and teacher preparation.[12] NCERT prints model textbooks (which many states adopt wholly or partially, translate, or otherwise utilize), carries out research, publishes journals on educational issues, and trains teachers.[13] Similar to NCTE, and often in collaboration given the responsibility of both entities for teacher training, a National Curriculum Framework (NCF) to guide primary and secondary education is periodically developed by NCERT.

NCERT has actively pursued UN mandates on human rights education in preparing resource materials, textbook reform, and teacher training. Collaborating with the National Human Rights Commission (NHRC), NCERT has published *Human Rights: A Source Book* (Dev 1996) and other supplementary guides for teachers. Additionally, at the behest of the NHRC, NCERT undertook a review of national-level textbooks "with a view to eliminating from them those passages that were inimical to human rights or that distorted them" (NHRC 1996). In recent revisions of textbooks—after substantial textbook controversies in the late 1990s and early 2000s rooted in the politics of religious communalism in India[14]—human rights issues can be found discussed in subjects related to caste, religious, and gender inequalities as well as other dimensions of rights (particularly in social sciences and history, but also in the subjects of Hindi and English through diversifying examples of literature). In 2009, NCERT also announced plans to develop an elective course for eleventh and twelfth standard students on human rights, although officials at the institution noted that finding qualified teachers for the subject may serve as an impediment to its actualization (Deccan Herald 2009).

NCERT's approach to HRE has been to integrate these themes across curricula rather than offering human rights education as a separate subject.

NCERT discussions on reform have previously noted that a "panic approach" characterizes demands for curricular expansion rather than a comprehensive strategy:

> The curriculum development process is often influenced by a "panic approach" in which the local, national or international developments with some socio-economic and political bearing influence the decisions concerning the curriculum without prior, careful, and structured planning. This "panic approach" of including new and temporal curricular concerns may often lead to an overloading of the curriculum. Whenever such new issues crop up and demand attention, it must be examined whether whatever is already present in the curriculum could be of relevance, and could effectively incorporate those new issues. At a time when concerns such as "literacy" "family system", "neighbourhood education", "environmental education", "consumer education", "tourism education", "AIDS education", "human rights education", "legal literacy", "peace education", "population education", "migration education", "global education" and "safety education" are making a case for separate place in the school curriculum, the best approach would be to integrate these ideas and concepts, after a careful analysis, in the existing areas of learning. (as cited in Panda 2001, 91)

As suggested above, NCERT has resisted human rights education and other new content areas as separate and required subjects. NCERT has, however, in recent years focused on "peace education" not as a separate subject per se, but as an umbrella for education about values, duties, rights, tolerance, conflict transformation, and mutual understanding. A peace education focus group was convened during the extensive National Curriculum Framework 2005 consultation process, and since 2005, a summer certificate course on peace education for teachers has been held (Roy 2008). In 2010, NCERT also released a resource book for teachers entitled, *Ways to Peace*. The education for peace initiatives are overseen by the Psychology department of NCERT, while the development of the eleventh and twelfth standard human rights elective course is being overseen by the Social Sciences department; this separation suggests that approaches to peace are seen as behavioral and approaches to human rights are seen as primarily content-driven. Such bifurcation among arguably related concepts suggests adherence to different sides of the "values" (peace education) versus rights (HRE) debate within India as noted earlier in this chapter; some conceptual coherence, however, is found in the 2005 National Curriculum Framework's articulation that "Peace cannot prevail if the rights of individuals are violated. Basic to human rights are the values of non-discrimination and equality, which contribute to building a culture of peace in society. These issues are interrelated. Peace education is thus a host of overlapping values" (NCERT 2005, 62).

NCERT has addressed larger debates about human rights in India in distinct ways. As seen in the case of textbook revisions, NCERT has not shied away from utilizing international examples and norms in developing the institution's vision of human rights. The Indian Constitution is presented alongside UN documents, and examples are provided from countries as diverse as the United States, France, South Africa, Nepal, Poland, and Chile. One senior official at NCERT highlighted this decision—resonant with a HRE for Global Citizenship approach discussed in Chapter Two—stating that, "issues have to be seen in a global perspective; the teacher is free to bring in local examples as necessary" (interview, April 2009). NCERT's increasing focus on critical pedagogy, as evidenced in policy documents and more attention to student-centered learning, also reflects shifts toward a more rights-friendly approach in the classroom.

National Human Rights Commission (NHRC)

Human rights education has to grapple with three important concerns: one, clarification of contemporary civilization dilemmas; two, intergenerational transmission of experience; three, acceleration of the process of transformation. The contemporary civilization faces several dilemmas arising from different contradictions. The development models have come to increasingly pre-suppose that self-interest alone can be the propeller of faster development of the productive forces. . . . A critical reflection of the past heightens the consciousness, which, in turn can create [the] necessary climate for not only democratic governance, but [also] a democratic way of life. This effort has to be continuously made at the individual, group, national, and international levels. Human rights education can be a catalyst in this process.

(Former NHRC Chairperson Justice S. Rajendra Babu, 2007)

India's National Human Rights Commission (NHRC) has increasingly sought to localize human rights, providing the Indian Constitution as the primary referent in the sample school-based lessons it has developed. The NHRC has interfaced with NCERT in the revision of textbooks and preparation of resource materials. Moreover, NHRC in its own right has been the most active national agency advocating for HRE nationally.

NHRC was established as part of the Parliamentary Human Rights Act of 1993. In addition to investigating violations and producing reports, the Commission is charged with spreading "human rights literacy among various sections of society" (Protection of Human Rights Act 1993, 9). The Act requires that members include retired judges and chief justices of the Supreme Court and High Courts across India, as well as civil society representatives with considerable experience with or knowledge of human rights. Since its inception, nearly coinciding with the start of the UN Decade for Human Rights Education (1995–2004), NHRC has promoted dialogue around HRE by sponsoring research, preparing numerous handbooks and publications for different constituents, holding seminars and symposia, and in recent years, convening a national consultation and taskforce on human rights education in schools. The HRE initiatives of NHRC have focused on three sectors: (1) higher education; (2) NGOs; and (3) schools.

In each of the documents produced by NHRC in these three domains, the Commission has tried to fuse international and domestic legal documents in an effort to "Indianize" human rights. In a lengthy manual for NGO staff entitled *Human Rights Education for Beginners* (2005) developed for NHRC by an NGO, the Karnataka Women's Information and Resource Center (KWIRC), NHRC's then-chairperson (A. S. Anand) noted the following in the introduction: "There has been a growing realization that human rights cannot be taught only from formal documents. Indigenisation of human rights education thus, can be one of the crucial components of human rights education in India" (NHRC and KWIRC 2005, preface). This vision is similarly contained in the report and module prepared by NHRC (2007) on *Human Rights Education for Teaching Professionals Imparting Education in Primary, Secondary, & Higher Secondary Levels* where a sample module is provided for teachers on the topic of "Human Rights and the Indian Constitution." As part of this module, the fundamental rights (enforceable civil and political rights) in the Indian Constitution are paired one by one with guarantees listed in the Universal Declaration of Human Rights, while the Constitution's directive principles (nonbinding rights) are matched with the UN's International Covenant on Economic, Social, and Cultural Rights.

NHRC has developed extensive resource materials that can be adapted for the university classroom on various dimensions of human rights (and movements toward them) in India. In the handbook mentioned above prepared by KWIRC, there are chapters on the following rights written by individuals integrally involved in advancing these struggles in India: the Rights of the Child, the Rights of the Disabled, The Rights of Dalits, Reproductive Rights, Human Rights and the Environment, Land and Housing Rights, the Rights of Home-based Workers, Gandhian Struggles for Land Rights, the Rights of Fish Workers, and the Right to Information (NHRC 2005). At the university level, in 2007, NHRC issued a comprehensive list of recommended changes to the

UGC's model curriculum on human rights. This nearly 300-page document updates the previous syllabi and course content with greater information on global debates about human rights and a field-based practicum component.

More important for this study, NHRC has consistently cited the importance of integrating human rights education into Indian schools although the Commission has no mandate to actually implement human rights instruction in schools per se. The NHRC has brought greater visibility to HRE as a national priority through repeated calls for school-based human rights education. In 2009, the Commission convened a national-level conference on HRE to assess the status of developments in the field. Representatives of various ministries, national bodies, and commissions attended, as did representatives of the Institute of Human Rights Education, the only NGO participants. There, NCERT announced plans to develop an elective course on human rights. Various arguments were presented for the need for teacher training, each state's responsibility in integrating human rights content in their respective textbooks, and the need for child-friendly approaches and pedagogy in the teaching of human rights. The ability of the NHRC to bring together agencies like the Ministry for Human Resource Development, the National Knowledge Commission, NCERT, NCTE, among others, as well as train state councils that prepare regional textbooks on human rights issues is indeed noteworthy. Similarly, the periodic trainings for teachers, judges, police, and other professionals have served to advance the "Indianization" of human rights and increase the integration of these norms into public discourse.

NHRC has also engaged other, larger debates surrounding human rights in India in multiple ways. As previously mentioned, NHRC has consistently tried to highlight the international *and* Indian roots of human rights. Regarding rights versus duties, the introduction of the 2007 report, which recommended revisions to the UGC curriculum, highlights the difficulty in naming HRE in India. According to NHRC, "Multi-level inquiries inherent in [the] human rights discipline also tend to create problems of nomenclature: whether the discipline ought to be [designated] as 'Human Rights—Duties Education', or 'Human Values Education', or simply 'Human Rights Education'" (NHRC 2007, preface). While NHRC does not directly express a preference for one term over the other, the Commission alludes to a preference for "human rights education" in line with the institution's mandate to promote "human rights literacy and awareness." Since NHRC has not been integrally involved in implementation, its position on whether HRE should be integrated or taught separately is difficult to ascertain. Nonetheless, members and chairpersons of NHRC have repeatedly advocated support for comprehensive human rights education. Former Chairperson Justice S. Rajendra Babu has noted, "human rights education should include a profound reform in the process of education, including changes in curriculum, textbooks, teaching methodology, class management, pre-service training and organization of the education system at all levels" (NHRC 2009).

National initiatives on human rights education offer policy approaches to cultivating a respect for human rights. Here, the scope for intervention is large, but the intensity varies. While these initiatives generally follow the HRE for Global Citizenship approach, they are not without their own internal tensions and contradictions. For example, the individual agency of chairpersons of different government bodies is reflected in their ability to put their own mark on the plans and visions of their institutions. These influences vary greatly across different tenures. The UGC's XIth Plan Guidelines noted that the UGC's human rights program under the previous chairperson's tenure became more about duties and values in line with the priorities of the ruling party in power at the time (UGC 2007b). The subsequent chairperson's interest in social exclusion cast a distinct imprint on the Commission's most recent efforts, though policies of frequent transfer and promotion of civil servants in India limit the staying power of any particular set of innovations.[15] Similarly, in other bodies, the term "human rights education" may be used, though policymakers and the officials charged with the day-to-day tasks of implementing policy operate under distinct meanings, definitions, and conceptions of HRE; hence, a decoupling (Meyer and Rowan 1978) of human rights education occurs through selective implementation and/or adaptation of meanings to fit with preexisting goals and values.

Exploring the range of national-level interventions also suggests how diverse agencies, councils, and commissions have responded to global and local pressures to engage human rights education. India's increasing interest in aligning with international educational standards and priorities occurred roughly around the time of economic liberalization in the early 1990s. Global discourses also frame and provide resources for NGOs advancing HRE, and accordingly, the next chapter examines the Institute of Human Rights Education's initiatives across India.

Chapter Four

Linking Laws, Liberties, and Learning: The Institute of Human Rights Education

The Institute of Human Rights Education (IHRE), part of the larger Madurai-based NGO People's Watch, has been the organization most active in promoting human rights education (HRE) in India. IHRE is a unique NGO that actively engages in teacher training, the development of textbooks, and the implementation of HRE in approximately 4,000 primarily government schools. In India and globally, few NGOs operate their own programs on the scale of IHRE, let alone without government funding. While global efforts of NGOs involved in HRE have included lobbying the United Nations to establish first a Decade (1995–2004) and now a World Programme for Human Rights Education to influence nation-states to adopt HRE, the Institute of Human Rights Education has primarily worked locally to demonstrate how HRE might be implemented. IHRE's programs now constitute a large-scale experiment spanning 18 Indian states. From its inception, the Institute has maintained that its eventual goal is government adoption of HRE as a separate curricular subject and that its role is to provide the evidence to convince state- and national-level educational authorities of the importance of human rights instruction. IHRE uses a Human Rights Education for Transformative Action approach, which prioritizes empowerment and social action as the outcome of instruction and differs from most government-led initiatives (as discussed in Chapters Two and Three). This disjuncture between government and NGO initiatives has led IHRE to be creative and strategic in finding ways to sustain their program over the past 15 years. IHRE's work squarely addresses the second premise of this book—that strategy as much as content and pedagogy influences HRE and its adoption. In particular, People's Watch and IHRE have used a strategy of "persuasive pragmatism" to enlist the support of a variety of stakeholders from government officials to headmasters and teachers and, ultimately, students for their goal of promoting respect for human rights. Analysis of their strategy also opens important windows onto the differing international, national, and local conceptualizations of HRE as well as the evolution of political support for human rights initiatives in certain institutions, agencies, and schools in India.

A vertical case study approach is particularly suited to understanding not just the *phenomenon* of HRE in India, but the *process* by which an NGO like the Institute of Human Rights Education has been able to leverage local, regional, national, and international institutions and sources of legitimacy to address, on a broad scale, violations of human dignity (from child labor to caste-based social exclusion and female infanticide). As such, data presented in this chapter come from a variety of sources. I interviewed 49 staff and advisory committee members of IHRE as well as their partners in different states about the approach and strategy of the organization. Additionally, I followed key events throughout the research period and undertook extensive document review to understand the workings and institutional culture of the organization. The latter part of this chapter also includes representative data from teachers (118) and headmasters (55) who were interviewed during the course of this research. IHRE and affiliates charged with implementing HRE (educational officials, headmasters, and teachers) have expanded human rights education through a strategy of sustained, persuasive, and pragmatic engagements with educational institutions and communities "on the ground" across the country.

STRATEGY OF PERSUASIVE PRAGMATISM

The Institute of Human Rights Education has employed what I term a strategy of persuasive pragmatism in scaling up and spreading its experiment with human rights education in a few schools in 1997 to a full-fledged national program that presently operates in approximately 4,000 schools. While scholars in various fields such as communications, social psychology, and philosophy have assessed and discussed the concepts of "persuasion" and "pragmatism" independently, I define *persuasive pragmatism* as a relational and situational strategy that seeks to identify individual and collective interests and appeal to them in advocating for the adoption of new attitudes and behaviors, in this case related to human rights.[1] The strategy of persuasive pragmatism varies depending on whether it is targeted at government officials, teachers, or students and reflects a deep engagement with the culture, norms, and micropolitics of the communities involved. A common feature of this strategy across groups is that persuasive pragmatism offers perceived and/or actual benefits to stakeholders, who range from policymakers to marginalized youth. As individuals grapple with the possibilities and challenges of human rights education, several pragmatic interests (e.g., who is advocating for HRE, what rewards might ensue for adoption)—often highlighted by IHRE in advancing their cause—play an important role in determining the outcome of this decision. Undoubtedly, the politics of deep engagement are not isolated to IHRE, though the organization's success with these methods is worth examining for its lessons.

The Institute of Human Rights Education's strategy of persuasive pragmatism has three significant components. First, persuasive pragmatism involves a relational and contextual approach that endorses the legitimacy of the bearer of human rights information. In other words, the messenger of human rights is often as important as the message in securing buy-in. Elements that lend to the credibility of the messenger include signals of legitimacy such as working through intermediaries who may make introductions or endorse the organization and its campaign for human rights education. In the case of IHRE, advisory boards with noted and respected individuals and dense networks across India facilitate the realization of this part of the institution's strategy. In this case, human rights are advanced primarily through human relationships.

Second, IHRE considers and addresses the multiple reasons why stakeholders may be interested in advancing or participating in HRE. Reasons may be rooted in similar goals that individuals share with the organization to promote human rights or rooted in perceived or actual elevated status through affiliation. Previous literature on global HRE has been largely prescriptive. Human rights education is presented in UN documents as a moral imperative grounded in appeals to the conscience of policymakers. In the NGO definitions reviewed earlier—directed primarily at targets of rights abuses—human rights education is thought to appeal to victims as an instrumental or necessary form of knowledge for the reclamation of rights that have been violated. A strategy of persuasive pragmatism moves beyond these traditional rationales for adoption and utilizes the diverse interests of various constituents to enlist their support for the program whether they have a preexisting interest in the human rights movement or not. The diverse motivations of government officials, headmasters, teachers, and students are engaged, or rather taken seriously as a matter of practical policy, to promote this strategy.

The third component of a strategy of persuasive pragmatism involves IHRE's creation and provision of an extensive network of supporters that can lend status and incentives to participants. While this third component is related to the second, reciprocity is what accounts for continued support and the retention of teachers since the sense or experience of elevated status offers an ongoing reason to stay involved even when time, resources, or the strict dictates of one's job may not require promotion of HRE. While methods vary and the individuals adopting, implementing, and developing HRE differ, the network affiliated to IHRE offers a connection to a larger community that may provide not only a psychological benefit of higher perceived status, but also tangible benefits. For example, one HRE teacher in rural Kanyakumari district in Tamil Nadu mentioned that the parent of a student of hers was being accused of murdering a neighbor in a land dispute that involved caste discrimination. Knowing the local IHRE coordinator, she called him. Because IHRE is affiliated with a larger human rights organization, staff members were able to launch an investigation that resulted in the release of the accused parent. This teacher noted that when difficult cases come to the local police, the police often send individuals to her—a teacher—since they believe she has more power and authority to resolve them—given her contacts—than they do.

In exploring IHRE's strategy of persuasive pragmatism, one that extends beyond simple moral suasion, I do not intend to diminish the organization's commitment to human rights education. To the contrary, IHRE's deep belief in human rights education and its benefits has driven their strategic innovation. As noted in Chapter Two, most literature on HRE to date notes the reasons for the spread of the reform, describes specific programs, or prescribes instructional models; little literature traces the evolution of political support for HRE. IHRE's model is instructive for theorizing how to expand the base of support for an initiative, here HRE, to individuals and groups who at first may not be inclined to support it, but after participating, may see the value of these efforts. IHRE's work is especially relevant in many national and local contexts where the term "human rights" is politicized in distinct ways—through affiliation with particular political parties, social movements, or in some cases, with criminal elements, where human rights groups are active on issues of detention and due process rights.[2] IHRE's strategies have not always been successful, but they explain how the program has been able to expand into thousands of schools over the past 15 years.

PERSUASIVE PRAGMATISM IN PRACTICE

Background of People's Watch and the Institute of Human Rights Education

The strategy of persuasive pragmatism is embedded in the very structure of the Institute of Human Rights Education. As the educational wing of the Indian human rights organization People's Watch based in the southern Indian state of Tamil Nadu, IHRE has developed the longest running human rights education program in Indian schools. The educational program of People's Watch began operating in 1997, when teachers asked activists at the organization how they might incorporate human rights principles in the classroom.[3] Starting as an experiment with a handful of schools in Chennai (formerly Madras), the organization developed a curriculum, delivered trainings for teachers, and attempted to translate and expand their human rights work (initially primarily on caste discrimination and police abuse) into a broad-based educational program.

Although human rights education programs were launched without knowledge of the then-ongoing UN Decade, strategic connections were later made and IHRE was able to gain support and funding by aligning with these international efforts. Funding for human rights education has primarily come from European organizations (Danish and German), with some support for national replication from US-based foundations. The larger organization, People's Watch, has been supported by Scandinavian and other European bilateral aid organizations, and private foundations in the United States and Europe.

In 1999, People's Watch decided to create the Institute of Human Rights Education to administer its educational work. The decision to create a distinct institutional arm was driven by the need, as the program scaled up, to separate People's Watch's work as a human rights organization—often critiquing abuses or demanding accountability from state- and national-level entities—from efforts as an educational institution seeking to work in government-run schools. In a report commemorating ten years of the Institute of Human Rights Education (PW 2008), the decision is described as follows:

> People's Watch faced a peculiar problem. . . . Many times, it was very tough for People's Watch to question the State and simultaneously to work with the State. In order to avoid this paradoxical situation and to ensure acceptance from the State for its human rights education program in all schools, People's Watch initiated a separate program called "Institute of Human Rights Education (IHRE)" and all HRE programs in schools and trainings were brought under it. (39)

There are an estimated 1.2 million NGOs that exist in India with a range of management styles and transparency (Kumaran 2008). As such, the decision to create a free-standing Institute or educational body reflects the evolution of People's Watch's thinking about strategy and persuasive pragmatism.

The Institute of Human Rights Education is chaired by a retired Vice-Chancellor of a university,[4] and has an advisory committee consisting of noted Indian educational and human rights experts. Endorsement by well-known experts is another strategy of IHRE to amplify its voice and deepen its impact. Also, whether unintentionally or a component of its strategy or in response to national debates on human rights, all of the Institute's staff and advisory committee members are Indian nationals.

The IHRE model offers breadth and depth in human rights education. IHRE has been able to enter into nearly 4,000 schools, mainly those serving Dalits and Adivasis—both groups comprising the most marginalized sections of Indian society. IHRE aims to secure two hour-long periods per week in which students in the sixth, seventh, and eighth standards are taught by teachers who are trained by IHRE staff and who use textbooks developed by affiliated curriculum experts. Textbooks and trainings include concepts related to general human rights, children's rights, and issues of discrimination based on caste, gender, religion, ability, skin color, and ethnicity, among others.

Since 1997, IHRE has offered more than 300,000 students a three-year course in human rights education and has expanded to 18 states across India working through partner institutions and organizations. Each state partner is encouraged to translate the language and adapt the content of textbooks to local realities. However, year one (offered to students in sixth standard) usually covers basic human rights in the Indian Constitution and international documents; year two (seventh standard) explores children's rights and realities of child labor and early marriage; and year three (eighth standard) delves into different forms of discrimination (caste, gender, religion, ability, skin color, nationality, etc.) and the right to equal treatment (see Table 5.1 in Chapter Five for more information on textbook content and pedagogical methods).

In many schools, IHRE utilizes periods that have no formal instruction for human rights education. In Tamil Nadu, for example, there are one to two periods scheduled weekly in government schools for "moral education," but for which the state has not provided books or a set curriculum. In many schools, the teachers utilize this period for HRE and, in some cases where headmasters are strong advocates of the program, they have even changed the name of the period for their school to "human rights education."

A key component of a school's excitement or reluctance regarding HRE involved the frequency of visits from IHRE staff. As part of IHRE's program, "zonal coordinators" visit schools periodically to deliver books and ensure that instruction is taking place.[5] Given the institution's genesis within a larger human rights organization, IHRE largely recruited staff (at least in Tamil Nadu where the program started) from the field of human rights rather than education, with local and regional coordinators often having been active in social movements.[6] In all states where IHRE's programs were operating, senior education experts (e.g., university professors, officials in education ministries) were involved at the advisory committee level and responsible for developing textbook curriculum, serving as presenters at trainings for teachers, and devising larger strategies for the program as a whole. Still, the individuals representing IHRE, who engaged with teachers most regularly, came to the job, for the most part, with interests in activism and social change. This staff typically viewed their jobs as an extension of the labor movement or other social movements, such as those seeking to combat caste and gender discrimination, that they had previously (and sometimes concurrently) been active in. A handful of the coordinators also ran their own NGOs in their home communities on the side.

The Institute has also developed several other mechanisms for advancing human rights education aside from committed staff, textbooks, and direct instruction, such as nonformal and supplemental education for human rights. IHRE started offering summer camps in 2008 for students to delve into human rights concepts and, while only a limited number of students can attend, those who do report that the experience was a transformative one (as will be discussed in Chapters Five and Six). Given many students' interest in continuing past the three-year course, IHRE has also been offering trainings for students and teachers to set up HRE clubs in their schools so that they can continue to learn and act upon human rights while in ninth and tenth standards.[7] In response to some teachers' resistance to teaching HRE since it is a non-examinable subject, the organization has also developed digital modules for students to be able to watch lessons on televisions available in many government schools. Another novel strategy, also part of an effort to ensure student interest, is the development of a compact disc with songs that relate to human rights (often written by students and teachers) in each state language. Students often take these materials home, choreograph dances to the songs, and learn them to sing at school and community events. These strategic interventions support what students are learning in the classroom and comprise a concerted approach to popularize human rights instruction for children through a variety of media.

ADOPTION AND EXPANSION OF HRE

Persuasive pragmatism is also important at the level of adoption and expansion of programs by government officials and advisory boards, not to mention implementation through headmasters and teachers. The process of advocating for official permission to carry out human rights education in government-run schools involves working through existing relationships and networks, often facilitated by IHRE's advisory committee members.[8] The organization has been successful at assembling advisory boards comprised of educational experts and well-known (often retired) civil servants in each state that it operates in, as well as a National Advisory Committee that oversees advocacy and policy efforts. The development of extensive networks that support and legitimize IHRE's work and the utilization of these relationships in advancing their goals form integral components of a strategy of persuasive pragmatism.

Role of Advisory Boards

The system we have developed for advisory committees is in every state. Yesterday we went to Kerala to consult our advisory committee member, former Supreme Court Justice Krishna Iyer, about expanding the program in the state. From our advisory committee members, we seek not only advice, but also blessings and guidance, as well as their adding their personal credibility and visibility to the program. When we are writing to the government for permission, it certainly helps to have these advisory committee members who have signed on.

(Henri Tiphagne, director of People's Watch,
Interview, February 2009)

The presence of well-known academics and officials on state- and national-level advisory committees, in part, accounts for how the HRE program has expanded into thousands of government schools. Advisory boards or committees are central to IHRE's composition. These committees are comprised of individuals who share IHRE's vision and commitment to human rights, some of whom have been previously involved through special events, conferences, or campaigns of the organization. Other individuals have little previous knowledge of People's Watch and its Institute of Human Rights Education, but are sought out or introduced by others to participate in some capacity. Oftentimes, advisory committees include retired or current government officials and noted experts (in education and/or human rights) who carry influence and lend credibility to IHRE's program.

While IHRE and its parent organization, People's Watch, are well-known in Tamil Nadu, they are less known in states where the program has spread; thus, the composition of the State Advisory Committee (SAC) has been essential in securing local support. For example, in West Bengal, the state's Women's Commissioner serves on the advisory committee for the human rights education program, and this, in part, has led to government permission for operation in selected schools and greater receptivity. In Orissa, some retired civil servants and senior professors sit on the committee and, as an IHRE staff member noted, such individuals "command great respect in the state. Many of the ministers have been their students or have been mentored by them." As a result, the HRE program has been introduced in all schools run by the "Tribal Welfare Ministry" in Orissa, an agency that specifically oversees the development and access to resources of rural, indigenous populations in the state.

The National Advisory Committee (NAC) has focused squarely on lobbying the government through various national entities concerned with education and human rights (such as those mentioned in Chapter Three) to advance and adopt human rights education. NAC members include current and retired Vice-Chancellors (presidents) of universities, retired and current senior officials and chairpersons of national government commissions, retired justices and members of the National Human Rights Commission (NHRC), and leading academics. Arguably, the high-level access of the national committee has also ensured that IHRE senior staff members have been participants in national-level consultations and meetings on human rights education—often the only non-governmental organization present. That the chairperson of IHRE, Dr. Vasanthi Devi, is also a retired Vice-Chancellor of a university and a former Women's Commissioner for Tamil Nadu state also legitimizes the educational expertise of IHRE's leadership and approach.

Committee members are motivated to contribute their time and energy through their prior knowledge of and commitment to human rights as well as some possible legacy effect. First, most advisory committee members have long-standing experience in education and/or human rights and see the organization as aligned with their commitments and beliefs. One prominent professor noted that IHRE's engagement with schools provides a practical application (by reviewing curriculum and serving as a trainer) of the work she has done over several years in developing the field of women's rights in Indian universities. Second, the networks by which individuals come to know about the organization lend it legitimacy and the relational quality of how new members are approached is noteworthy. A retired government official who had held senior posts and has written extensively on issues of caste discrimination noted the following:

> My commitment to human rights *education* is the consequence of my being in
> human rights *action* for more than half a century. I was giving a lecture at a
> college when Vasanthi Devi [Chairperson of IHRE] came to the dais and set
> up a time to meet me. One or two days later, she came and met me along with
> another common friend. She proposed that I should join this National Advisory
> Committee, which I gladly accepted. Here we are talking about the rights of the
> Scheduled Castes [Dalits], rights of the Scheduled Tribes, rights of the "backward" classes, women, children. . . . We have to create the conditions which
> will strengthen the communities from the bottom, whereby they will be able to
> get their economic rights, educational rights, their security, their social dignity
> through legislative measures, administrative measures, and then democratic
> mobilization measures. At the same time, discriminatory ideas have become
> so deep-rooted; this poison of caste, caste based inequalities, and superiority-
> inferiority is injected into the child from as early as possible in the family and
> subsequently in the peer group. How do you counteract this venom which creates such a mindset? This is where human rights education comes in. (Interview,
> November 2009)

A strong sense of civic obligation may also explain the participation of retired senior civil servants. As noted above, for those who are retired (for civil servants in India, retirement is mandatory at age 60), the chance to be part of a vibrant organization that advances shared goals can indeed be deemed a productive use of time and energy. Many senior and/or retired academics and officials served as advisory members, speakers at special events held by IHRE, and as presenters or "resource persons" at teacher trainings. Many also contributed to the development of HRE textbooks as well. Thus, whether because of shared commitments or a relationship with someone in the organization (or both), advisory committee members were active in contributing to the development of textbooks, training of teachers, and advocacy with government officials.

The presence of senior officials and renowned experts on the National Advisory Committee also created a knowledge base that could inform IHRE's strategies and approaches. NAC members held a diverse set of views on how best to expand HRE. For example, members differed with regard to (1) whether the program should be taught as a separate subject or be integrated into existing subjects, (2) whether exams and papers should be made mandatory on human rights so that students and teachers were certain to take it seriously, and (3) whether differentiated approaches and content should be directed at marginalized and privileged students.

Government Officials as Sympathetic Bureaucrats

While officials already interested in human rights were natural supporters of IHRE's program, persuasive pragmatism is perhaps most illuminating in reaching individuals whose personal and professional interests were not necessarily aligned with human rights. Advisory committee members regularly liaised with government officials whom they knew or may have mentored in order to introduce IHRE, but other reasons—such as political ambitions— often motivated officials' interest in advancing the program as well. This study identified three groups of "sympathetic bureaucrats," or government officials whose support at various levels has allowed for the expansion and spread of HRE, namely: (1) those already committed to human rights; (2) those who knew staff or advisory board members of IHRE; and (3) those whose political careers could improve through promotion of human rights or association with IHRE.

The first group of "sympathetic bureaucrats" were those whose political or personal beliefs aligned well with IHRE's work in advancing human rights and who occupy senior positions at local, state, or national levels. Lant Pritchett (2009) refers to such officials as "reform champions" (37), since their authority can result in policy changes or support for programs ranging from the provision of government services to, in this case, human rights education. Pritchett, however, also cautions about the limited life of such reforms given the regular transfer of civil servants.[9] Several examples from IHRE's history in Tamil Nadu and other Indian states suggest that the institution's ability to scale up has been dependent on "human rights-friendly" officials who champion the cause of HRE and who may or may not have had any previous contact with the organization. These officials can be ministers or high-level authorities at the state level, commissioners of corporation schools in urban areas, or District Collectors—the highest authority in rural districts who oversee all aspects of the district, including schooling. While no funding for HRE has been granted by these officials to date, their ability to lend credibility to the program by sending memoranda to headmasters requiring the program, excusing teachers for trainings, and allowing IHRE personnel to visit schools, has offered needed support for ensuring the implementation of the program.

Certainly, personal background, commitment to social justice, and/or political leanings may all influence why an official without prior connection to IHRE's leadership may be receptive to advancing human rights education. For example, a commissioner in Tamil Nadu for a state-level ministry concerned with the welfare of Dalit or Scheduled Caste populations noted the following:

> Education liberates Dalit children from their shackles. Without education, they are always bound by invisible chains. I come from that community so I can say this confidently. I realized how important it is for education to bring about social changes. In this climate where there is a lot of caste-ism, this [HRE] book gives the children awareness on what are their rights and what are their responsibilities. This book helps Dalit children at the initial stages to know how to claim their rights, and for non-Dalit children to know about human rights since [those communities] have perpetrated atrocities; such children can challenge the discriminatory practices of their parents and elders. (Interview, February 2009)

This high-ranking Dalit officer and other officials from historically marginalized communities supported the HRE program in schools and initiatives under their jurisdiction, as in the case of an educational official who introduced human rights into an adult education program she coordinated in Karnataka state. However, there were also some officials from similar backgrounds who did not want to support HRE for fear of being associated with human rights groups in the state. The latter category of officials generally included early career civil servants concerned that promotions and professional advancement may have been dependent on avoiding any perceived influence from a particular group.

While not necessarily from minoritized groups, some young officials also shared a desire to promote new ideas, like HRE, in their capacity as District Collectors. For example, one staff member of IHRE noted, "there are some dynamic young Collectors who were so receptive to this kind of program since they found it interesting and were willing to grant us permission to introduce it in all the schools in the district" (Interview, January 2009). In these cases, the Collectors, though not usually considered educational authorities, could grant access and permission for the HRE program to be carried out in schools in their locality.

The second channel for officials to come to know of and support HRE was through relational networks. For example, IHRE had several contacts at key ministries and commissions made through the senior leaders of IHRE's many years of involvement in the fields of human rights and education in India. These relational networks ranged from individuals having heard of senior staff at IHRE to close personal relationships that facilitated the advancement of IHRE's program. For example, the Chairperson of IHRE, a former state-level commissioner, had a certain amount of notoriety. Other representative examples that emerged from the data included persuading visiting officials—for example, the former Chairperson of the National Human Rights Commission, a UN official visiting IHRE programs, and others—to write letters of support for human rights education to state- and national-level authorities to endorse efforts at expansion.

While IHRE cultivated and sought after these professional relationships, at other times, such connections emerged accidentally and resulted in unexpected support from officials. For example, in Chhattisgarh, one particularly motivated teacher who actively attended and participated in HRE trainings, unbeknownst to IHRE or its local partners, was the brother of the Minister of Education for the state. Through this relationship, the Minister gave permission for human rights education to be introduced in several districts (although funding has constrained widespread expansion) and included two chapters on human rights in the state's social science textbooks. In another serendipitous turn of events, IHRE's Chairperson, Dr. Vasanthi Devi, narrated the following:

The former secretary of the Adi Dravidar Welfare Department[10] (in Tamil Nadu) was very much interested in our HRE program. We had a big state level conference here; he came and sat through the whole day and he gave so many suggestions and was very excited about our program. Soon after, he was transferred. I ran into him one day as I was coming back from Delhi and lamented that, "We have lost you" since his being there was a very big help. He said, "Oh Madam, why do you say this? I am now overseeing all the corporation (urban) schools. You have another avenue opening up. Why don't you come into all the Chennai schools?[11] I can place all of them at your disposal." So that's how our HRE program is in all the Chennai schools. Such accidents also sometimes happen! (Interview, February 2009)

Whether through social and professional networks cultivated by staff, advisory board members, or accidentally discovered, IHRE utilized these relationships in line with their strategy of persuasive pragmatism to advance opportunities for human rights education.

The third manner of securing the support of government officials involved approaching individuals who may not be committed to social justice initiatives nor have any connection to members or affiliates of IHRE; instead, such individuals viewed affiliation with human rights and/or a human rights organization as beneficial to their career interests and professional ambitions. While this category may not have been the most common variant of "sympathetic bureaucrats," understanding this group's newfound interest in HRE provides a glimpse into a unique component of IHRE's strategy. The Executive Director of People's Watch, Henri Tiphagne, explained the following approach in securing permission to enter into Madurai corporation schools in the late 1990s as the program first began scaling up:

> This man had just become the mayor of Madurai. We approached him to grant permission to introduce HRE in some 20 schools and he didn't have any idea about what the program was. We said, "You have become the mayor and we want you to do certain things which will improve your image, not just in this small city of Madurai, but nationally." We had just learned about the UN's efforts and the Decade for Human Rights Education (1995–2004), so we said, "There is this national program of human rights education which is part of the UN Decade so your schools will become the first of any in the entire country officially taking a position on this." So he asked, "What should I do?" We prepared a circular to be sent to the schools and he took his pen, signed it, and then passed it on to the chief education officer to implement. . . . The idea is to do all these things in a manner to make sure that the initial hesitations that people had were not given scope. (Interview, February 2009)

"Bureaucrats" may also become "sympathetic" to a program that could advance their standing, even without any prior knowledge of it. Certainly, such support does not exist in a vacuum. The worldwide diffusion of "human rights" concepts and norms facilitates these endeavors being recognized as something worthy of promotion (Ramirez et al., 2007; Meyer et al., 2010). The example of local officials being influenced by perceived global trends and movements is a variation of Keck and Sikkink's (1998) argument about the "boomerang effect," wherein global transnational advocacy networks influence national policy; in the example provided above, the possibility of elevated status through being affiliated with a forward-looking reform already valorized at the national level provided sufficient impetus for action.

Data also pointed to cases where a strategy of persuasive pragmatism was not effective. IHRE's attempts to expand and scale up a program to almost 4,000 schools nationally have also been met with resistance. International and national educational efforts are primarily focused on achieving universal enrollment in primary schools, and less concerned with curricular interventions like human rights education. Education ministers at the state level have resisted the adoption of the program based on limited funding or a desire to maintain a focus on enrollment (as will be discussed further in Chapter Eight).

Role of Headmasters

The role of headmaster—though circumscribed by official mandates and government programs—nonetheless contains considerable autonomy and flexibility with regard to the operations and practices within a given school. Headmasters can be complicit in reproducing unequal social relations and practices in their schools just as they may promote transformative action.

Rural schools presented more cases of headmasters operating in unlawful ways and to the detriment of students than urban schools located closer to agencies and officials charged with oversight. In schools particularly designated for Adivasi or "tribal" students—often quite far from government offices and infrequently visited by government inspectors and officials— cases of negligence repeatedly emerged in teachers', students', and parents' accounts. The first type of abuse related to the basic presence of teachers and headmasters. As mentioned in Chapter Three, absentee rates in India average 20–25 percent (Kingdon and Banerji 2009; Kremer et al., 2005) and are considerably higher for remote schools that Adivasi students attend.

"Tribal" schools are often considered the least desirable posting for headmasters and teachers. Even when present, quality of instruction and simple engagement can be significant problems since some headmasters and teachers do not necessarily conduct meaningful teaching and learning while there. According to one IHRE staff member:

> When I reached the school to discuss the HRE program, I was so surprised because the headmaster was sleeping on a cot under a tree in the schoolyard. It was during the school hours and he was sleeping in his *lungi*.[12] When I arrived, he woke up and said, "No problem, sir. Welcome." He then got up, pushed the cot away, and showed me into his office. (Interview, February 2009)

Various other forms of abuse aside from negligence and absence emerged from the data. Not infrequent practices included sexual abuse of adolescent girls and siphoning off foodstuffs provided by the government for mid-day meals to sell for extra profit. Certainly not all headmasters were engaged in these types of practices and some, indeed, were very good educational administrators. However, the repeated accounts of abuses that emerged in this study highlighted the lack of oversight and accountability that affected the well-being of students, particularly those from marginalized communities.

In this context, the Institute of Human Rights Education sought to secure headmasters' support for the implementation of the program despite having been granted higher-level permission to teach HRE. First, a day-long training/orientation session was offered where noted speakers and IHRE staff discussed the importance of human rights. This relational approach high-lighted the sanction for human rights of noted educationists and public figures and often proved convincing for headmasters. Second, the memorandum from the respective official who had given permission, such as a local District Collector or state-level authority and other supportive individuals, such as members of the National Human Rights Commission or UN officials, were sometimes read out to remind participants of the support of authorities for the HRE program. Third, headmasters, teachers, and students from other schools (sometimes in other states) where HRE was in operation spoke in favor of the program and attested to its benefits. As one respondent noted, in India (and likely elsewhere), "there is power in the precedent," suggesting that demonstration of previous implementation and acceptance was useful in convincing headmasters to support the program. Teachers often become headmasters, and headmasters often become educational officials at the district, and sometimes state, level. As such, headmasters may have previous exposure to the program, and some of the most supportive headmasters had been HRE teachers themselves.

Several headmasters found that human rights education resonated with their personal beliefs or, after undergoing training, were convinced about its relevance and benefit to students. One headmaster who was a strong champion of the reform designated an entire room as the "human rights classroom" at a girls' secondary school in Tamil Nadu, where images of leaders, reports from different organizations, and student work related to human rights were displayed, and where the human rights class and club could meet. Another noteworthy headmaster in rural Orissa, after attending a training session, took human rights education to the whole school, encouraging students to educate their fathers about the dangers of excessive drinking and the illegality of domestic violence, both common practices in the community. Other headmasters set up bulletin boards, carried out special assemblies, and supported school events for International Human Rights Day (December 10) or other global days.

Several headmasters overseeing human rights instruction in their schools had previously been human rights teachers, especially in Tamil Nadu where the program had been operating for over a decade at the time of this research. One headmaster at a school for "tribal" or Adivasi children in Tamil Nadu noted the following:

> Normally headmasters are authoritarian—they come and go as they please and no one questions if they are absent. I have started practicing certain things like if teachers are going for training, they tell me, and if I am going out of the school,

I tell them. I ask the teachers if students have come to school, have they come on time, has anyone dropped out. With all the information, I can inquire and encourage children to come to school, speak to their families, and stay involved. Also, if any teacher goes for a training, I make them share the knowledge with the other teachers when they come back. All these changes have come about through human rights education. Earlier, headmasters didn't have that kind of relationship or contact with teachers and students in our school. But now I've built up these relationships and many more tribal children are staying in school rather than dropping out to work in the tea plantations like they used to. (Interview, January 2009)

As teachers who have been impacted by human rights education advance into positions of school leadership, they carry their learning into institutional structures to change the dynamics that facilitate the abuses mentioned earlier in this section. This can help counteract practices that disempower marginalized youth.

Yet even committed headmasters and school leaders faced several challenges in adopting human rights education. One headmaster in West Bengal who was very supportive of the program and had attended trainings pointed out that unless the material was included on exams, other headmasters would not take HRE seriously since there were no consequences for non-implementation. Similarly, in Orissa, some state authorities did not encourage human rights education in schools where the exam results were poor. One teacher noted, "only 40 percent of our tenth standard students passed last year so now the headmaster is answerable to the authorities. He is not giving importance to anything else but exam-related subjects now" (interview, July 2009). Another issue affecting implementation and support for HRE was the frequent transfer of headmasters that sometimes resulted in inconsistency and varied support. While these challenges affected all schools, there were also headmasters who were not convinced by the trainings in HRE or the high-level support they saw afforded to the program.

Some headmasters actively resisted HRE and the involvement of an outside organization in school-related matters. These headmasters were sometimes those involved in illicit practices and an outside organization visiting and getting involved with students and teachers was seen as a threat to the status-quo. Structural issues related to school management, lack of oversight, and absenteeism also impeded the effective implementation of HRE, despite efforts at persuading school leaders about the program's importance. Unsurprisingly, in schools where teacher and headmaster absenteeism was extremely high, headmasters did not actively promote the HRE program even if teachers were interested. In one such school in Orissa, the teacher reported that he would be interested in teaching the subject since he had attended the training, but that he was covering so many classes for absentee teachers that he could not find the time. As such, many variables had to fall into place for human rights instruction to actually reach students.

Teachers

The interpersonal relationship and human connection between us, as the IHRE staff, and teachers, raises the chances of success since our program depends on the teacher's attitude towards HRE. We give importance to the teachers' lives. I go to the school, drink coffee with them, and ask, "How is your husband? How are your children?" Then, only lastly I will come to the subject; "Have you finished the topics? How useful is it for you?" So many other programs don't have that attitude as part of the product. Even in the training, after the session, we sing together and play games. That builds the human bond; that rapport building with teachers is very important to this program.

(IHRE Staff Member, Interview, February 2009)

Teachers are a key component of any successful human rights education program and IHRE employed a variety of strategies to secure their support and change their practices. Teachers, too, had a variety of reasons for supporting human rights education programs (the corresponding impact of HRE on teachers will be further discussed in Chapter Seven).

IHRE recognized the crucial role that teachers played in the implementation and impact of human rights education. Senior staff of IHRE repeatedly encouraged coordinators to develop strong relationships with teachers; for example, at staff meetings, the executive director of People's Watch often stated, "We are friends to the teachers," encouraging frequent contact and visits to schools. Reiterating this importance of teacher support, as one state coordinator noted, "Wherever there is a supportive HRE teacher, the process has gone far beyond what we could have expected" (interview, December 2009). Many coordinators regularly communicated with teachers by telephone and had developed lasting friendships with them through the time spent together at trainings and the opportunity to socialize while away from their homes.

One aspect of IHRE's persuasive pragmatism as directed at teachers included holding a three- to five-day training once teachers were first selected by their schools to teach the subject. These trainings were often held in retreat centers in beautiful natural surroundings and provided an opportunity for teachers to travel to places in their state that they may not have visited before.[13] "Refresher" trainings were held after each school-year for one to two days in the summer holidays for teachers to get together, share methods and experiences, and provide support for the upcoming year.

The structure of these trainings included lectures and participatory sessions led by IHRE senior staff (some of whom were retired college professors and senior administrators) and outside experts who were sometimes well-known celebrities. For example, at one teacher training in early 2009, a noted musician, who often appeared on television, taught teachers how to have students design and make puppets to stage shows about social issues like domestic violence. As part of the training, he led teachers in songs, had them participate in the show he put on for them, and gave helpful advice on how to design the props and puppets. The active format (that differed from most teacher trainings in India that were more didactic)—coupled with exposure to local celebrities—engaged teachers and provided, according to their accounts, a unique and memorable experience. IHRE also provided avenues for motivated teachers to stay involved in their networks, associations, and campaigns. For example, HRE teachers in the state of Tamil Nadu spearheaded an effort to have the state teachers' union advocate for HRE as part of their platform in 2009. While these efforts had not resulted in state-level action at the time of this writing, the recruitment of teachers in advocating for human rights education was a deliberate part of IHRE's persuasive pragmatism.

IHRE's strategy of securing teachers' interest was multi-pronged and teachers' reasons for participation varied. For those teachers who became interested—certainly there were those who didn't—there were multiple and overlapping reasons for promoting HRE and associating with the Institute of Human Rights Education, including: (1) viewing human rights education as an avenue to promote their own interests in education; (2) witnessing the benefits of HRE in their classrooms; (3) identifying IHRE as a resource and provider of assistance; (4) seeing HRE and IHRE as providing new opportunities for teachers and students (e.g., travel to conferences); and (5) affiliating with IHRE as a marker of status and a way to be exposed to noted experts.

In most schools, headmasters asked teachers to volunteer to attend the HRE training and be the designated HRE teacher, thus attracting teachers with previous interest in the subject matter. In some schools, the youngest or newest teacher was assigned to attend the training since it was seen as an additional burden and time commitment. In both cases, however, these teachers often found the trainings resonant with their interests and/or recent teacher education. Having a concrete subject with textbooks and trainings offered teachers a chance to explore "their own interest in social work," as one teacher put it. Another teacher in Orissa became so interested that, after retirement, she would attend trainings voluntarily to learn more and offer younger teachers advice on how to implement HRE, noting that, "teachers want to do something like this, but they never before had a forum" (interview, July 2009). Some teachers were inclined toward social issues, but human rights gave them a framework for channeling their interest into local campaigns and projects. Several teachers discussed becoming active in their state human rights commissions or other local organizations after attending trainings and becoming cognizant of human rights issues.

Other teachers, often without previous knowledge of human rights concepts per se, observed certain outcomes after HRE, such as greater confidence among students and increased closeness between students and teachers, and sought to continue advancing the program. Many teachers entered the profession with a desire to effect social change, but were socialized into the norms that characterize many government schools, norms that tolerate teacher absenteeism, corruption, corporal punishment, and/or discrimination. HRE offered interested teachers a chance to connect with students through a subject that involved exploring and analyzing their own social realities rather than memorizing textbooks. As a result, nearly all respondents noted an increased closeness between students and teachers. One teacher even noted, "children are now closer to us than their parents because they can speak freely" (interview, May 2009). Teachers also noted an increase in confidence, greater integration among students of different classes, religions, and castes, and more participation among students. These benefits often influenced teachers' continued participation in trainings and periodic special events related to human rights education.

The third area motivating continued teacher interest in HRE was the network of support and assistance that IHRE offered teachers in addressing their own and their students' hardships. For example, teachers often discussed taking problems they faced in their own lives or at school to the IHRE coordinator, and that staff member utilizing People's Watch's contacts or resources to bring resolution to the issue. These issues ranged from personal situations of domestic violence to abuse students faced at home or at school to policy changes that teachers sought to effect but were unable to without an organization that might amplify their voices. For example, in an urban school in the city of Bengaluru (formerly Bangalore), a HRE teacher facing domestic violence solicited the help of the IHRE state coordinator who assisted the teacher in getting legal and medical support. Another teacher in Bengaluru utilized IHRE to find a residential home for one of her students who was being sexually abused by her stepfather. Similarly, in Tamil Nadu, a teacher reported a case of sexual abuse happening in his school to IHRE who then drew on People's Watch's legal staff to file a case against the teacher who was abusing the child and taking on the teachers' union that was defending the errant teacher. Less severe cases of abuse involved teachers utilizing the network of teachers and IHRE staff to advocate for changes to district officials, such as offering rooms for lactating teachers to breastfeed, allowing them to come back to work sooner or miss fewer classes than if they had to go home to feed their children. Such support to teachers and students who were either victims or witnesses of abuses or unsupportive policies provided teachers concrete evidence that affiliation with IHRE could result in benefits and positive changes that improved their and their students' lives.

IHRE also offered new opportunities to teachers and this contributed to teachers' desire to stay connected to the organization. New opportunities included travel to national and regional events, as well as the opportunity to participate in trainings and events with noted individuals. Dozens of HRE teachers and students from across the 18 states in which IHRE operates attended the Indian Social Forum held in New Delhi in 2006; this was cited as a particularly exciting opportunity for many of the participants. For one teacher in rural Tamil Nadu, the trip was memorable because it was the first time he visited Delhi and because it was the first chance his students had to leave their village:

> We traveled continuously for three days in the train to reach Delhi and it was a new experience for the students and for me. The students were really very happy and their parents too because they have never even gone anywhere beyond 10 kilometers of their village. The children got a chance to speak in front of 3,000 people and meet so many different children from all over India. They were endlessly smiling and laughing together. (Interview, February 2009)

The chance to transcend social boundaries and take advantage of unique opportunities facilitated continued participation by many students and teachers. Many remarked how unusual and special it was to travel to events or trainings, or to interact with noted individuals at events or have them come visit their schools, suggesting that greater exposure to people from different social backgrounds—rather than HRE content per se—may be a factor in generating interest in the program. In West Bengal, government school teachers noted the unique opportunity to learn new content and teaching methods from IHRE's state partner—a well-known and award-winning private school in Kolkata (previously Calcutta)—and befriend teachers of different social classes. Many teachers commented on how much they enjoyed trainings where there were "brilliant senior people teaching us" (interview, January 2009). Teachers and students repeatedly mentioned how fortunate they were to meet senior officials, ministers, and experts they would never likely have contact with otherwise. One student, for example, talked about a photo that still hangs on her family's wall from a visit by a UN official from Geneva to her school.

New opportunities were integrally linked to the elevated status that HRE teachers had through affiliation with the Institute. By attending trainings or events inaccessible to others, HRE teachers gained status through the special opportunities and treatment they received. This sometimes turned the extra onus of teaching an additional, non-exam related subject into a special privilege. One teacher in Gujarat state noted how after returning from a regional training on human rights in the city of Ranchi, she happened to mention it to a judge she saw afterwards:

> I ran into a judge from the civil court and I told him I got all these materials and learned about human rights at the training I went to. The next morning, he came by my house while I was cooking and asked me to lend him the materials that I had got at the training. I had 11 books, which he took and photocopied. After a week, he returned them to me and told me to share any materials I get with him if I attend any trainings in the future. It was really nice. (Interview, December 2009)

To be considered an expert on human rights in the community meant many things given the varied receptions of global discourses of human rights. Given the diffusion of human rights (and despite decoupled understandings of the field), in many circles, "human rights knowledge" carried currency and was prized. Particularly for civil servants, such as police officers or judges, who may be subject to trainings on the topic, greater information on human rights might result in career advancement or other professional benefits. In the case mentioned by the teacher in Gujarat—and the case previously mentioned of the teacher in Tamil Nadu who the police viewed as an expert in resolving complicated cases—affiliation with a human rights organization (made visible through attending trainings and interacting with visiting staff and experts) was noticed by community members, thus elevating teachers' status in the community. Similarly, teachers in various states highlighted their identity as a "human rights teacher" and the value of the networks of other teachers, staff, and experts they had met through trainings. In Vellore district in Tamil Nadu, a group of HRE teachers even formed their own association to advocate for child rights and provide material support to underprivileged students.

CONCLUSION

IHRE's strategy of persuasive pragmatism addressed varied interests, legitimized them as messengers of human rights, drew on relational approaches, and incentivized participation to diverse constituents. Taken together, these elements facilitated the expansion and sustenance of a broad-based human rights education program across India. Certainly there are stakeholders who lost interest or refused to participate based on resistance to the subject matter and/or the organization's approach. While global human rights discourse has given legitimacy to human rights education from above, the Institute of Human Rights Education has simultaneously broadened the base of support for HRE from below, creating a large-scale experiment with a diverse set of participants and supporters within and beyond the traditionally defined human rights community in India.

Chapter Five

From "Time Pass" to Transformative Force: Human Rights Education for Marginalized Youth

We had a training for staff from the DIET (District Institute for Education and Training). We showed them the modules we had developed for human rights education and how they might utilize it. They were so happy, but later they sent a note saying these modules focus more on the affective domain, not the cognitive. They asked why there was so much of a focus on violations rather than on positive elements. I told them that in the field of human rights that we are in, we are working with victims so naturally we'll focus on the affective domain. Here, the children we are working with in [government] schools are so happy to see this book because a lot of the examples are from their own lives. They know first-hand about drunken fathers beating mothers. For those students who see themselves in the book, the impact is strong.

(Dr. Devasahayam, IHRE Director, Interview, January 2009)

In this chapter, I argue that social location mediates and contextualizes how human rights education (HRE) is understood by students. In examining the impact of HRE in India, social location also mediated the impact HRE had at the personal, household, school, and community levels. For the purposes of this book, "victims" are defined as those who suffer from a particular abuse and seek to counter it through some form of action. I utilize the term "coalitional agent" as a way to identify those individuals who act in solidarity with others in speaking out against an abuse that does not directly affect him or her. These boundaries are provisional to the extent that the same individual may, in one instance, be a victim (of say, caste discrimination), and in another moment, be a coalitional agent (say, as a male child standing up to parents because of unequal treatment of his sister in the home). Distinguishing between the experiences of marginalized youth or victims of human rights abuses and coalitional agents in the following chapter demonstrates how social location influences HRE and how it is in turn understood and enacted. These distinctions can also help highlight diverse rationales for HRE from moral imperatives in the global citizenship approach to direct and enlightened self-interest in a transformative action approach. The material conditions of students' lives also mediated how human rights learnings were understood, internalized, and acted upon.

This chapter draws on various sources of data to contextualize the experiences of marginalized youth with human rights instruction. First, analysis of human rights textbooks by topic and pedagogical method offered a way to understand IHRE's approach toward centering the experiences of marginalized youth. Second, while not extensively utilized, a subset of the quantitative data collected for this study is presented to underscore differences in understandings about human rights for HRE students and youth from similar communities not partaking in the three-year course offered by IHRE. Survey questionnaires asked students to define human rights, identify situations of abuse, and agree or disagree with a series of statements related to local examples of human rights. Third, semi-structured interviews and focus groups with a total of 625 student respondents from 6 states provided considerable data on youth responses to HRE.[1] The data categories emerged through inductive analysis, with codes being generated through reviewing the data. In a highly examination-driven system of education, the introduction of a non-examinable subject that is overseen by an NGO presumably might seem to students and teachers like an exercise in "time pass," a term used locally to refer to something that has no relevance to preparation for the exams or one's future professional pursuits. Surprisingly, however, a majority of students and teachers identified substantial impact, ranging from increased content knowledge about human rights to students citing HRE as an extremely positive experience—a "transformative force"—that has influenced their lives greatly. Data also revealed, however, that marginalized students faced challenges in implementing HRE because of their limited social status.

CONTENT AND PEDAGOGY OF HRE

As discussed in the epigraph to this chapter, the Institute of Human Rights Education's (IHRE) approach of Human Rights for Transformative Action (as detailed in Chapter Two) offered students—often those who were Dalits and Adivasis (indigenous)—a framework to situate their own experiences. The three-year course in human rights discussed issues of social inequality based on gender, class, caste, language, skin color or religion, among others.

IHRE's approach to educational reform vis-à-vis human rights differs greatly from conventional Indian education, especially in government schools where rampant human rights abuses occur. These abuses range from corporal punishment to caste discrimination in seating and mid-day deals (Nambissan and Sedwal 2002) to insufficient and dilapidated facilities, such as the absence of toilets which often leads to girls dropping out after they reach puberty (Nambissan 1995).

In the three IHRE textbooks for learners in sixth, seventh, and eighth standards, of the hundred and fifty-three real-life examples presented (primarily from historical stories and newspaper articles), 86 percent relate to social inequalities based on gender, caste, religion, income level, ability, age, or place of birth (see Table 5.1); of these, 21 percent present specific examples of individuals and/or movements that have brought about social change through individual or collective action.[2] The representative examples of human rights violations chosen for national or state-level textbooks in government or private schools typically do not reflect the graphic descriptions of caste and gender discrimination, child abuse, and social inequalities that fill the pages of IHRE's textbooks. However, for students who witness and hear about such incidents in their daily lives, naming these abuses and providing a framework in which to interpret and condemn such practices indeed proves to be meaningful.

The analysis in Table 5.1 draws from the English translation of the textbooks first developed in Tamil Nadu, though the three textbooks have been adapted in distinct regions to focus on local problems. For example, in the states that comprise India's Northeast, HRE textbooks include more examples of discrimination against Adivasi communities and collective action relating to the region's struggle for human rights amidst state violence.

Students across states repeatedly mentioned the unique character of the human rights textbooks, which were the primary materials utilized in HRE. Many respondents noted that other books and subjects were exam-oriented, whereas this subject and its books were related to their lives and offered important information for their futures. One eighth standard girl noted, "In

Table 5.1 Frequency of Topics and Methods Utilized in HRE Textbooks

Topics	Methods
(In order of frequency, from highest)	*(In order of frequency, from highest)*
Poverty/ underdevelopment/ class inequalities	Reflective/ participatory in-class exercise
Gender discrimination/need for equal treatment	Illustrated dialogue or story
Child labor/ children's rights	Community interviews and/ or investigation and research
Caste discrimination/untouchability/need for equality	Small group work and discussion
Social movements/examples of leaders and activists	Creative artistic expression (drawing, poetry, etc.)
Religious intolerance/need for harmony and pluralism	Class presentation
Rights of tribal/Adivasi communities	Inquiry questions & essay writing
Rights of the disabled and mentally ill	Role play, dramatization, song-writing
Democracy	Letter writing to officials
Environmental rights	School or community campaign

math, we only get formulas, but in HRE, we are reading about ourselves. We are reading about the kind of society we can create if we take this awareness to other people" (student focus group, June 2009). As such, teachers and students noted that many children kept these books with them at all times, read them multiple times, and shared them with friends and family. IHRE encouraged state partners and advisory committees to annually review the components of textbooks that might be changed. This also left room for real-life stories of HRE students to be included in the text and, in some chapters of the textbooks, examples of actions taken by human rights education students related to opposing abuses (such as infanticide, early marriage, or child labor) were offered as a way to inspire current human rights learners.

ANALYZING IMPACT

The Institute of Human Rights Education provided the "input" of HRE through textbooks, teacher training, summer camps, special programs, and since 2009, through the establishment of human rights clubs in schools. Another important dimension involved "output," or how HRE was received by youth. By and large, children valued the opportunity to place what they witnessed in society into a larger framework, namely by understanding issues such as discrimination and violence in a way that determined legality and offered clear directions on what to do to address such instances.

Previous studies have identified a general familiarity with the term "human rights" among Indian students (Dev, Sharma, and Lahiry 2007), though typically, a more involved understanding of concepts and concomitant action among these students has been limited. As a part of this study, thousands of quantitative surveys were administered to HRE students and students of similar age in the same neighborhoods who were not involved in the HRE course across five states. Survey data suggest that the regular syllabus (absent specific human rights instruction) did not have a significant impact on students' responses to human rights abuses. While non-HRE students were able to measure up with HRE students for a few of the general knowledge questions, HRE students were more knowledgeable about nuanced questions concerning human rights. For example, in the state of Karnataka, when asked, "If a man is beating his wife, I should remain quiet and not let anyone know," HRE students (n = 1488) in the Institute of Human Rights Education's program had a higher mean for answers indicating their willingness to take action, distinguishing them from their counterparts not taking the HRE course (n = 1437).

HRE students, according to survey data, were also more likely to question and be critical of discriminatory beliefs and practices based on their human rights learnings. In terms of the common practice of dowry— which is illegal and results in gender-based violence in many instances—HRE students had a higher mean in correctly identifying it as an abuse. HRE students also questioned the common belief that "children only drop out of school because they aren't intelligent," with a majority of the HRE students disagreeing with this statement as compared to their peers not receiving the human rights course. Passive acceptance or resignation to one's fate also obviously limits actions to address human rights violations. HRE students, when compared to non-HRE students, had a higher mean for disagreeing with the statements, "Poverty is due to fate" and "Disability is a punishment from God." In general, for a majority of questions, HRE students had a higher mean (for rights-friendly responses) than their counterparts.

Qualitative data from interviews and focus groups with over 600 students provided rich accounts of their responses to human rights instruction. Student reaction (across schools and states) fell into four areas, with action and intervention in an ongoing abuse being the most common (though not always the most effective) response by students. Students repeatedly narrated experiences in interviews and focus groups indicating the impact of instruction in human rights on their lives; teachers and parents also corroborated these accounts. The real-life impacts that students offered can broadly be categorized in four areas that emerged from the data, the first three of which were action-oriented responses: (1) intervening in situations of abuse; (2) reporting or threatening to report abuse; (3) spreading awareness of human rights; and (4) attitudinal and behavioral shifts at home or in school that were more aligned with human rights learnings. Although these categories were determined through an inductive approach to data analysis, they broadly correspond with scholars' articulations of what human rights education should consist of: namely, a combination of information, values/behavioral changes, and active responses.

The first category of impact involved students intervening in situations of abuse to assist or advocate for victims, be they household or community members. Examples of this type of impact included trying to convince a peer involved in full-time remunerated work to return to school or visiting a family in the neighborhood to convince them not to kill a female baby given the common practice of female infanticide in many of the communities in which this study was carried out. Several students also mentioned trying to stop the practice of early marriage of their classmates, in which adolescent girls' marriages were arranged soon after they hit puberty, because this impeded their right to education.

The second category of impact consisted of students who, after learning about human rights, identified and reported an abuse—or equally effective, threatened to report the abuse—to an authority, such as a headmaster, village-level leader, or the police; child labor, marriage under the age of 18, and female infanticide are all illegal practices in India. The primary difference between category one and two is that in the first, students directly intervened in situations, and in the second—and perhaps more strategically given the ages (11–15) of HRE students and often low caste or gender status—students sought an intermediary with (or at least with the specter of) greater authority to induce changed behavior on the part of those they identified as violating rights.

The third category of impact was more preventative and included educating others or spreading awareness in some way about human rights based on what was learned at school. Students reported sharing their human rights education books or learnings with parents, siblings, neighbors, and/or friends, as well as seeking out venues to teach about human rights, such as in community self-help groups (often organized around microfinance) that their parents belonged to or in other settings. Students who were slightly more affluent or socially privileged often engaged in more awareness-raising, though some marginalized youth did as well if abuses were not immediately visible in their households or communities.

The fourth category of impact related to personal changes or shifts in behaviors or attitudes at home or in school that resulted in greater respect for human rights. Students discussed renegotiating household norms related to gender, caste, and/or religion. A class seven boy, for example, noted that he cleaned his own plate after eating rather than having his sister wash all the dishes as was previously done. Students interacted with classmates of different backgrounds more readily than before HRE, a notable phenomenon given caste strictures against "impurity" and contact with members of lower castes, even if it meant discontent on the part of parents, grandparents, or neighbors since many villages in rural India are still largely residentially segregated by caste, subcaste, and religion.

Figure 5.1 illustrates student responses to the focus group question, "Have you taken any actions after learning about human rights?" Taking the affirmative responses to the question, data on the types of actions are presented by gender.

While all four areas were consistently mentioned by students, the majority of responses involved students' attempts to intervene in situations of abuse in some way—whether successful or not. Boys in general were more likely to directly intervene in abuse (around 69 percent) whereas girls were slightly less likely (49.5 percent) and had a greater propensity toward community education and charity (nearly 23 percent) in comparison with their male counterparts (less than 10 percent). Boys and girls were roughly equal in reporting (or threatening to report) abuses and personal changes. The higher number of boys engaging in direct action is ostensibly related to the relative social status of boys versus girls as will be discussed in the following chapter.

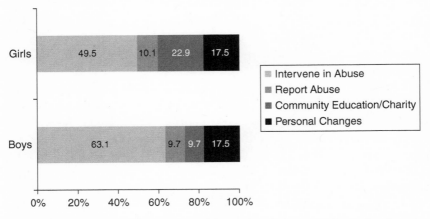

Figure 5.1 Responses to the question, "Have you taken any actions after learning about human rights?"

Nonetheless, the high number of both boys and girls claiming to act in the face of injustices suggests that students, through human rights education, developed a sense of agency to intervene and confront violations. All four types of impact were noted at household, school, and community levels. Additionally, marginalized youth inspired by HRE often had to strategize how to intervene collectively or with an adult since their limited social status could frustrate their attempts at intervention.

INDIVIDUAL ACTIONS

The most common type of action—whether in the household, at school, or in the larger community—that students took were individual efforts by students to influence change (approximately 61 percent of all student actions were individual and 39 percent were collective). However, individual actions were much less likely to be successful especially for marginalized youth who often did not hold the social position or status to induce change (see Figure 5.2). Those acting in solidarity (coalitional agents) were more successful in enacting change individually as will be discussed subsequently, but for Dalit and Adivasi children, as well as girls facing discrimination, acting on their own behalf individually did not always produce the desired results.

Several young women studying HRE did mention standing up for their right to equality so they could play outside or limit their household work since their brothers were free from such responsibilities, albeit not always successfully. One student from Tamil Nadu, Uma,[3] who had participated in three years of HRE as well as a residential summer camp for HRE students and was now in class eleven, noted that she had argued with her parents to let her participate in dance programs at school. The family felt that this was "dishonorable" and after she participated in one at school without permission, they beat her severely at home. Uma persevered and eventually convinced her parents to let her participate, but she still reported that her father's drinking and conservative views limited her ability to act freely. Uma's experience demonstrates the way that students utilized human rights messages to stand up to their families, going against many of the hierarchical, gendered, and age-structured traditions that are part of many Indian communities. These changes were sometimes slow and incremental, but students' persistence, based on their belief in what human rights teachers and books—both sources of knowledge deemed legitimate and authoritative—were advocating, sometimes resulted in greater freedom from restrictions that limited their lives.

Many students were less successful than Uma in changing unequal household or community dynamics. For example, several female students discussed arguing unsuccessfully for a more equal proportion of food at mealtime or to be allowed to go outside and play instead of carrying out household chores. One Dalit student discussed telling the local priest to allow him to enter the temple because he had read that discrimination was wrong, but his request was ignored. Similarly, a Dalit student in seventh standard discussed using a tap to wash his plate one day and getting yelled at by a village elder from a higher caste. He defended his right, but he and his family were threatened with violence.

Resistance to and backlash toward marginalized youth utilizing their new learnings came from two distinct quarters: their own families and those whose power was upset by their actions. Parents often rely on higher-status community members for employment and students' actions to change social relations could disrupt the livelihoods of families. For instance, one parent noted that there was considerable caste discrimination in the village, but that "if we stay quiet inside our homes, it is better instead of going and intervening in the problem. It's better just to keep quiet and we can lead a peaceful life that way" (interview, January 2009). Thus, for marginalized youth to speak out against an abuse in itself is an act of resistance given the dominant pressure to conform to unequal norms and practices. At times, students faced violence and backlash for attempting to change practices. Several students noted physical attacks as a result of trying to make changes at home or in the community or being subject to corporal punishment for attempting to stand up for something they felt was wrong at school. One sixth standard student, learning about human rights for the first time, went to the headmaster to complain that he had not received a uniform to which he was entitled; as punishment, he was caned and threatened with expulsion.

Given resistance and backlash, students then had to consider other options, one of which was to desist from taking any action or postpone action until they were older and had more status. After trying to take action in line with the human rights learning in their classrooms, and after not seeing desired changes, some students did feel discouraged and resigned to facing violations. As has been discussed in previous chapters, caste and gender discrimination often permeate schools with teachers as perpetuators of unequal attitudes and practices. The following account by a Dalit student in ninth standard, Shyam, conveys his discouragement:

> In my school, the teachers make us lower caste children eat the food that was left over by them on their plate and then wash their plates. There were ten teachers and if we didn't wash all the plates, they would yell at us and hit us. My teacher also asks the Dalit children to wash all the toilets in the school. They give us some

bleaching powder and some brooms and we have to clean up the toilets. They never make the higher caste children do this. We don't want to be on the bad side of the teacher since they are powerful, so we can't say anything. I want to go and stop human rights violations in the future, and I'm certain that when I grow up, I can do something about all the violations that are happening around me. Now I am too small to do anything about it. (Interview, May 2009)

Shyam did not receive regular instruction in human rights since his teacher just distributed the books to students. Perhaps correspondingly, Shyam did not have a favorable view toward the power of individual or collective action to confront the abuses he faced at school. In either case, he did discuss effectively challenging an unequal practice of a rope separating Dalit and non-Dalit villagers when receiving compensation for a rural employment scheme,[4] but felt he could not speak out against the practices he saw at school given teachers' authority and power. His response was to wait until he was older to take action. Other student responses were to be strategic about how to intervene more effectively utilizing textbooks, teachers, and their peers to enhance their status in confronting abusive practices.

STRATEGIZING AND COLLECTIVE ACTION

Repeated examples emerged from the data of students with limited social status who were discouraged by the reactions to their individual efforts and who subsequently turned to collective strategies. These alternative strategies included utilizing their human rights textbooks, enlisting teachers and/or parents, or organizing in collective peer groups to intervene in situations of abuse. Collective action as defined in this study included students' actions that leveraged the social status of peers, the authority of textbooks, and the support of teachers, parents, and/or staff of IHRE or other individuals with higher status to make change.

Figure 5.2 illustrates that, for all students, collective action was more successful than individual action in securing desired changes in behaviors or practices aligned with human rights principles. Despite this, students tended to engage in individual actions (perhaps related to the way lessons focusing on singular human rights "heroes" such as Mahatma Gandhi and Dr. B. R. Ambedkar were presented)[5] with nearly double the frequency of collective efforts.

Collective action was organized horizontally—with other peers—or vertically—with students enlisting sources of authority, usually higher status teachers and parents. In certain cases, students leveraged the authority of their human rights education textbooks to inform violators of their knowledge of

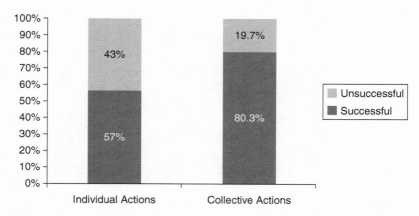

Figure 5.2 Efficacy of Individual versus Collective Action (all student respondents)

avenues for recourse. For example, one 12-year-old student in Tamil Nadu noted telling his father, who was seeking to withdraw him from school to work to support the family, that he would report him to the authorities listed in his book if he tried to discontinue his education. The student was then allowed to stay in school.

More typically, the textbook alone did not offer sufficient authority to secure respect for human rights. Usually, students needed assistance from committed human rights teachers willing to intervene directly in situations. In an urban Bengaluru school where HRE was being offered, a young woman, Chitra, discussed confronting her stepfather who was sexually abusing her:

> Before, I used to think I was the only person undergoing these problems at home. But after reading this book, I learned about my rights and that there are so many boys and girls around the world whose rights are also being violated. I realized we should not keep quiet. I used to think that nobody was out there to help me and whatever torture I was facing in my family, I thought that it was my fate and I deserved it. But once I started reading the human rights education books, I knew I had to stand up and fight for my rights. So one day I told my stepfather to stop and showed him the books, saying that I would report him to the authorities listed in there. He got scared and my teacher helped find a residential home for abused girls for me to go live in. When I got there, I started teaching all the other girls about human rights with my HRE textbooks. In the future, I want to be a social worker so I can tell everyone about human rights. (Interview, June 2009)

Chitra's prior feeling that whatever treatment she was experiencing was fated and shameful resonated with the accounts of many marginalized youth.

Chitra realized that other young people may be facing abuses as well, making her experience less isolating and also providing a framework in which reporting an abuse to the police or other authorities was sanctioned rather than seen as bringing shame on her family. For such youth, HRE served to counter some of the assumptions that have facilitated unequal caste and gender relations for centuries.

Students often discussed their socialization into unequal social relations primarily through parents' messages, school processes, and the limited space to question practices related to "tradition" and "culture." For example, female students sometimes did not want to get married at young ages but had little authority to question arrangements and customs that preceded them. Larger or dominant Hindu belief systems related to *karma* and rebirth dictate that the results of one's previous lives impact current circumstances such that inequality and mistreatment are justified as the victim's fault. One educational official noted in an interview that, "things [like child labor] are because of them only. If one suffers [as a laborer], it is because of the things they have done in their young age or in the previous birth. Whatever we did, we have to suffer" (interview, February 2009). Such beliefs often limit action aimed at challenging the status quo and realizing greater access and equity.

Many Dalit students, experiencing social exclusion in schools and communities, internalize ostracism. For example, a Dalit student in sixth standard in his first year of human rights education remarked that he was not allowed to go into his classmates' homes (because of common beliefs about "pollution" and "purity" as discussed in Chapter Three). Prior to HRE, he had assumed something was wrong with his personality leading to other students' dislike of him. The simple act of learning about human rights in schools, from their teachers, and with supporting evidence in textbooks, in many student accounts, provided a framework for analyzing discrimination as a negative social force, depersonalizing ostracism and helping to remove a sense that these behaviors were their fault. The learnings also helped students work against such discrimination through the inspiration provided by quotes and examples of notable historical and contemporary activists.

Teachers' own transformed views about human rights and equality (as will be further explored in Chapter Seven) also influenced their involvement. Often, children would be pulled out of school if the father, the usual breadwinner, passed away or left the family, or if the student's performance in school was not very promising and the family felt the time would be better spent on income generation. An estimated 8 million children remain out of school, despite substantial efforts and a decrease from 13.4 million in 2005 (as cited in Mukul 2009). Many student actions—whether individual or collective—also involved encouraging out-of-school youth to return. Without a consideration of the family's financial needs, individual student actions alone usually were not enough to secure a child's return to school. The most successful of these student responses usually involved teacher support or collective action by students to creatively address the family's needs.

Children pulled out of school to support their families often had trouble resisting the family's pressure to work on their own and required assistance from fellow students, community members, and teachers. Nearly all the students interviewed for this research came from low-income families and, as such, knew of students removed from school to support their families. Students cited examples of children doing factory, construction, or domestic work and working in restaurants or making bricks. Such work was poorly remunerated, but often was the only option that allowed families to survive. Velmurugan, a student from Tamil Nadu, recounted how his family wanted him to leave school, going against his human rights learnings:

> I am the oldest son and after my father died, we didn't have any money. I thought the only way I could support my family was to work in the tea stall and not come to school anymore. My friend and classmates asked me, "Why are you working in this tea stall? Come and study along with us. You should get an education—it's very valuable." My classmate went and told his father, explained the situation and about human rights, and brought him to convince my mother to let me keep going to school. His father came and asked me, "Why are you doing this work?" Then he talked to my mother and convinced her to work in the tea stall so that I can finish my studies at least until 10th or 12th standard. My mother is now working and our relatives are also helping out. (Interview, February 2009)

The authority of Velmurugan's classmate's father assisted in shifting his family's perspective about the role of schooling in his future and generated the solution to have Velmurugan's mother work in the tea stall, an unusual job for women in some rural areas of India. By intervening—first alone and then with a parent—the HRE classmate was able to assist Velmurugan in devising ways to reconcile his family's financial needs with his right to an education.

Students in West Bengal also collectively sought to educate their community in situations where children were pulled out of school at a young age to work as embroiderers (often at significant cost to their eyesight in later years). Here also, students often had to face parents' questions about replacing the economic contribution of a child's labor. In these cases, students had mixed results for their efforts.[6] Similarly, getting a child back to school did not always result in sustained attendance given the persistence of the same factors that led to the students' initial decision to drop out.

Students used instruction in human rights to confront abuses, such as corruption, mismanagement of government schemes intended for their own benefit, and discrimination by teachers that they saw in their schools. As a collective, students still faced the possibility of backlash, but by acting together and wherever possible, leveraging the authority of their human rights teacher, students often had notable successes in addressing human rights violations. For example, a group of human rights education students related the following incident that occurred the first year they were learning about human rights in class six:

> In the school mid-day meal scheme, the food was not good—there were insects, flies, and stones in the food. Before reading HRE, we used to take those insects out and then eat since we are not getting any food from home. The teacher also didn't care about the noon meal scheme, what's going on, he did not bother about that. But after going to the training, after teaching this HRE to us, we learnt about the basic right to food, right to clothing, right to have clean water. What we did one day in sixth [standard], we got the food from the cook. We brought the food to her and said, "See this food, insects and stones are there, how can one eat this food? We won't have this food; we also have rights. We should have clean food and water. But you are not providing clean or good food for us." Then, what she told us was, "I am working for the past 27 years. No one has ever asked me any single question. You children are asking me like this?" We told her, "Yes, we have the right. See this book." We also complained to the headmaster. She had to realize the mistake she was doing. Now we are getting noon meal from her and we are having good meals. (Focus group, February 2009)

Whether for fear of losing her job or a genuine belief in students' right to clean food, the cook changed her behavior. In this case, student success was predicated on a responsive and supportive headmaster, not a given factor in every school. In another case, the headmaster, rather than supporting the students' demands against the cook, beat the children who were complaining and threatened to expel them.

Headmasters' and human rights education teachers' interest in the subject and willingness to support student action were also important factors in students' ability to influence change. Predictably, there were also tensions between the HRE teacher and other teachers who benefitted from existing social arrangements. For example, the Institute of Human Rights Education reported a case where the attendance of Dalit students in a rural district in

Tamil Nadu was irregular. The HRE teacher, citing her training in human rights and motivated to find out the cause of the problem, investigated why her students' attendance was erratic. She found that other teachers were using the students as unpaid domestic servants for cleaning, cooking, and other tasks in their homes during the school-day when their parents thought they were at school. The HRE teacher took action and reported this issue to the authorities. The headmaster—perhaps out of fear of sanction or his own rejection of this practice—prohibited teachers from engaging in this and consequently, this practice stopped. The teacher did note, however, the anger of her colleagues in response to her actions (PW 2008, 102). HRE teachers who attempted to intervene to stop corporal punishment or other abusive and unlawful practices felt similar backlash. Eradicating school-level abuses was thus greatly dependent on support from higher authorities.

CONTINUUM OF IMPACT

There was a continuum of experiences with HRE. School-level factors and students' and families' social location played key roles. On one end of the continuum, students found the program to be a "time pass" based on their inability to enforce their knowledge of human rights in meaningful ways whether for reasons of lack of agency or inability to engage in collective action, or based on some teachers'/headmasters' resistance to implementing the program. At the other end, students repeatedly reported that HRE was a "transformative force" in their lives. Figure 5.3 presents individual- and structural-level

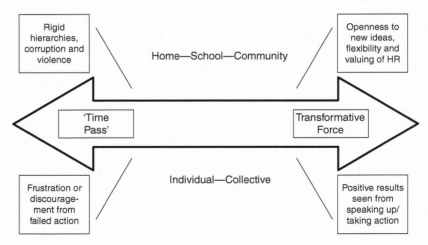

Figure 5.3 Continuum of Impact of Human Rights Education

factors that shaped impact, such as the rigidity or openness of households and schools in responding to change.

At the structural level, the openness of adults in the household, school officials, and community figures to new ideas influenced the level to which marginalized youth felt comfortable challenging social relations. In situations where rigid hierarchies, high levels of corruption, and violence predominated, youth struggled more to believe in the applicability of human rights information contained in their textbooks. At some rural schools in Orissa visited as part of this study, HRE students and teachers reported rampant corruption. For example, not uncommon practices included watering down of rice and *daal* (lentils) in the mid-day meals of students (so that, according to reports, teachers and headmasters could earn extra money from selling the foodstuffs that came from the government). Given their remote locations, these schools were rarely visited by government officials. During my fieldwork, the roads had been nearly washed away under heavy rains, making it difficult for even dedicated officials to reach some schools. This minimal oversight undoubtedly contributed to the incidence of corrupt practices, including allegations of sexual misconduct. Under such conditions, a group of HRE students understandably noted, "when we are grown up, we will share human rights in the community" (focus group, July 2009), suggesting their discouragement in viewing the efficacy of immediate action.

Rigid hierarchies that were sometimes rooted in tradition proved difficult to overcome through student action. Those resistant to intervening in, for example, early and arranged marriages, typically invoked culture and custom as a counter-weight to human rights norms. Conversely, those students with families open to new ideas—for example, rural and illiterate parents who valued the knowledge brought home by children from school—were most affected by human rights information at the household level.

The interplay of structural and individual factors sometimes led students to experience HRE as a "time pass," receiving little benefit from the information presented. Students were sometimes discouraged after failed attempts to address discrimination and aggression, an unsurprising phenomenon given extreme levels of violence and inequality they faced in their households, schools, or communities. Fear of backlash or retaliation also stifled further action in examples involving school corruption.

At the level of school and community, for the program to be a transformative force, teachers and headmasters who were willing to comply with officials and the NGO to carry out the program were needed. When rigid hierarchies, entrenched corruption, insufficient time, or a simple lack of interest dampened the motivation for teachers and headmasters to take on a new program or be open to students' demands about their rights, the program seemed to remain at the level of "time pass." For example, in one school, a now class ten student noted students' response to the subject matter given the teacher's approach:

> In the beginning, teachers were not giving lessons properly. "There is no exam for this subject; this is for you to read only," the teachers were saying, and they didn't give the lessons. They just gave us the books. Teachers were not teaching us, so we thought, "Why should we read the books?" We would just read it for time pass sometimes. (Interview, May 2009)

In such schools where teachers hold similar attitudes or where teacher absenteeism results in overcrowded classes, the program and its benefits remain contained in closed books in the corner of the classroom.

Alternatively, students achieved some success where there was an openness to new ways of interacting based either on genuine belief in the value of human rights or fear of punishment from authorities if such legal guarantees were not respected. Where students—through collective and strategic actions—were able to influence some sort of change, their identity as human rights education students and budding activists was solidified, resulting in further action and campaigns. Thus, many students drew on their peers, textbooks, teachers, parents, or other authorities to strategically counter abuses that they witnessed in their homes, schools, and communities. As a result, many students noted that the program was indeed a transformative force—"I will never forget [it] in my life," as one student commented,—based on the positive changes they were able to effect through speaking up and taking action.

A number of ingredients contributed to the more transformative results achieved by the HRE program. These involved reciprocal actions by both the schools and the NGO implementing HRE (i.e., IHRE or its state partners). The factors that facilitated impact included (a) close contact between the school, teachers, and IHRE; (b) frequent visits by IHRE staff and participation in regional programs; (c) teachers' interest in nurturing student activism; and (d) teachers' willingness to intervene in situations of inequality or abuse in schools, students' homes, and the broader community. There were also schools where teachers and headmasters were supportive, but where differing individual and household circumstances influenced students' interest in the program. Indeed, social location and power dynamics proved to be important factors in assessing the impact of HRE, an important caveat to nation-state centered models of educational reform.

As illustrated in this chapter, students' social location, gender, and realities in their homes and schools influenced the ways in which they mediated and understood human rights education in line with this book's third premise. The actions of marginalized students in response to HRE demonstrated both the promise and peril of this type of learning. The use of collective strategies (whether horizontally with peers or vertically with higher-status adults) enhanced Dalit, Adivasi, and female children's ability to change unequal practices, though reaction, backlash, and the challenges to implementing HRE bear further formal scrutiny. For marginalized youth, respect for their human rights was in their immediate self-interest. Even if no actions were taken, instruction that allowed students to consider their equality may produce attitudinal and behavior shifts in the future vis-à-vis the refusal to accept unequal relations and practices.

The following chapter continues exploring the notion of social location as integral to understanding the conceptualization and practice of HRE. Chapter Six explores the experiences of youth who serve as coalitional agents, those students who seek to influence changes that may not directly benefit them.

Chapter Six

Building Solidarity and Coalitional Agency through Human Rights Education

This chapter explores the ways that human rights education (HRE) inspired action on behalf of others and how youth develop such empathy and solidarity. As discussed earlier, a coalitional agent can be thought of as someone who acts together with or on behalf of a victim of abuse, but who is not directly targeted him or herself. Because the Institute of Human Rights Education (IHRE) operates in government schools serving marginalized youth, Catholic schools serving students from varied socioeconomic backgrounds, and a handful of elite private schools in some states, there are a number of variously positioned students who can serve as coalitional agents. Indeed, the distinction between a "victim" and a "coalitional agent" can often be situational and fluid. Depending on the situation, a coalitional agent could be someone from a disadvantaged social group who, in a particular moment, is not the target of abuse. Coalitional agents could be male students in all schools (relative to their female counterparts), students of slightly higher-caste background or from dominant religions, or students with considerably higher socioeconomic status.

Coalitional agency can include solidarity with victims in one's midst, advocacy on their behalf or for creative solutions to unequal practices, or charity efforts that alter rigid class hierarchies. These categories emerged through data analysis of the interviews and focus groups with students not directly affected by abuses. Data were coded using various descriptors, one of which determined whether a student's account of taking action involved him or her as a victim or coalitional agent. Thus, the same student, depending on the situation, could be a victim in one account and a coalitional agent in another, but the unit of analysis for this coding strategy was the action not the individual.

Social location mediated how human rights information was received by coalitional agents. The same HRE textbooks, for example, for some could offer a framework for abuses that were witnessed first hand in their communities and for others could offer a window into an unknown world that was completely separate from lived reality. In either case, substantial impact was documented among coalitional agents who were often more successful in transforming situations of abuse—whether individually or collectively. Collective action could include peer action among coalitional agents, solidarity and action together with victims, or enlisting the help of parents, teachers, or other authorities to utilize the moral bases of human rights or fear of sanction to change behavior. In a society deeply divided along caste and class lines, more privileged or higher-status youth typically faced less backlash in addressing human rights violations. Conversely, lower-status students more often appreciated the severity and urgency of some of the worst violations of human dignity, and stood in solidarity with victims, no doubt due to social location.

IHRE's strategy involves securing the interest and support of students who, through human rights education, are compelled to take action and intervene on behalf of siblings, friends, and community members. IHRE's approach of persuasive pragmatism demonstrated considerable success in convincing students that human rights is an important cause, whether their response is understood as one of charity or solidarity. HRE often produced a form of coalitional agency that proved effective in creating change at the level of individual social interactions. The third premise of this book is that HRE must be understood in terms of relationships of power and, in this study, social location was key to understanding the impact of human rights education.

The previous chapter documented the effectiveness of collective action (whether through horizontal or vertical alliances), even though students showed a greater propensity toward individual action. This chapter focuses on the efforts of coalitional agents who, as a group, were more effective than victims in addressing abuses they encountered in their homes, schools, and communities. While 625 student respondents were involved in this study, Figure 6.1 presents a total number of actions (not respondents) to the extent that ascertaining the exact numbers of victims and coalitional agents,

Successful Individual Actions (% by actor)

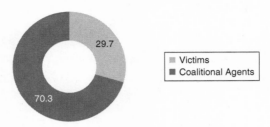

Figure 6.1 Individual Actions as Percent of all Successful Actions

given the shifting nature of these categories, is impossible. In analyzing all the actions taken by students as a result of HRE, more than 60 percent of them involved individual efforts. Of this, as Figure 6.1 demonstrates, just over 70 percent were taken by coalitional agents, not the victims themselves. While victims or targets of abuse were not as effective as coalitional agents in intervening in isolation, both groups were more likely to succeed if they acted collectively with peers or adults.

The issue of status, even for coalitional agents, is important to consider and is often absent from discussions of human rights education. The moral imperative of human rights assumes that HRE affects children in uniformly positive and beneficial ways regardless of their backgrounds, without consideration of their different roles as victims and coalitional agents. Power dynamics and status certainly amplify some voices more than others. Even if not victims of mistreatment, distance from an abuse and gender influenced others' responsiveness to students' actions. Oftentimes, male student responses to violations of the rights of female youth were more successful, just as interventions from higher-caste youth on behalf of Dalits and Adivasis carried more weight.

GENDER AND AGENCY

Despite the greater efficacy of individual interventions, gender often limited the actions of coalitional agents. Even in cases where girls were not the ones targeted, their actions carried limited authority. As a group, the young women interviewed in this study reported less efficacy in intervening in abuses. Boys, especially ones of higher caste and socioeconomic backgrounds, were nearly twice as likely to see positive outcomes based on their interventions than girls. While HRE may inspire them to act, young women who attempted to act alone or who could not enlist support from peers, teachers, and parents, were often frustrated in their efforts to help.

Human rights education sometimes offered students an idyllic presentation of guarantees and how change might be achieved through intervention without a concomitant analysis of the structural constraints to their efficacy. Students who were inspired to act when seeing abuses in real life that they had just studied sometimes encountered first hand such constraints as they attempted to take action. This was particularly true for young women who attempted to act individually. Saranya, a student now in eighth standard, related the following incident that happened during her first year learning about human rights in sixth standard:

> Nearby my house, there was a family and the husband was beating the wife, saying she hadn't brought enough dowry when they got married. I had just started studying HRE and had learned that dowry was illegal. I went and spoke to these neighbors—the woman's in-laws and husband who were all living together—and told them this is a human rights violation. I told them, "See, we are reading about this in our books." What they responded was, "You are a small child. What do you know about that? You should not interfere in our family problems. You just close your mouth and get out." One day, what they did was they poured some kerosene on the wife, burnt her, and killed her for not bringing more dowry. I didn't know at that time where to give a complaint since they were not listening when I tried to tell them that this is wrong. (Focus group, May 2009)

Saranya went on to say that if she encountered a similar situation, she would find the appropriate authorities to call and report what she saw; she no longer saw direct intervention as a useful strategy for countering abuses in her community. For some, the idealism inspired by human rights education motivated actions that, because of their limited status, did not prove effective. Yet, lower status itself was not indicative of the lesser value of teaching human rights to young women. For some students, such experiences resulted in frustration; other girls sought different strategies, some of which were successful and some of which were not.

Young women, even when acting as coalitional agents, often needed additional support to effectively intervene in cases of abuse. Mathangi, an HRE student who at the time of this research was in ninth standard, related the following incident that occurred in her neighborhood when she was in seventh standard:

> My friend's father used to get drunk and beat her mother and the children regularly. He wasn't happy because the mother didn't give birth to any male children and he blamed her. One day, my friend came over and told me what was going on

and asked for my help since she knew I was studying human rights and I used to share some of the lessons with her. I went to talk to her father and he slapped me so hard, even my neck was hurting after. I told my parents and they tried to talk to him, but he was too drunk to listen. I told my human rights education teacher and she said he should be taken to a rehabilitation home, but she didn't want to get involved further. One day, the father came home and beat my friend severely and she could not bear the problem anymore. She committed suicide. The case was even in the newspaper. (Interview, May 2009)

In Mathangi's account, her friend's father was very difficult to reason with or convince, and though she sought to enlist the help of higher-status individuals like her human rights education teacher, the teacher just provided advice rather than coming in person to help. In the absence of a counterfactual scenario, we do not know if the outcome would have been any different if Mathangi was a boy. Nonetheless, in the cases offered, greater effort was required on the part of girls to secure the support of others (whether peers who were girls or boys, parents, and teachers), even for those not directly affected by a particular abuse.

As noted in the students' accounts as well as in Figure 5.1 from Chapter Five, this limited efficacy in intervention may have, over time, limited girls' interest and belief in the power of intervening in abuses. 49.5 percent of all girls interviewed reported intervening in rights violations as compared to 63.1 percent of all boys. Some girls, in response, gravitated toward charitable actions and community education as a way of addressing abuses in the present and future. Many instead became more strategic in their interventions by working collectively with male peers and adults with higher status to increase their chances for success. Young women's human rights agency was often contingent on coalitional solidarity, whereas young men's favorable social position allowed them—individually or collectively—to become human rights defenders in their communities.

LEVELS OF INTERVENTION

As previous sections have indicated, collective groups of coalitional agents—with at least some boys—were the most likely to be effective in addressing human rights abuses. Though the range of coalitional agents spanned Dalit boys and affluent children in elite schools, their responses to HRE were often distinct and merit discussion here. Categories emerged after all the data were collected and in the analysis stage. Figure 6.2 maps how responses were shaped and enabled by social location and dynamics of power.

Figure 6.2 Types of Response by Social Location

The actions of coalitional agents fell into three categories as shown in Figure 6.2. The closer the abuse was (i.e., in the same household or community), the greater likelihood that a response would be intervention and direct solidarity, putting the coalitional agent oftentimes at risk for physical violence and backlash. If the agent chose to not intervene directly, and to educate or lobby for consideration of human rights-inspired alternatives to the practice, actions were identified as "advocacy." As the social distance from abuses grew (even if the physical distance was not great as in the case of domestic workers in affluent households), students' HRE-inspired actions resembled charity or material assistance. The same curriculum was utilized, but students' social location mediated the response and actions taken.

The data that follow illustrate these three broad areas of response by students not directly targeted by human rights abuses. The data involving acts of charity included a handful of elite schools in a few states and Catholic schools in various states where a mix of middle class and poor children on scholarship attend. Students closer to the everyday incidence of human rights abuses tended toward advocacy on behalf of and physical solidarity with victims of abuse.

Human Rights and Charitable Action

While ideology can influence what goes into human rights education, as Chapter Two highlighted, social location can shape—though it does not determine—the influence of HRE on students. In schools where students came from more affluent backgrounds, human rights education and events related to the program inspired reflection about and action challenging previously held beliefs and common social practices. For example, several students noted that getting together at regional events or trainings allowed them the chance to meet students from Adivasi communities with whom they otherwise would never have had contact given their geographic isolation. Other students from privileged backgrounds reconsidered their reliance on domestic servants with one seventh standard student, Mohan, stating, "In the human rights day function that People's Watch organized for HRE students, after lunch we took our own plates and washed them. I realized then that we should clean our things ourselves and not rely on others. Since then, I've been washing my own plate after meals" (focus group, January 2009). This section focuses on the charitable actions that HRE inspired among coalitional agents.

For many middle- to upper-class students, a small proportion of the students that IHRE served at the time of this research, human rights education forced a reconsideration of their and their family's relationships to those individuals from lower class and caste backgrounds in their midst. This sometimes meant reconsidering relationships with students from less affluent backgrounds in their own schools (particularly in Christian institutions where scholarship programs resulted in diverse socioeconomic groups attending the same schools). In one such school in Tamil Nadu, half of the students were from an orphanage run by the parish and the other half of the student body were fee-paying middle-class students. A result of HRE was greater student integration; previously, the two groups were separate. The more affluent students also organized donations and drives for their classmates from lower socioeconomic backgrounds. Teachers noted the greater willingness of students to share food and create friendships across these previously fixed boundaries at the school.

In more affluent schools, human rights action often included domestic staff and other workers they interacted with regularly. For example, in one private school in Tamil Nadu run by a trust,[1] many students came from families who had large agricultural holdings. One 12-year-old student in seventh standard, Santhosh, noted the following, which was representative of other affluent students' accounts:

> Some parents are not sending their children to schools, but are taking them to the farm to work, like the one owned by my family. I told them that their children have a right to education and helped raise money for school supplies for them.

One woman whose husband works on the farm came home to seek help because she said her husband was continuously beating her. I had been reading my human rights textbooks to my mother after school and she remembered that there were some phone numbers there to report any problems like domestic abuse. She told the laborer's wife that, "You should go and complain about this to the human rights commission and they will take severe action against your husband." (Focus group, February 2009)

While this student utilized his influence as the child of the landlords/employers to emphasize his human rights-related advice, his intervention also helped support a woman seeking refuge from domestic violence. Santhosh's willingness to speak up based on his human rights learnings offered an avenue for support that was legitimized by his family's higher socioeconomic and landed status.

Students from a range of class backgrounds discussed providing assistance to individuals or organizations as a result of human rights education. For example, in West Bengal, students at an all-boys school identified out-of-school children and raised money to get backpacks and school supplies for them, with the help of their teacher, in order to encourage them to come back to school. In Tamil Nadu, a student from a government school discussed volunteering to help disabled children at an institution near her home. Another group of students from Tamil Nadu discussed teasing a boy because he always used to come to school with torn clothes; after learning about human rights, they instead raised money to help him buy new clothes his family could not afford. A group of students from a low-cost private school in Kerala discussed their human rights club's activity of tutoring the children of migrant laborers from Bihar in the local language of Malayalam because not knowing this language was an impediment to their schooling. In Andhra Pradesh, a group of human rights education students in a Catholic school raised money for victims of floods in other parts of the state. Such efforts were organized by HRE students, sometimes inspired by teachers or human rights clubs in response to the needs they identified.

In West Bengal, IHRE's state partner is a unique private school that has service to the underprivileged as a core tenet. The Loreto Sealdah School, run by Sister Cyril Mooney, has offered education and housing to streetchildren in Kolkata since the 1980s. The school formally adopted HRE and became a state partner of the Institute of Human Rights Education in 2006. Half of the children at the school are from extremely poor backgrounds and are on scholarship, while the other half are fee-paying students from largely elite families in the city. As the nodal point for HRE in West Bengal, the school has expanded the HRE program to other Loreto schools (the most well-known institutions having long served Kolkata's elite) as well as dozens of government schools in West Bengal. As such, affluent students were exposed to human rights instruction whether or not their school was directly engaged in the educational projects for streetchildren. One eighth standard girl in another Loreto school, Nisha, noted the following about actions she had taken since learning about human rights:

> Some of my classmates have started to keep packets of biscuits in their cars, and when the beggars come to the window to ask for money, they give them the packets instead. Sometimes the domestic workers who work in our house want to study and get educated. For example, my maid wants to learn some English. She goes to a person who is teaching just for the heck of getting money, but I have advised her instead of going to that person, she can spare at least half an hour with me everyday and I can teach her new things. She has improved a lot on her English. I figure if I can waste time on my own entertainment, I can at least take this time out to help make her a more important part of society. In class, our teacher made us write down at least one way in which we can help our domestic servants or anyone who works for us like visiting their family or teaching them something. The idea is to just make them feel a part of the world and feel more important so that's why we all did that. Some students also started collecting donations for different charities. (Focus group, July 2009)

Though the charitable acts mentioned appear quite different than the actions taken by students faced with extreme violence discussed earlier, a child from an elite family offering a domestic servant English instruction or visiting their family on a regular basis was nonetheless an extremely unusual disruption of traditional hierarchies and social relations. The humanization of domestic workers, while not a radical transformation of social inequalities, was perhaps a useful socialization into an alternative way of interacting with employees, especially since these children, ostensibly, would occupy positions of continued privilege as adults.[2]

Welfarism or "asistencialismo," which Paulo Freire described as charitable actions by elites that promote dependency among the poor (as cited in Schugurensky 2001), is not an ideal response to HRE in that it often eclipses the agency of victims of abuses in acting on their own behalf. Arguably, however, charitable acts are still better than ignoring or tolerating dehumanizing conditions that perpetuate social inequality. The nature of solidarity as developing and cultivating others' ability to act on their own behalf is often confused with paternalism and actions for groups that further marginalize them. This study classified the responses to HRE among coalitional agents, but further research to parse these notions in greater detail would be productive.

Though not sponsored by IHRE directly, the Loreto Sealdah School in Kolkata had also begun to work with elite schools on a project to help affluent students become community educators to address child labor. An estimated 50,000 children, 86 percent of who are girls (Save the Children 2009), work as child domestic servants in the homes of wealthier Kolkata residents. This program sought to have students identify these children, request employers to release them for after-school programs, and ultimately educate the children about the need to reenroll in schools and the employers about the illegality of hiring child laborers. Students who had studied HRE utilized such instruction to tutor these child domestic servants after school or engage the employers in conversation that shaded into advocacy efforts as will be discussed in the next section.

Advocacy for More Equitable Conditions

Students who did not necessarily witness extreme abuse regularly but identified inequitable practices at home or in school generally utilized human rights learnings to engage in advocacy strategies to address these practices. The line between advocacy and solidarity was often blurred. Advocacy did not usually involve the risk or sacrifice required by solidarity efforts; the latter often jeopardized safety and privilege. Students of somewhat higher status advocated—both individually and collectively—for changes in policies or practices that would result in more just treatment for their classmates, peers, and neighbors in homes, schools, and communities.

Household. Students often advocated for change in homes and in their extended families. Usually the "abuses" were not necessarily extreme or violent, but were related to unequal practices and customs that had not previously been challenged. Students not directly affected by the practices could suggest alternative models and leverage their voices to encourage reconsideration. For male children, their voices were often amplified by cultural norms that held sons in high regard and thus afforded them more authority in households. Young men equipped with human rights knowledge thus could influence family decisions and norms in a variety of ways.

Boys who had studied human rights could sometimes intervene and advocate on behalf of their sisters or other female family members for greater freedoms or rights. This included advocating for an equal share of food to be given to their sisters, for them to be freed up from chores by taking on some themselves, and delaying early marriages of adolescent girls. Even if the boys were unable to delay arranged marriages until their sisters could choose for themselves, certain advocacy efforts did allow for greater flexibility. Many accounts emerged from the data related to boys' advocacy on their sisters' behalf. For example, Parthiban learned that the marriage of his 18-year-old sister was being arranged to his uncle (as was the community's custom)[3] after she finished twelfth standard, even though she wanted to continue on to higher education. Most schools and colleges were reluctant to have a married girl (regardless of age) continue on with her studies and, oftentimes, these young women soon had considerable domestic responsibilities related to cooking, cleaning, agricultural activities, and childrearing. Parthiban, however, related the following action he took on behalf of his sister, inspired by what he had learned in his human rights class:

> My eldest sister was about to complete 12th standard, when the groom's side came to see her. My mother asked them to come and told my sister, "You do not have to go for higher studies; you should get married." I was studying human rights in seventh [standard] when they came to arrange the date for the marriage and when all this marriage talk was going on. I went and talked to my uncle and told him that my sister really wants to continue studying and asked if he could support her in her studies and get married after she finished her B.A. Now she's in the final year. Because of what I studied in human rights education, I could help make it better for my sister. (Interview, May 2009)

While Parthiban could not necessarily stop his sister's marriage, and while the sister's choices regarding her own marriage are not a given, he utilized his human rights knowledge to at least encourage the family to consider alternative options in which her desire to pursue higher education would be fulfilled. Some alternatives, like the one proposed by Parthiban, presented a different option without radically shifting the practices and norms in the household. Students were also able to suggest alternatives at the school and community level to encourage behavior in line with human rights.

School. Many human rights problems were identified at the school level. Students acting as advocates for others at the school level generally involved cases that only affected some of them, and where the others had some power to offer creative alternatives to a situation at hand.

Disabled students face tremendous obstacles to their participation in social life in India, not least when physical infrastructure prohibits their access to schooling. The Right to Education Act passed by the Indian Parliament in

2009 specifically highlights the need for schools to be accessible to all children, and the disproportionately high out-of-school rates for disabled children.[4] The following action taken by students in Kerala reflects creative thinking that was inspired by human rights education related to the issue of accessibility:

> We have started speaking up more because of human rights education. There is a student who walks with a handicap and his classroom is on the third floor. He has to walk up the stairs really slowly and with some help everyday to get to class. Some of us in the human rights education class went to talk to the headmaster about this problem and asked him if that student's classroom could be moved to the ground floor so that he doesn't have to walk up and down the steps everyday. Nobody thought of doing that before, but the headmaster agreed so now another class is upstairs and this boy's class is on the ground floor. (Focus group, December 2009)

The human rights education students, seeing examples about disabled children and their right to equal access and opportunity in their textbooks, took action based on an issue they identified in their own school. In this sense, the creative solution they brainstormed did not have any adverse consequences and the headmaster was amenable to their suggestion. These students felt empowered by their ability to effect change in the school and benefit a fellow student.

Other students also sought to improve their schools in more informal ways. For example, a young male student encouraged female students in class to speak more, telling them, "You girls know so many more things than us boys. You should speak up more." Given gender dynamics in the larger society and in schools, this advocacy counteracted many girls' reticence to speak. For a young man to say and believe this was important and contributed to more equal relationships.

Community. One way that students could advocate for their peers was by getting out-of-school youth back in school. As discussed in the previous chapter, despite significant efforts made through India's domestic SSA (education for all) program, recent estimates put the number of out-of-school children at around 8 million (as cited in Mukul 2009). A group of seventh standard students in a rural district of Karnataka state, inspired by the messages they received at a human rights summer camp run by IHRE in 2009, identified several out-of-school youth in their community. These students together advocated for these children to be let back into school (even if they didn't have a mandated "transfer certificate" from a previous school), spoke with the children's family to convince them about the importance of education, and even raised funds for backpacks and other school supplies:

> After the camp, we went around the village and found many young boys working in hotels, restaurants, factories, and shops. For example, this boy here (*points to student*), he dropped out after fifth standard and was working in a brick factory for three years. At first, his parents did not want to send him [to school], but we raised money for his school supplies and also told the parents that this is illegal for a child under 14 years go to work. We told them, "We are going to tell Maggie Aunty (IHRE state coordinator) and the police if you don't send him." This other boy was working in a restaurant cleaning the tables and getting food for people. He would go everyday from 7 in the morning until 8 o'clock at night, and would earn 500 rupees per month (roughly US $11). We convinced his parents to let him come back and now they are thankful because we collected enough money for books and pens for him. We have identified a few more child laborers that we are now targeting to bring back to school. (Focus group, June 2009)

The example above had elements of charitable action, advocacy, and even solidarity; students put themselves and those they were trying to help at risk of backlash if employers saw them as a threat to their source of cheap labor. Still, the creativity in devising strategies to go out and speak with children and parents directly, as well ensure that the school would allow them to reenroll is notable.

Students also engaged in other types of advocacy, such as community education and devising plays and street-theater performances on human rights issues like caste discrimination, dowry, and child labor. Students and teachers also organized performances at festivals or other venues to spread the message of human rights more broadly. Some students discussed sharing information on human rights in other settings, whether one-on-one or in more formal settings. A few students discussed advocating for better treatment for neighbors or classmates who were darker-skinned given pervasive societal beliefs that lighter skin is more desirable; a lesson in the human rights textbook discouraged such discrimination. Other students discussed sharing human rights information at their parents' self-help (microfinance) group meetings or meetings of the local *panchayat* (elected village-level council). These educational efforts also sometimes turned into advocacy campaigns on a particular issue.

Students across the states noted that alcoholism (and related domestic abuse after their fathers had gotten drunk) was a major problem in their homes and communities. Many students tried to intervene on behalf of their mothers (in solidarity and risking physical harm). Others tried to read their HRE textbook to their fathers, seeking to educate them about the illegality of domestic violence under Indian law. In rural Karnataka, several students and their teachers decided to hold a protest and marched to the local liquor store, demanding that it shut down given the negative consequences in their households and community. A staff member from IHRE related the following incident:

> When this teacher started teaching human rights and sitting together with the students, they identified the problem of alcoholism and domestic abuse in their homes. The men work in agriculture and will usually get their wages and spend it all on alcohol. Whatever he earns goes straight to the liquor shop. So for those reasons, the children made the decision to get together and go on a march to the liquor shop. Along the way, the village women joined them. They did this many times, shouting slogans and all. Slowly, that shopkeeper got irritated and he closed the shop. So now there is no liquor shop in this village. (Interview, June 2009)

Students used their new human rights learnings to advocate for community changes on a broader scale. While the efficacy of shutting down a local business may be questioned, for students it represented a way to remove one barrier to their family's financial well-being and their mothers' physical safety.

HRE and Solidarity Action

I link the reasons for the adoption of advocacy efforts versus solidarity actions to the immediacy of violence—be it direct violence (such as corporal punishment or infanticide) or severe discrimination related to structural violence, such as caste or gender discrimination.[5] The possibility of backlash was also greater in solidarity actions given students' proximity to the violations. There were a vast number of responses that fell into the category of solidarity actions by coalitional agents. This section is divided into three thematic areas: (1) caste discrimination, (2) gender discrimination, and (3) the violation of children's rights.

Caste Discrimination: "You can keep your caste outside, don't bring it inside here"

Several student examples of solidarity actions involved practices of caste discrimination in primarily rural areas. While Adivasi communities are residentially segregated and fairly homogenous, Indian villages have a variety of caste and subcaste groups with historical disenfranchisement reflected in current land holding patterns as well as unequal social relations (Ramachandran

1991). Despite the illegality of these practices, caste discrimination permeates schools and society, especially in rural areas where residential and employment patterns make one's caste identity more visible than in urban settings. In many accounts, students mentioned utilizing knowledge related to human rights discussed in HRE textbooks to interrupt such practices. For coalitional agents of higher-caste status, such solidarity often challenged long-held traditional beliefs and the authority of elders.

For children in schools, even those schools specifically designed for increasing the access of Dalit and Adivasi students, discrimination often played out between administrators or teachers and students, and among students as well. Headmasters, teachers, and students themselves often replicated these distinctions in schools, with Dalit students being barred from taking part in school activities or being made to clean the school while other children were in class. After beginning HRE, students reported changing behaviors inside and outside of schools related to caste. One male student in class eleven, Murugan, from a slightly higher subcaste than some of his peers, narrated the following:

> Before, I wouldn't go into lower caste people's homes, and I wouldn't allow them to enter into my home because my grandmother would scold me. When human rights education was introduced, I thought, "I won't be interested in this." Our HRE teacher used to be very harsh; she used to beat us by using the stick. But after attending this HRE training program, she came and told us, "Hereafter I won't beat you people because you are also human beings." Then she told us about the human rights education book. When we were taking the class, there are some lessons related to caste discrimination. So during that class I realized that we should not discriminate [against] people on the basis of caste. So now we are all mixing, but my grandmother still scolds me if I'm playing with that [Dalit] boy or going to his home. But I don't care about that because I am learning human rights education. I know that everyone has their rights. (Interview, May 2009)

While Murugan noted his grandmother's resistance to his new learnings, he persisted in acting on what he believed in based on what his teacher and human rights textbook had taught him. Here, the teacher's changed behavior as a result of human rights education inspired Murugan to take the content of the HRE textbook seriously. His decision to, and success in, standing up to family traditions may have been related to the fact that as a son of the family, he had greater flexibility to challenge tradition than a young woman would, though the absence of a counterfactual scenario for each family makes ascertaining the gendered dimension of such action difficult.

Many students discussed going into other children's homes when they previously would not have, having them over, or generally playing and eating together, which challenged traditionally held beliefs about caste that held that if someone from a lower caste—especially a Dalit—came near, the higher-caste individual would become "polluted" or "defiled" (HRW 2007a). In one twelfth standard classroom, a group of youth who had taken human rights education from sixth to eighth standards declared collectively that they now believed in inter-caste marriages and would not allow their families to arrange their marriages with someone in their own caste as per the community's custom.

Social segregation was one aspect of caste discrimination with another dimension being the violence that ensued for violating its norms. During the time of this research, there were many news stories of caste-based violence in villages, including "honor killings" by families or vigilante justice by members of the higher-status group killing both members of couples involved in inter-caste relationships because such unions violated customary rules (Biswas 2010; Wax 2008). After learning about human rights, students often attempted to act upon their new learnings upsetting elders who had not authorized such changes. For example, the following incident related by a non-Dalit eighth standard student, Elangovan, from Tamil Nadu is illustrative of solidarity acts related to caste violence:

> We were all eating our lunch and one of our classmates went to wash his plate in that water tap near the street. A woman from the village, who is from a higher subcaste, started yelling at him and beating him saying, "Why are you washing your plate here? You will pollute this tap!" So I went over and raised my voice to her saying, "Why are you doing this? He has a right to wash in this tap. This is a common tap. He is a kid in this school and everyone is equal here. You can keep your caste outside, don't bring it inside here." (Student focus group, February 2009)

Several other students, especially in Tamil Nadu—but also in Karnataka, Gujarat, and some parts of Orissa—discussed taking action when their classmates were targeted for transgressing caste norms. As noted in Chapter Three, many students discussed witnessing community realities that belied their lessons in equality. For example, in one district where human rights education was being offered in Tamil Nadu, an electrified wall was erected by upper-caste families in order to separate their residential areas from the Dalit area of the village (Viswanathan 2008). Some villages also had armed militias to enforce caste norms, resulting in violence and tension that several students discussed in their focus groups (Gayer and Jaffrelot 2010). Human rights education offered coalitional agents a framework for rethinking abusive practices carried out by community members (sometimes even their own family members), and standing up for victims, known and unknown.

Gender-Based Violence: "Why are you beating your wife like that? . . . This is a violation against the Domestic Violence Act"

Social inequalities manifested themselves in students' homes and communities not only along caste, but also gender lines. Students repeatedly discussed various types of gender-based violence that they witnessed or encountered across class backgrounds and regions. From domestic violence to female infanticide, students were often confronted with situations that contradicted what they had learned in their human rights lessons. In Tamil Nadu, for example, students often discussed the issue of female infanticide. Some overheard discussions held by neighbors, deliberating about whether to kill a newborn. One group of sixth standard children (ages 10–12) in Chennai living in fisher communities discussed routinely happening upon plastic bags that came ashore with dead girl babies that families had thrown into the sea. In Orissa, a group of seventh standard students discussed witnessing severe domestic violence when one of the student's uncles tied his wife (her aunt) to a tree and beat her in front of the other villagers. All of these practices of course reflect a sense of women and girls as burdens rather than family members with equal status. Gender discrimination featured prominently in HRE textbooks and was the second most frequent subject of lessons (see Table 5.1).

Coalitional agents who witnessed gender-based violence were able to identify these practices as an infringement of both the right to equality and in some cases, particular those involving female infanticide, a violation of the right to life. The following incident was narrated by a group of human rights education students (boys and girls) now in standard twelve, but who had taken the HRE course in their middle-school years:

> After reading human rights education in sixth standard, we overheard in our area that a neighbor was planning to kill their newborn girl baby. We formed a group of classmates and we went to their home. We explained to the lady [that this is wrong], but the father didn't accept. He scolded us and slapped us. We told [him] that the child also has a right to life; you should not kill the child. We said, "If you are going to kill the child, we will complain to the police. We also have contact with human rights organizations. We won't move from this area. We will stand here and watch what you are doing with this child." Often we used to go to that

home and watch that child. But now that child is older and is even studying in school. (Focus group, May 2009)

These students felt a great deal of pride in having influenced this family's decision not to kill their child and used their own intervention as well as the threat of reporting them to the police to influence the abuse they saw. It remained unclear, however, what the status and treatment of the child was in her family where she was reluctantly allowed to live.

Many students (and teachers as will be explored in the subsequent chapter) discussed seeking ways to intervene in domestic violence in their own and in neighbors' homes. The Indian National Family and Health Survey (2006) found that 37 percent of Indian women aged 15–49 reported having experienced physical or sexual violence in their homes, with high levels of social acceptance of the practice across socioeconomic groups. The following incident reflects the way in which a 15-year-old girl, Kavita, acted as a coalitional agent to a neighbor who was being beaten by her husband:

In my house, my parents give the back part for rent to a newly married couple. About three months ago, they started quarreling with each other a lot. The husband was being pressured by his parents to demand more dowry so he started beating her and demanding that she bring more money from her parents' home. He would slap her so hard that her face would look like there was a rash from where the fingers had left red marks. One day, I went and asked the man, our tenant, "Why are you beating your wife like that?" He said, "You are a small girl. Don't interfere." I told my father and he also said not to get involved. This went on for weeks. I asked my father one day, "What would you do if that woman was your sister and was being tortured like this?" I showed my father the human rights lessons in the textbook. So my father and I went and told the woman she could stay in our house if her husband was beating her, and she came for one week to stay with us. During that time, we also told her husband, "Brother, if you keep beating her like this, my father and I will go to the police and file a complaint against you. This is a violation against the Domestic Violence Act." So finally that man realized that this was wrong and people were there to raise questions. The situation has gotten better—he is not beating his wife anymore—and I believe he has changed. (Interview, May 2009)

Kavita's experience trying to intervene in an abuse unsuccessfully and then having to educate her father to help amplify her voice against the abuse offered her instructive lessons about her ability to make change. Ultimately, she went out of her way to make the situation better for her neighbor and serve as an ally to her. Whether it was the threat of reporting his illegal behavior or the fact that the abusive husband's landlord was housing his wife for lengthy periods, the husband, according to the student, treated his wife better. Certainly the support of the HRE student's father made a significant difference. Kavita's persistence and ability to enlist the involvement of a higher-status coalitional agent contributed to the efficacy of her intervention. IHRE's strategy of persuasive pragmatism at an organizational level bears fruition in the many micro-strategies of students like Kavita who use creative means of enlisting support for an identified cause. As discussed earlier, girls had different levels of social power and often had to seek strategic alliances with male peers or adults in order to effectively intervene in situations of abuse. This was also true with situations of solidarity that involved protecting children's rights.

Violations of Children's Rights: "Beating is the wrong way to treat students. You should use words rather than the stick to control students"

Many children were motivated to recruit out-of-school youth back to school after learning about human rights. As discussed earlier, the conceptual difference between categorizing efforts as advocacy versus solidarity involved the possibility of backlash and the vulnerability of lower-status coalitional agents. In many cases, parents or employers did not fear any sanction and instead retaliated against the coalitional agents, making their actions riskier.

At school, efforts to protect children's rights also included speaking up against the common practice of corporal punishment. Instances of violent punishment abound in Indian schools—both government and private. In some private schools, corporal punishment was seen as a key tool in securing high scores on exams, which in turn would make these schools competitive and able to recruit future students. Corporal punishment also caused psychological damage. In 2010, a class eight-level student of an elite private school in West Bengal committed suicide after harsh beatings from the headmaster and teachers (NCPCR 2010). A national study found that despite the outlawing of corporal punishment, 65 percent of children reported still being beaten in schools, not to mention other forms of punishment (Bunsha 2007). In 2009, Indian news outlets widely reported the case of Shanno, a class two student, who was made to stand with bricks on her shoulders in the searing Delhi heat as a punishment and died later that day after collapsing from exhaustion (Bhowmick 2009). Efforts by HRE students and teachers to stop corporal punishment often went against the socialization and training of many teachers.

HRE textbooks discussed the difference between violent and nonviolent disciplinary methods, favoring the latter. When students encountered corporal punishment in their schools, they often tried to stop these practices. One student, Nalini, who had participated in several human rights events, was known at her school as someone affiliated with an outside organization. Because of this perceived special status, she was spared from beatings by teachers. Nalini also acted as a coalitional agent for other students and discussed utilizing this status to help her peers:

> I attended an IHRE training and we had a debate on corporal punishment. My group came to the conclusion that we shouldn't allow children to get beaten by their teachers. In my computer class, the teacher is very strict. She used to scold the students loudly and beat them with a stick. But she knows I was selected to go to the regional training on human rights and I am always raising questions in school, so she never used to beat me. I told her, "You should not do this. Beating is the wrong way to treat students. You should use words rather than the stick to control students." Other students also got courage from my saying this and started also telling the teacher the same thing. I think the teacher felt afraid because I raised a question against her and, if it went to the headmaster, she could get in trouble. After that, she didn't beat the students and spoke more softly to all of us. (Interview, May 2009)

Nalini used her privileged status at school as a means to help other students; the teacher—whether for fear of being reported or genuine conviction in what her student was arguing—stopped punishing her students violently. Nalini's experience with influencing change at school gave her more confidence, resulting in a greater commitment to promote rights and stand against abuses.

Another form of solidarity that related to protecting children's rights (also related to earlier discussions of advocacy) involved the intervention in parents' decisions to pull children out of school. A lot of advocacy with parents, employers, and school officials was required to secure students' return when children were already out of school. Conversely, standing up to parents or families at the moment decisions were made to withdraw children from school also carried the threat of backlash. Allies sometimes risked their own safety to convince families about the adverse consequences of dropping out of school. Senthil, a 13-year-old boy in Tamil Nadu, discussed being a coalitional agent in one's own extended family, but facing violent resistance as a result:

> My cousin was in school and his father decided to pull him out of school to work in a mechanic shop to help support the family. My uncle used to drink heavily and

when I went to ask him to not take my cousin out of school, he hit my head so hard that it was bleeding. I even went to the school and got all the paperwork for him to re-enroll, but my uncle refused. My cousin only studied up until fifth standard in the end. (Focus group, February 2009)

The lack of success of this effort could be related to both the uncle's reluctance or Senthil's limited social status, primarily related to age in this case. It is uncertain whether collective attempts or further strategizing might have further assisted or whether the uncle was impervious to change. Social location and power proved to be important considerations for coalitional agents in structuring their responses to rights abuses they encountered in their families and communities.

CONCLUSION

This chapter offered further evidence that social location mediates the impact of and responses to HRE. Previous studies of HRE have not engaged the differentiated social positions and status of learners in a comprehensive manner. Relationships to individuals and institutions that hold power in local communities certainly affect how human rights issues are experienced and thus, how HRE reconstitutes students' understandings of social phenomena. Whether victims or coalitional agents in distinct situations, students and teachers navigate and internalize HRE within the context of complex social processes that may serve to facilitate or impede action in distinct moments.

This data showed a widespread embrace of human rights norms even by coalitional agents who did not benefit directly from rights protective actions. Coalitional agents may not always have been strategic in their interventions. Yet, their stories make important points about the value of human rights education, not to mention human capacity to act beyond one's own self-interest. The distinctions provided above offered an understanding of different levels since a child intervening in a violent fight between a neighbor, putting his or her own safety at risk, is a different form of intervention than raising money in an affluent neighborhood for an NGO. This by no means is meant to diminish the importance of all actions, although questions of charity and advocacy dwarfing the agency of victims need to be considered in further studies of educational interventions, such as HRE. Arguably, the advocacy efforts of affluent and higher-status youth may resonate further in a society deeply divided along caste and class lines, bringing greater visibility to human rights principles and their importance.

Thus, the greater activism of students at all levels is notable, but must be cultivated in a way that considers strategic (often collective) interventions that do not put students at risk for violence, frustration, or disillusionment if their attempts at change are met with hostility. This does not mean that students should only engage in action when they are guaranteed success, but that teachers and students together devise interventions that consider the larger social conditions and material realities surrounding their efforts.

Chapter Seven

Teachers and Textbooks as Legitimating Forces for Human Rights Education

Human rights education has created a lot of change in the school itself. Earlier, there was this big tree behind my school and if you take a stick from that tree, and hit someone on the hand or anywhere, the place will swell up a lot. We used to get beaten black and blue with those sticks before human rights education. Once we got the book, our teachers came and told us, "hereafter, we are not going to touch the stick." That really took us aback and we were shocked, in fact. That increased our interest and curiosity about the entire book because they became so different. After that, they never took the stick once. They believed that they could teach us just by affection and love. The teachers became so friendly that we could go and even stand close to them, which we couldn't do earlier because you would not know what kind of mood they are in, and if they were just going to hit you and take it out on you. Now we even go into the staff room and ask any questions we have. All the teachers have changed because the human rights education teachers mingle with all the other teachers. And they not only impart the knowledge on the students, but they also share it with the rest of the teachers. If there are any administrative decisions they have to make among the teachers, it always comes to them through the human rights teacher. So we really like school now.

(Eighth standard student, Tamil Nadu, interview, May 2009)

As suggested above, the personal transformation of teachers played a central role in students taking human rights education (HRE) seriously. Chapter

Four offered information on how the Institute of Human Rights Education's (IHRE) strategy of persuasive pragmatism engaged teachers to promote HRE in schools; this chapter focuses squarely on teachers' personal experiences of change, an area of relative silence in the literature on HRE to date. Teachers are the obvious catalysts and messengers of HRE. In this context, their training is an intermediate step in the process of imparting knowledge of, and attitudes and behaviors in line with, human rights principles among young learners.

The previous chapters (Five and Six) in this book have emphasized the impact of human rights education on students and how a particular non-governmental organization, IHRE, based in the southern Indian state of Tamil Nadu, has expanded its program to nearly 4,000 schools nation-wide. This chapter argues instead that teachers' *own* transformation should be central to discussions of the educational reform, particularly in the global South. This section presents data from the teachers involved with IHRE. Utilizing terminology consistent with student responses to HRE, teachers may be "victims" of abuse in their own lives and can be "coalitional agents" for their students and/or members of the community.

Teachers are central to an analysis of HRE for two reasons: the role of teachers in propagating and sometimes addressing human rights violations in their immediate spheres of influence as well as the ripple effect of teacher practices in the larger communities around them. In this chapter, I explore two related themes: (1) teacher transformation and corresponding action, and (2) the (pragmatic) leveraging of existing hierarchies—here the privileged social position of teachers and textbooks in semiliterate communities—as a means of addressing violence and oppressive practices in these places. In many cases, teachers are the *cause* of human rights abuses or are indifferent in the face of them, and human rights education could, to a certain extent, counter these through personal changes that transform teachers' own abusive practices in schools. Once teachers become allies to students, they could work to provide community education, material assistance, and intervene in abuses they encounter in schools and the broader community. Teachers' experiences with training (as also discussed in Chapter Four) were critical in the motivations for teachers' transformations with regard to human rights.

The authority of teachers (and to a certain degree, textbooks) was another perhaps surprising source of power in relation to students and their communities. Many semiliterate communities hold teachers and textbooks in high regard. In this context, their advocacy can have an instrumental role in equalizing social relations by promoting respect for human rights beyond the school walls, the ultimate aim of the HRE project (Flowers et al., 2000; Tibbitts 2002). Students could also utilize teachers as resources in confronting abuses by leveraging their authority against current and would-be violators. In many students' accounts, textbooks complemented teachers' authority suggesting that the status afforded to the printed word (in India and perhaps beyond) offered human rights norms legitimacy and credibility for students and teachers seeking to intervene in situations of abuse. The findings of this study corroborated the way that social hierarchies privileged teachers' actions when confronting abusive social practices.

PERSPECTIVES ON TEACHERS AND HRE

Chapter Two highlighted developments in human rights education to date. Indeed, teachers figure prominently in scholarship and practice as the messengers, models, and mediators of rights instruction. Scholarship on HRE frequently takes up teacher education as a means of developing awareness and practices of respecting and protecting human rights, typically through teacher knowledge, pedagogical skills, and behaviors in their classrooms (Osler and Starkey 1996, 2010). However, little previous scholarship on HRE has examined teachers' own transformation and their corresponding actions as a result of learning about human rights. This study sought to address this gap through an in-depth examination of teachers' experiences with HRE. Teachers' personal changes and subsequent actions played an instrumental role in students' utilization of teachers as resources in countering injustices. Analysis of the data on Indian HRE teachers suggested that personal transformation as well as the relative social positioning of teachers had a significant influence on social change efforts.

Many scholars have focused on the need to examine pre- and in-service training in human rights for educators (Flowers et al., 2000; Magendzo 2005; Osler and Starkey 1996). Looking at that training, commentators have differentially focused on the development of a more critical pedagogy that can give teachers confidence to stand up for human rights in the community (Magendzo 2005); the emphasis on the affective dimension of human rights learning (Müller 2009; Osler and Starkey 1996); and the fostering of networks among trained teachers and resource centers to support them (Cardenas 2005). In these ways, human rights educators differ from conventional teachers when they are provided additional content knowledge on human rights history, norms, and standards, as well as participatory pedagogical techniques in line with the goals of creating classroom communities that respect human rights.

Approaches to teacher training and human rights education also vary. Audrey Osler and Hugh Starkey look at how non-governmental organizations have run courses just for teachers, such as those offered by the Geneva-based International Training Centre on Human Rights and Peace Teaching (Osler and Starkey 1996). Nazzari, McAdams, and Roy look at the use of short courses for educators and human rights activists, as seen with the International Human Rights Training Program run by the Canadian NGO Equitas (Nazzari, McAdams and Roy 2005). University departments have also developed (in some cases compulsory) courses and certificate programs in human rights for in-service and pre-service teachers. The Council of Europe has facilitated such initiatives in the region through publications and support of training programs in HRE.

Empirical research offers insights into perspectives on national-level initiatives toward incorporating human rights concepts into textbooks and schools (Meyer et al., 2010; Müller 2009). In a recent study, Lothar Müller (2009) examines German teachers' attitudes toward human rights education since the 1980 recommendations by a national educational body (*Kultusministerkonferenz*) for the introduction of human rights content. In the teacher component of his study, he finds that educators who were able to name human rights standards identified the media and personal interest as sources of such information rather than teacher training. Teachers were more interested in the emotive or affective dimension of human rights, but as Müller notes, the challenge lies in deciding "where an educationally fostered motivation to human rights activism is legitimate and where it oversteps the boundaries of the school's mandate" (20).

Other scholarship worries less about the line between education and activism and focuses instead on providing techniques and tools to teachers. The Human Rights Education Handbook (Flowers et al., 2000), for example, places considerable responsibility on teachers, stating that,

> To teach about and for human rights requires more than knowledge about human rights and experience in facilitating learning. The human rights educator must have a deeply felt commitment to human rights and a belief in their necessity for building a just and democratic society. (23)

The authors pose four personal challenges to HRE teachers in order to be effective. First, following from "the challenge to learn," HRE teachers must be willing to become learners in their classrooms and cultivate an environment in which all participants engage in critical inquiry and learn from each other. Second, pursuant to "the challenge of the affective," learning about human rights should go beyond content and require the educator to engage the feelings and responses of all learners. Third, under "the challenge of self-examination," educators must critically examine their own prejudices and biases and be open to changing them. Finally, according to "the challenge of example," educators must be willing to align their behavior and attitudes with human rights principles in order to be credible (23). Questions remain regarding whether overburdened and, in many national systems, underpaid, teachers would assume the additional responsibility for democratizing classroom relations and changing their own practices in line with human rights principles without the provision of additional status or other incentives.

TEACHERS AND HRE IN INDIA

Institute of Human Rights Education (IHRE)

As discussed in Chapter Four, the Institute of Human Rights Education (IHRE) has expanded to operate a three-year course in human rights education for middle-school level students (standards six through eight) in approximately 4,000 schools in 18 states across India. IHRE's model operates by securing government permission, asking each school to send one to two teachers for a three- to five-day residential training, and then having those teachers identify two periods per week in which to teach lessons on human rights from textbooks prepared in local languages by IHRE's team and affiliated curriculum experts. After the initial training, "refresher" courses are given each year and teachers are incorporated into ongoing activities of the Institute in their area.

The data presented in this chapter come from a variety of sources over the 13-month fieldwork period. A total of 118 teachers were interviewed and represented a range of subject areas, years of experience, genders, and ethnic/linguistic backgrounds. Almost all of the teachers interviewed were offering or had offered HRE at some point, though in many of the 60 schools visited during this study, other teachers also wanted to participate and were interviewed primarily about the impact of HRE on their schools. I observed teacher trainings on HRE in Tamil Nadu, Orissa, and Gujarat, and attended and conducted interviews at a National Conference on HRE, where teachers and students from all 18 states were represented. Textbooks and other documents were also reviewed for the latter part of this chapter and data are also presented on how students and other respondents utilized HRE textbooks outside of the classroom. An inductive approach to coding provided the themes deemed representative and presented in this chapter.

As discussed briefly in Chapter Four, teachers come to the trainings with different levels of interest in and knowledge of human rights. Some teachers reported volunteering to become the human rights teacher out of a previous commitment to the topic. Other reasons included being assigned by their headmaster because they were the most junior teachers or because no other teachers could attend. Once at the trainings, IHRE provided teachers a unique experience: retreats were held in beautiful locations; notable speakers led sessions for teachers; and participatory methods engaged teachers in ways unconventional in Indian teacher training and professional development.

Given the identification of teachers as a key component in the efficacy of HRE programs, teacher training was often foregrounded in state and national advisory meetings held by IHRE. Current problems of teachers' involvement in discrimination and other abuses were central to designing training that would be transformative as one advisory committee member, a retired senior government official, noted:

> Many of the teachers are part of the system which is promoting and perpetuating discrimination. There are studies which show even in *anganwadis* (pre-schools), Dalit children are seated separately and made to feel unwelcome, so they don't go there. Teachers are a part of society and come with all those prejudices, so our intervention has to be well-calculated to take into account their backgrounds. We of course respect teachers, but we have to acknowledge that a good section of teachers are also among the active promoters and perpetuators of these human rights violations. (IHRE National Advisory Committee meeting, June 2009)

In this context, the Institute of Human Rights Education sought to engage teachers as more than passive conduits of content. Careful attention to social location, context, and strategy was devoted (as discussed more extensively in Chapter Four) to catalyze teachers' transformation—a goal equally as important to securing support for teaching HRE to students.

Teachers had varied motivations for promoting HRE and affiliating with the Institute of Human Rights Education. For some teachers, the opportunity to participate in a larger movement aligned with their previous interests in human rights or social justice issues influenced participation. For others, attending a training was their first exposure to human rights and the changes they witnessed in their classroom provided motivation for continued participation. Other teachers viewed the unique opportunities to attend trainings (sometimes in other parts of the country) and become a local expert on human rights (as discussed in Chapter Four) as a motivating factor. For yet other teachers, perhaps those with political inclinations, affiliation to a large

NGO working at the national level with many noted individuals on its advisory board, provided an opportunity for elevated status in the community and could lay the groundwork for future professional aspirations. Some HRE teachers did indeed go on to political roles at the village and district levels.

Teachers' Responses
The role of training
Trainings were central to the process of teacher transformation. Trainings offered the means for teachers to learn, integrate, and act on their understandings of human rights in their homes, schools, and communities. The residential training was some teachers' first contact with concepts of human rights and all teachers' first contact with the Institute of Human Rights Education. As mentioned, trainings were designed to convince teachers of the importance of human rights and inspire them to carry out instruction. Of the teachers interviewed for this study, the majority noted the distinctness of the training and how it helped them develop an interest in human rights. Reasons for these successes included sessions with noted speakers, introduction to new material, the participatory format, or even the opportunity to visit a new part of their state and the desire to stay connected to an organization providing such opportunities. For example, in discussing a session by the former Vice-Chancellor of a university (now the chairperson of IHRE) and a senior government officer who serves on IHRE's advisory board, one teacher noted, "This training was very useful. I met those [notable people] as equals. They were very humble to come down and be with us together, though they are so [well-known]" (teacher focus group, January 2009).

While HRE trainings and notable trainers may be the reason some teachers found these messages legitimate, other factors included their newfound conviction that practices, such as discrimination and corporal punishment, were detrimental to their school community. Though the practice has been outlawed, teachers in many Indian schools accept corporal punishment as normal and often argue that beatings offer needed motivation and discipline. Corporal punishment emerged repeatedly in students' accounts of their schooling experiences, with one respondent even noting that his teacher beat him so severely that the stick broke his arm (student focus group, February 2009). Other discriminatory practices found in society at large crept into classrooms (NCPCR 2008). Examples of such practices included discrimination against Dalit students through segregated seating or forcing such students to clean the school-grounds or bathrooms while other students were in class. Scholars and investigative bodies have noted these practices throughout India (Nambissan and Sedwal 2002; NCDHR 2008), and as has been discussed, respondents repeatedly highlighted discrimination in schools, particularly in Tamil Nadu, Karnataka, and Gujarat. While not all teachers reported enthusiasm for human rights even after attending trainings, almost all participants highlighted becoming aware of the illegality of practices such as corporal punishment and discrimination.

Personal changes

Teachers' transformation was a central goal of the NGO-run training and human rights education program in India. IHRE sought to put teachers "on the spot" to protect children's human rights given many teachers' complicity in the most common and worst forms of discrimination. Mr. Madan, a teacher in a rural area of Tamil Nadu, noted the significant impact that training in human rights had on his approach to teaching:

> After attending this training, I could understand the students from their point of view. For example, when I go to class, if I see a boy sleeping on the desk, I used to have the tendency to beat him or be harsh on him, without knowing if he may be hungry, without knowing anything about his family background. Maybe he is sleeping because he is having some problems in the family; maybe his father was drunk at night and beating his mother. So after attending this training, I have come to ask the children their problems instead of beating them; I try to understand the children, be friendly, and respect them. The students have started moving more freely and talking to me more also, so the distance [between us] is much reduced. If anything happens in their homes, any family problems, they are also sharing with us. Even the District Education Officer has noticed these changes . . . because a lot of teachers attended the training in human rights. (Teacher focus group, January 2009)

Mr. Madan indicated the transformation of his approach to teaching after instruction in human rights and the closeness he developed with students.

These changes, needless to say, benefited students. In addition to spending considerable time in teacher trainings on the issue of corporal punishment, IHRE textbooks contain a chart that explicates the difference between "discipline" (nonviolent) and "punishment" (violent), seeking to make children and teachers aware of laws around corporal punishment and offer alternative practices.

In addition to allowing teachers to become allies for children at school, human rights training often took on a more instrumental role in resolving problems in their homes as well. For example, domestic violence was a significant problem for women teachers, despite their economic contributions to the household. Several female teachers reported that after attending trainings in human rights, they were able to stand up against abusive practices in their own homes. One teacher in the state of Karnataka noted that after the training, she showed her husband the human rights textbooks and explained to him that domestic violence was illegal. Whether for fear of being reported or a genuine conviction that his previous behavior was wrong, the teacher noted that her husband stopped hitting her. Mrs. Devanesan, a teacher in rural Tamil Nadu, similarly noted the following:

> Before there were so many problems arising in my home, misunderstandings between husband and wife. After learning human rights, I saw that there were rights for women also. The commissions are also listed there [in the textbook]. Phone numbers are given there. So I could say, "you don't beat me." Nowadays there is no problem. (Interview, February 2009)

Other women teachers discussed standing up to their mother-in-laws who treated them in abusive ways—whether physically or psychologically—in the extended family household context (often related to dowry demands or the birth of daughters rather than sons). One teacher noted, "Earlier I used to feel I have two girls, why is there no boy? Now I know girls are also valuable" (interview, January 2009). Importantly, many male teachers also discussed not beating their wives after attending human rights trainings and one teacher even encouraged his wife to reenroll in high school since she had dropped out after the ninth standard to get married.[1]

The household and school-level changes discussed above—involving matters such as gender dynamics and corporal punishment—were widespread and notable. In addition to this study, an evaluation carried out by IHRE of its own work in 2008 surveyed 350 teachers, 89 percent of whom reported rejecting corporal punishment as a practice after learning about HRE (PW 2008, 81). For teachers, these changes represented the most significant type of response to human rights education. Categorized as "personal changes," these transformations also included attitudinal shifts with regards to caste or religion and increased interaction with colleagues and students of different backgrounds. Many teachers also reported changing their attitudes toward teaching after human rights education. Previously, as one teacher noted, "we'd come to school, give the lesson, and take the salary" (interview, February 2009). He further noted that HRE had given him the impetus to get further involved in students' lives and advocate for human rights in school and beyond. Figure 7.1 shows that personal changes were those most consistently mentioned by the 118 teacher respondents in this study. Other responses to human rights training and teaching included the imparting of education in

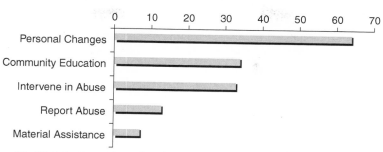

Figure 7.1 Distribution of teachers' interview responses to the question, "What impact, if any, has HRE had on you?" (n = 118)[2]

community settings, intervening in abuses, reporting abuses, and in some cases, providing material assistance to students. Notably, after a personal change or transformation occurred, teachers more willingly engaged in pro-active steps to counter abuses or educate others about human rights.

Community education

After learning about human rights, teachers often sought to share their new knowledge with others. Human rights educators were charged with teaching two periods of human rights weekly as part of the IHRE-sponsored program, but several went beyond that responsibility to deliver instruction on human rights in other settings. Examples of this included teachers organizing sessions on human rights for village leaders, women's microfinance groups, and for parents and children more broadly. Sometimes these sessions focused specifically on domestic violence, child labor, caste discrimination, or dowry, among other topics. Teachers repeatedly mentioned working together with students to organize and perform street-plays on human rights themes as well as community celebrations of international days, such as Human Rights Day (December 10), Women's Day (March 8), and the Day to End Child Labor (June 12).

Some teachers developed unique and alternative ways of promoting HRE. IHRE began recording songs on human rights (sometimes written by teachers themselves) and distributing CDs to schools a few years back. One teacher, Mr. Kumar, discussed taking this compilation of songs to a nearby temple and asking them to play the CD during a village festival. He also bought prizes with his own money and organized competitions related to public speaking and singing about human rights in his community. Like Mr. Kumar, Mr. Ganesan became an advocate of human rights since his first HRE training in 2002. After serving as a teacher for many years, he was promoted to the position of "warden" at a residential school. He decided to teach all the students in the hostel about human rights in weekly lessons in the evening. Mr. Ganesan also founded a community organization to protect children's rights and raise money for out-of-school children to make it easier for them to reenroll. These teachers' interest in human rights was sparked through IHRE's training. Further activities were also facilitated through regular contact with IHRE and its staff.

Intervening in abuse

Another type of response that grew out of teachers' own transformation with regard to human rights was the desire to take action and confront abuses they saw in their own or students' lives. Teachers repeatedly mentioned that human rights education provided them with a framework to understand the legality of social problems and determine strategies to intervene when they saw abuses. Given teachers' status, this intervention often proved instrumental in changing situations of abuse. The types of situations that teachers intervened in ranged from child labor and gender, caste, or religious discrimination to early marriage, corruption, and female infanticide. Students often identified such issues occurring in their communities and sought out their teachers' help in addressing them after learning about human rights.

In the eastern state of Orissa—the poorest state in India with 46.4 percent of residents below the national poverty line (see Table 3.2 in Chapter Three) and with a large population of Adivasis—IHRE operates in all schools run through the government's Tribal Welfare Ministry. The remoteness of these schools often allowed widespread forms of corruption. Mr. Patnaik, a seventh standard HRE teacher, noted:

> After attending the human rights training, I've brought 13 drop out children back to school. I go village to village with the HRE students, sit with the community, and convince the parents. I ask them, "Why are your children going for work? Send them to school. It is a government school, it is free." Parents think school is expensive and how can they afford it; no one has told them it is free and the children are provided books, uniforms, and school meals. It is the district's job to inform the parents and encourage them to send their children to school, but the headmasters don't want that. Their idea is to show the government false enrollments and then accordingly, [extra] facilities and funds are given to the school. They don't have any interest in getting more children to school. (Interview, July 2009)

Several other HRE teachers in Orissa as well as in other states said they sometimes faced resistance to HRE from headmasters and other teachers implicated in corrupt practices in schools (such as pocketing funds sent for students' meals, uniforms, and books).

Many HRE teachers across several states discussed being able to get students back to school through talking with parents and convincing them of the value of education. Depending on the type of violation, one form of intervention was the reporting of abuses to authorities, which teachers also noted doing as a result of human rights training.

Taking action and reporting abuse

Despite newfound desires to intervene in abuses, teachers' authority sometimes proved insufficient to transform situations. Here, reporting such abuses to local or state authorities became necessary. While officials didn't always respond, the threat of police action or actual reporting to the police often offered another way to stop abuses that children and teachers identified in the community.[3] Especially for young students of HRE, enlisting the help of a teacher was sometimes necessary before confronting adult neighbors and would-be violators in their communities. Mr. Gopal from Tamil Nadu related the following incident, emblematic of several others offered by teachers who reported an abuse:

> In the first year of human rights education, my student, Kuruvamma, overheard from a neighbor that if their child was born a girl, they would kill it since they already had three female children. The child was born a girl and what they planned to do was make the baby lie down on the ground without putting any bed sheets and put the pedestal fan on high speed in front of her. The baby can't live—she would not be able to breathe and then she would automatically die. Kuruvamma told me and together we gave a complaint in the police station. The family got scared and didn't kill the baby. Now that girl is even studying in first standard. Kuruvamma is now in high school. (Interview, January 2009)

In many communities in Tamil Nadu and other states where HRE is being offered, female infanticide is a common practice, though illegal. Throughout the research, however, students and teachers reported encountering evidence of infanticide or overhearing about cases such as the one above. While there are other socioeconomic reasons, such as rural poverty, that factor into an explanation of practices such as early marriage and female infanticide, students' identification of abuses and the help of teachers willing to report or intervene, were critical components in making human rights come alive for students.

Material assistance

The last type of response motivated by human rights training discussed by teachers involved the desire to provide material assistance to children or others in need. While less common than the other responses discussed, several teachers, inspired by human rights, donated food, uniforms, books, or school supplies to students. Students in Indian government schools are generally from lower class and caste backgrounds than the teachers who teach them; of the more than 100 teachers interviewed, not a single one sent their own children to government schools. One teacher noted that after HRE, instead of throwing a party for his son's birthday, he bought gifts and sweets for his students. In a context where government school teachers generally view their students as "other people's children" (Delpit 2006), the desire of teachers to treat them as their own children and provide care and material assistance to them was indeed a radical shift in thinking. One teacher in Karnataka state sought corporate donations and raised money in the community to build school latrines, additional classrooms, and a school well so that children would have drinking water at school. Whether through increased closeness, a desire to intervene in their problems at home, or the provision of food or related items, the humanization of lower class/caste children in teachers' eyes as a result of HRE was indeed noteworthy. The following section discusses the ways that students utilized teachers as community resources within existing hierarchies to influence change in parts of India.

TEACHERS AS LEGITIMATING AGENTS FOR HUMAN RIGHTS

One of my cousins was made to work and drop out of school after 5th standard. I was in seventh [standard] at that time and learning about human rights. I went to his home and spoke to his parents. I quoted some of the examples from the human rights textbook, and told them, "Why you are not allowing your child to come to school? This is a violation. You should send him to school." The father told me, "What do you know about our family? You are talking nonsense. Go away." He slapped me and I left. I kept going for a week trying to convince them. I showed them the human rights books, the lessons on child labor being illegal. But they are illiterates so couldn't read what was in the book.

Finally, I told my HRE teacher what had happened. The teacher called the boy's parents to school by saying that she had to give him a certificate since he had dropped out. Then, our HRE teacher spoke to my cousin's parents, saying, "What you are doing is obviously the wrong thing. At this age, children are getting education for free. Because you didn't stay in school, you are now doing hard labor, menial jobs. Let him study. Later, he can go for a job and he can take care of your family. Why are you doing the same wrong thing that your parents did to you?" She counseled them for half an hour. Finally the father realized and sent him back to school. And now that boy is the first in his family ever to go for higher studies.

(Rajesh, former HRE student, Tamil Nadu, interview, May 2009)

As noted in the epigraph above, a combination of student action and the legitimacy of human rights concepts afforded by teachers—and sometimes textbooks—allowed many meaningful interventions on behalf of students. Here, the status of teachers in the community and the reverence given to them by parents lent credibility to the advice they gave. In the interaction between the parents and teacher highlighted above, the role of HRE in creating the conditions for Rajesh to tell the upper-caste teachers about his cousin's predicament was significant. Also, the clear hierarchy between the educated teacher and illiterate parents, backed by printed information in textbooks, allowed the teacher's voice to be heeded, though perhaps not reflective of a broader equalization of social relationships.

Teachers' elevated status and greater connections, as well as the power of information contained in textbooks, at times also transformed an abusive situation. In rural India, many young women are pulled out of school to get married during their middle-school years. Mr. Prakash, an HRE teacher in the state of Orissa, narrated the following case of his student:

Last year one of my students, Radhika, who was in seventh standard was about to be forced into marriage by her parents. She appealed a lot to her parents saying, "I'm only 12 years old, my physical and mental development are not yet complete. I want to study and be something in the future." But this didn't affect her parents at all. They fixed the date for her marriage. She had her human rights book with her and she took a friend with her to report this to the police. But the police just told her to listen to her parents. Radhika told the police, "We are studying human rights education and we can approach our human rights teacher and the institutions listed in this book if you don't help." Then the police changed their attitude and called her parents and made them understand what they were doing was illegal. They called off the marriage and now she's studying in eighth standard at our school. (Interview, July 2009)

As described above, the perceived weight of "human rights authorities" spurred police action on behalf of the student who was going to be forcibly married. While police are supposed to enforce the law, early marriage remains a common occurrence in rural India. Marriage in India, for purposes of the law, requires both parties to be over 18 and to both consent to the union. A recent study analyzing data from the Indian National Family Health Survey found that of 22,000 women aged 20–24, 22.6 percent were married before age 16, 44.5 percent were married between ages 16 and 17, and 2.6 percent were married before age 13 (Lyn 2009).

Students, teachers, and parents reported throughout this study that the police were often complicit in ongoing abuses, indifferent when cases (of early marriage and other violations) were reported, or motivated to act only through the provision of some form of bribe. However, the threat of well-informed teachers connected to outside institutions (i.e., highly visible NGOs located in state capitals or state-wide human rights commissions) that might take action against local police, often spurred change. The fact that students had access to the phone numbers and even names of such institutions printed in their textbooks and could perhaps actually contact them, inspired action by authorities in several accounts. In the example of the two teachers who stood up to their abusive husbands provided earlier in this chapter, both referred to information in the human rights textbooks to demonstrate their knowledge of outside authorities to whom they could report happenings, which directly led to changes in their husbands' behavior.

BEYOND THE CLASSROOM—TEXTBOOKS AS COMMUNITY RESOURCES

Human rights education textbooks had a life beyond the classroom and were being used in a variety of ways by distinct stakeholders. Several incidents in this chapter, as well as those in Chapters Five and Six, involved students and teachers utilizing textbooks as part of a strategy to stand on one's own or on another's behalf in the face of an abuse. The use of printed information (on human rights or otherwise) in semiliterate contexts as a source of authority has also received scant attention in studies of HRE; as such, the following section seeks to explore the role of HRE textbooks as community resources.

Students often shared their textbooks with siblings, parents, and friends. Many students discussed teaching their families what they learned once they reached home. One student mentioned buying sweets with his spending money and gathering younger children after school to offer human rights lessons. Younger and older siblings often took interest in the books and would read them in addition to their subjects, often lamenting not being able to partake in human rights instruction themselves. One student, Lakshmi, mentioned showing her father the book. As the *panchayat* (elected village council) president, he then gathered the other community leaders to teach them about what was in the textbook.

Students like Lakshmi also took their learnings directly out into the community. Some students talked about taking their textbooks along on their National Service Scheme (NSS) or scouting activities, where youth undertake community service projects. One participant noted:

> As part of the NSS project, there were a few illiterate women from a nearby village and we were teaching them how to read and write. I brought the HRE textbook, narrated some of the stories that are there, and told them about their rights. They really enjoyed that and said, "You are such a small girl, and you are teaching us so many useful things." (Focus group, February 2009)

Additionally, one of the most frequent pedagogical methods utilized in the human rights education textbooks was interviews or research in the community. As such, individuals engaged in this way often asked about what course was prompting such questions since conventional Indian textbooks rarely contained this participatory and community-oriented element. These questions provided an opening for students to share lessons and information informally and formally.

Teachers also shared the textbooks with individuals they knew, ranging from relatives to neighbors and friends. As mentioned in Chapter Four, the teacher who provided copies of her HRE training materials to a local judge in Gujarat state offered evidence of how materials spread to others. One district-level Chief Education Officer in Tamil Nadu had the children's rights (seventh standard) textbook on her shelf and mentioned utilizing the book in any training or workshop she had to give to teachers and other officials because she felt the information was important for them to know. In Karnataka state, one teacher noted that her sister-in-law who was also a teacher saw her book, copied it, and started teaching it to her students in another school not affiliated with the IHRE program.

The HRE textbooks have also inspired different approaches to teaching human rights in a variety of settings. The head of a Dalit women's organization discussed utilizing the books to develop literacy materials for rural women's education programs. A state education official involved with the advisory committee also discussed utilizing the books to develop materials for literacy programs for out-of-school adolescents. In Bengaluru, a staff member from an affiliated organization who had served as a trainer at various human rights education workshops, discussed utilizing the textbooks to inspire the following unique approach:

One day on the bus, I was riding and a boy pulled out his human rights textbook. I had given the teachers training so I was so happy he was carrying that book and he told me that it is his favorite subject. I ride the bus at the same time everyday with all these children, aged 12–14, and we always ride the same bus, 293K. At first, we started singing songs and gradually it became a human rights club on the bus. I read some lessons or stories, or the children tell me about any problems in their schools related to corporal punishment or anything. A really positive thing is that the bus conductor is very helpful to us. We even put posters up related to human rights in the bus. All the passengers know that this is a human rights bus and no smoking is allowed, people have to give up their seats for any disabled passengers, pregnant women, or small children. It has been school holidays now, but some of the kids are already talking about making badges and pamphlets on human rights to give the passengers. (Interview, June 2009)

The creative use of the bus as a space for human rights instruction was inspired, in part, by the textbooks. The textbook as a source of authority, legitimizing human rights principles and participatory education offered children and adults a useful chance to engage with the materials in a variety of settings.

CONCLUSION

This chapter argued that teachers' own transformation is an essential component of HRE. Resting on the book's third premise, this chapter also explored teachers' and textbooks' unique social location, examining how their authority offers legitimacy to human rights information for students. While teachers may democratize their classrooms through HRE, their authority offered human rights credibility in the wider society, even more so in the context of semiliterate rural and urban areas in India, which allowed teachers the opportunity to effectively intervene in situations of abuse. While the previous chapters have explored how strategy influences how teachers and students learn about HRE as well as its corresponding impact, the following chapter examines how HRE fits into larger debates and social projects.

Chapter Eight

Divergence and Decoupling: Indian Human Rights Education in Focus

Previous chapters have explored the diverse meanings and functions of human rights education (HRE) at multiple levels in India. Chapter Eight situates the Institute of Human Rights Education's (IHRE) efforts in wider policy discussions and national political projects. Taking a broader view of those involved in educational policy, including those who do and do not locate themselves under the banner of HRE offers a picture of significant adaptation or decoupling that occurs between international, national, and local levels (Meyer and Rowan 1978). Decoupling of HRE in India can take the form of equating human rights with other concepts as diverse as religious morality, hygiene, and communist political beliefs. The final section of this chapter considers how stakeholders domestically equate HRE with its most vocal proponents, either accepting it or rejecting it accordingly. Individual and organizational sites of resistance to HRE are also identified and analyzed to shed light on the limits and possibilities for the expansion of HRE in India.

This chapter draws primarily on interviews, focus groups, observations, and fieldnotes. As part of this study, I interviewed many policymakers, some supportive of HRE and others opposed. Additionally, I met with staff and leaders of a variety of NGOs broadly working in the areas of human rights, citizenship, and peace education. Data that follow come from interviews with teachers (n = 118), officials and staff of various NGOs (n = 80), and some student data (n = 625). During the data analysis, certain themes emerged related to how respondents were modifying and adapting "human rights" as a term or a concept to their own meanings or projects, whether intentionally or unintentionally. Thus, this chapter explores how IHRE's work is situated within a larger context of the indigenization of human rights in India.

DIVERSE FORMS OF DECOUPLING

The diffusion of educational reforms has concerned scholars of International and Comparative Education as a key component of increased globalization in recent decades (e.g., Ramirez et al., 2007; Steiner-Khamsi and Stope 2006; Taylor 2009). Specifically, the role of human rights principles and human rights education has been discussed as a core component of a "world society" through the (at least nominal) convergence toward similar curricular reforms among nation-states (Ramirez et al., 2007; Meyer et al. 2010). As Ramirez and Wotipka (2007) have argued,

> The world society perspective assumes that nation-states vary with respect to how much access they have to the appropriate scripts and norms. The latter facilitate the sense making that paves the way for adherence to a given standard or norm. The more nation-states are embedded in the broader world . . . the more they will learn how "to talk the talk" and maybe even how "to walk the walk." (315)

Perhaps not surprisingly, the rise of human rights education has mirrored India's integration into the global economy and emergence as a key player in regional and international policy discussions.

The concept of decoupling is particularly useful in understanding the intermediation of human rights education by ideology, context, constituency, and locale. As discussed earlier, the term "decoupling," as it emerged in new institutional theory, refers to the existence of discrepancies between formal policies and actual practice and local adaptation of these norms to diverse ends (Meyer and Rowan 1978). The term has been applied to organizational studies as well as practices in schools, agencies, and other entities. A world society perspective on decoupling and human rights holds that even though countries may sign treaties or agree to adopt HRE because it is the "expected, rational, and legitimate" thing for countries to do (Bromley 2009, 40), the level of commitment of governments to enact these agreements vary. Similarly, in India, there has been ample "policy talk" regarding human rights education (Tyack and Cuban 1997), and some, though substantially less, "policy action" at the national level with regard to textbook reforms, a proposed elective course, and the development of supplemental materials on HRE, as discussed in Chapter Three.

While most neoinstitutionalist educational scholars have looked at the decoupling of national-level action from global discourses, my research on Indian human rights education reveals the selective "coupling" of local agendas with global discourses to gain credibility/authority, bypassing or utilizing the national government's reticence as part of a legitimizing strategy. For example, in discussing an early recognition of the Institute of Human Rights Education's program, the director of People's Watch, Henri Tiphagne, noted the following:

> The first year [1997–1998] after we implemented HRE in nine schools in Chennai, we held a valedictory celebration. It was during the UN's Decade for Human Rights Education, and since India is a signatory, some efforts were taken by national agencies like UGC (University Grants Commission) and NHRC (National Human Rights Commission). We invited the Chairperson of the NHRC to be a guest at our celebration and since the government has a mandate to implement HRE, but had not done much thus far, he came and delivered a speech at our function. So the state-level officials saw that we had high-ranking national officials endorsing this program. (Interview, February 2009)

Utilizing the international UN Decade as a rationale for their efforts, IHRE was able to draw in national authorities to convince state-level officials about the importance of human rights instruction. Ultimately, state officials granted permission for only a partial scale up and to select schools, but the alignment of local efforts with inter/national (Vavrus 2005) forces assisted in advocacy efforts. This is somewhat similar to the "boomerang effect" referred to by Keck and Sikkink (1998), though the case of HRE in India highlights the state level at which most educational policy decisions are made rather than the national level, which the authors emphasize in their analyses of the adoption of human rights norms globally.

Similarly, in approaching state-level officials for permission to enter government schools, one strategy (as briefly discussed in Chapter Four) included highlighting the UN's mandate for HRE that state-level authorities were morally obligated to follow. While the UN's proclamations around human rights education are not binding per se, the securing of letters from visiting UN officials in support of the program, which were then forwarded to state-level officials, provided them evidence of the program's legitimacy despite relative inaction at the national level for widespread school-based implementation.

Under the aegis of human rights education, this study found that further "decoupling" occurred at state levels for reasons related to the worldviews of IHRE's implementing partners and participants. IHRE's decision regarding what to include in human rights education textbooks (see Table 5.1 in Chapter Five) reflected an expansive view of diverse forms of social exclusion (poverty, caste, religion, gender, ability, skin color, "tribal" status, among others) and international and domestic guarantees that such practices violated. The general content of textbooks by and large adhered to international definitions of what human rights education is and ought to be, as discussed in Chapter Two. In localizing instruction, however, teachers and sometimes students added their own "flavor" to what they understood by human rights. Each of the three themes discussed below were factors in the implementation of HRE across states. These areas involved the alignment of instruction in human rights with other goals held by participants, whether intentionally or not. Human rights were also sometimes deliberately coupled with other messages, for example, prominent themes in Hinduism, to garner greater interest.

HUMAN RIGHTS AS RELIGIOUS MORALITY

Several participants, who were offering or receiving human rights instruction, conflated HRE with concepts found in public discourses about Hindu morality. While certainly some concepts overlap, teachers and students sometimes misunderstood human rights as a character-building exercise that sought to instill respect for elders and good behavior. For example, a district-level official charged with overseeing HRE in schools under her jurisdiction, related the following about why she supported the program:

> Human rights education is necessary because some children don't have any moral instruction at home. . . . Students should be taught what is good for them and what is bad for them. All of these bad things, like anger and jealousy, have not been given by God but have been created by humans. We have to teach children and give them some practices like meditation; they have to do it at least 10 minutes per day . . . So gradually, if we teach them spirituality and also human rights, they will become good citizens. (Interview, February 2009)

During the Bharatiya Janata Party's time in national office (1998–2004), values or duties education was emphasized and, as briefly noted in Chapter Three, the previous National Curriculum Framework issued in 2000–2001 sought to "Indianize, nationalize, and spiritualize" education nation-wide according to Hindu fundamentalist doctrines (as cited in Lall 2005, 5). Here, this conflation between values and rights education could have been related to viewing such directives from higher authorities as similar without having extensively reviewed the content of the HRE curriculum.

Nonetheless, common associations between values education and HRE were held by some officials, teachers, and perhaps students (although in-depth engagement with the textbooks tended to provide distinct information about human rights as a way to challenge rather than dutifully obey authority). These similarities relate back to the larger debate between duties and rights discussed in Chapter Three regarding which of the two should hold priority in Indian HRE. These attempts also involved efforts, such as those by national entities, to fuse the understandings of rights and duties to highlight their complementarity, sometimes for their own political reasons or to further the acceptance of HRE.

While not necessarily part of a political project, some teacher trainers *deliberately* sought to teach Hindu tenets (since most teachers in government schools shared this religious background) and to relate them to human rights to ensure support for the program. Some professionals who led teacher trainings discussed utilizing Indian and Hindu texts as a way to highlight past abuses. For example, in Karnataka state, the following example of how to engage teachers as well as communities was provided:

> Sometimes before we start the workshop, we talk about what happened in Indian mythology, like the story of Dhruva. He was denied attention by his father because of his stepmother's preference for her own son. There are so many examples of children who are mistreated. In our culture, [people] are very familiar with mythology so automatically they will start responding and saying, "Yes, they did wrong to him." Then we can talk about how this is still happening in our society and how we need to protect children's rights. (Interview, June 2009)

Utilizing known stories as a starting point for engaging teachers or community members in popular education efforts was one strategy for enlisting participation and engagement. In the example above of the story from Hinduism, the child Dhruva then went into the forest and achieved spiritual heights, which as the trainer quoted above noted, suggests how children should be well-treated since they have the same dignity and spiritual potential as adults. Religious texts can provide fertile ground for lessons rooted in understandings of human equality provided participants are willing to critically engage stories rather than accept them as fixed truth.

Other teacher trainers and state advisory committee members sought out examples of respect for, rather than violation of, human rights in the writings of historic figures in the region and/or from religious sources. The need to convince teachers of the alignment of human rights education with Hinduism was particularly evident in a state such as Orissa, where, given reigning political consensus, even students in government-run schools carry out Hindu prayers at school each morning, even though these schools are nominally secular and contain many students who are Christian or practice religious traditions of Adivasi communities. In these schools, students touched their teachers' feet each morning as a sign of respect, a common practice rooted in Hinduism to indicate that teachers are considered a form of God. In Adivasi areas of Orissa, students showed respect by bending their knees and walking lower when they saw teachers and administrators. Ironically, students also bent their knees when they walked in front of a poster adorned with human rights quotes and the image of the seminal Brazilian educator Paulo Freire that IHRE, the authority in this example, had placed in all affiliated schools in local languages (see Figure 8.1).

In this context, the need for engaging Hindu or local sources was paramount to some, as one advisory committee member noted:

> Unless they are convinced, teachers won't accept what we say. The first day of the training program is always difficult. In India, people think human rights have come from the West, but it was also there in our mythology. For example, at the end of the Ramayana, Sita wasn't getting justice from her husband (who accused her of being unfaithful), so she left and went down into the earth. This is a protest on her part where she is claiming her rights as a woman. We have collected such type of evidence and stories from mythology and we let the teachers know that human rights principles are not a new thing. These are a part of our culture. We also discuss a famous poet from Orissa who talks about a woman's right to choose whom she marries. We place these types of examples from our culture in front of the participants so they know that human rights are also our concepts and that we can adopt them. (Interview, July 2009)

Such strategic approaches to human rights and teacher training proved useful in securing interest among teachers and advancing the program. In line with IHRE's strategies of persuasive pragmatism, the way that human rights education was "decoupled" from international- and national-level discourses then, could actually be a source of benefit and help promote the expansion and implementation of the program.

While not the majority religion in any state where HRE was offered, some institutional partners also utilized Christian principles to encourage adoption of human rights education and foster aligned behavior. In Tamil Nadu

Figure 8.1 IHRE Poster with Paulo Freire's Words (in Hindi) and Image

and West Bengal, the implementing organizations were linked in some ways to Christian organizations (either through staff's personal affiliations or institutionally in the case of the Loreto Sealdah School in Kolkata run by Catholic nuns). This resulted in local Christian educational institutions sometimes volunteering to adopt human rights education at their own expense and offering the course to their students. Adoption of the program and teacher training, in such cases, reiterated the Biblical origins of concepts related to human rights such as social equality and service to the poor. As such, at the level of delivery, there was sometimes an intentional effort to match human rights concepts with Christian or Hindu ideals. At times, human rights was also similarly confused with other international development programs.

HUMAN RIGHTS AS HYGIENE AND "PROPER DRESS" IN ADIVASI COMMUNITIES

Development efforts in rural communities, particularly those serving Adivasi communities, have long focused on health, hygiene, and sanitation. Getting children to school is still a considerable challenge in many of these communities, and once there, teachers and NGOs utilize their presence to impart lessons related to public health. This included education on matters such as adopting hygienic practices and preventing infectious diseases. Health data provides the rationale why Adivasi communities are targeted for such messages: the mortality rate in Adivasi communities for children under 5 is much higher (96 per 1000) than the rest of India (74), while the incidence of long-term malnutrition among Adivasi children is notably greater when compared to other Indian children (55 versus 42 percent) (Das et al., 2010).

As such, several teachers and students conflated human rights education with these other programs, like hygiene campaigns, also present in their schools. In residential schools serving Adivasi children in Tamil Nadu and Orissa, HRE has been implemented in all the schools, which seek to boost the dismal rates of post-primary education among Adivasi youth (just 23 percent compared to nearly double that for the rest of India). One teacher in Tamil Nadu stated the following with regard to Adivasi students' realities: "the children come from a very remote area and they have no idea about how to clean their room and sanitation. They also don't know how to interact with other children. After imparting this human rights course, they understand what discipline is and why it is necessary to maintain hygiene" (teacher focus group, February 2009). Another teacher in Orissa similarly noted that one of the outcomes of the human rights camps (that some students were selected to attend during summer holidays) was that "students gained confidence and also learned about cleanliness" (interview, July 2009). While HRE textbooks did not contain messages about hygiene specifically, there were subjects on the right to clean water and development that may have aligned with other initiatives. Alternatively, teachers receiving a variety of programs to implement may have assumed that they were all connected despite different trainings, materials, and curricular content.

Students sometimes also utilized the prominent focus on the "right to education" in HRE to encourage their parents to take schooling more seriously in a variety of ways. One common way that many students mentioned was telling their parents that they could no longer miss school for work, harvesting, or cultural events as many children often did. One teacher noted the following about his students after learning about the right to education:

> Students used to not come to school neatly and neither would their parents if they came for a meeting. The parents would come to school in *lungis* (a long cloth worn by men, oftentimes to sleep). After this education, the students used to go to their parents and say, "We have to follow school discipline and this is the dress code we should use when coming to school." So students and parents have changed this practice. (Interview, February 2009)

The perceived increased respect for education resulting from human rights education perhaps reflected other factors. Most teachers came from outside the community and, as such, other prejudices may also have been operating with regards to conceptions of cleanliness and proper dress.

Students from rural communities also mentioned the inability of human rights messages to counteract the larger forces at play in their communities. These were not "decoupled" meanings of human rights but instead larger structural limits and belief systems that impeded the realization of rights in their communities. In parts of rural India, many human rights education students discussed the role of superstition in driving practices that violated rights. For instance, there existed strong beliefs about the impurity and need for segregating girls who were menstruating, either for the first time or in some cases, every month (a belief held by many communities not just Adivasi groups). These beliefs obviously impeded adolescent girls' right to education. Practices such as the lack of provision of latrines for girls in most schools also contributed to differences in educational attainment as reflected, for example, in the significant differences in literacy rates between men (82.1 percent) and women (65.5 percent) at the national level (GOI 2011). Kanipriya, a 15-year-old, explained the following:

> The exams were happening at school when I had just started menstruating so I went to school. No one would sit or come near me. My teacher said to them, "You all are reading HRE, right? You should realize that this is discrimination. You are hurting her dignity." So after she scolded the students like that, my classmates treated me better and I was able to complete my exams. (Interview, February 2009)

While Kanipriya's account had a positive ending based on her teacher's rejection of the practice of segregating menstruating girls and intervention, some realities that students encountered did not have such easy resolution.

At a school in Orissa, several students discussed the practice of child sacrifice that exists in some Adivasi communities. An advisory committee member in Orissa explained it as follows: "In some places, a tantrik [mystic] will tell you to kill and there will be a good harvest or you'll have more property" (interview, July 2009). As such, children at one school were abuzz with concerns that a child from their community would be sacrificed for the "auspicious" start to a construction project that was to get underway. The students approached their teachers and the staff of IHRE for assistance in dealing with the situation, but abuses related to superstition abounded in many communities.

Another force that surrounded students' realities in Orissa and nearby states was the Maoist armed insurgency or Naxalite movement that claims significant support from Adivasi communities across the "red corridor," comprised of parts of India's poorest states of Bihar, Jharkhand, Chhattisgarh, Andhra Pradesh, Orissa, and West Bengal. Students and teachers reported that members of these groups sometimes slept in their schools at night, fleeing state forces. Human rights reports have noted how these groups "are targeting and blowing up state-run schools. At the same time, police and paramilitary forces are disrupting education for long periods by occupying schools as part of anti-Naxalite operations" (HRW 2009, 1). Many Adivasi communities are sympathetic to the Naxals because they seek to resist—albeit through violent and excessive means—the usurpation of collectively held forest lands by mining companies seeking to extract natural resources.

As a result, students witness conflicts between their own indigenous communities, armed insurgents (from within and outside of their community), and police and state-aided paramilitaries who have been responsible for abuses ranging from damaging property to rape and killing of suspected Naxalite sympathizers (HRW 2008). Anand, a seventh standard student in Orissa, highlighted the following in relation to questions about his human rights learning: "Killing is a violation of our right to life. That happened here. A boy from this school was killed by the police during the firing on villagers nearby here" (focus group, July 2009). Anand was relating an incident that happened a few years prior when community members occupied land that the government was trying to buy for less than market value in order for a steel plant to be built. In this case, the police fired on protestors and a student walking home from school was killed in the crossfire. Students were trying to interpret how the state's obligation to protect their rights matched with the day-to-day realities they witnessed in a complex and brutal sociopolitical environment that included the charged dealings of state forces, armed insurgents, large corporations, and nonviolent community activists.

When schools are being occupied by either side in an armed struggle or children and villagers are getting killed, human rights education sometimes offers mixed messages to students about their basic rights and who to look to for protection of them.[1] Armed Maoist rebels are an extremely controversial movement that does not represent the diversity of parties and perspectives of the Indian left, as discussed in the following section.

HUMAN RIGHTS AS LEFT POLITICS

Whereas in other contexts human rights may not be associated with left politics, in India, several members of the many active Communist parties and social movements advocated for human rights. Teachers and staff of human rights organizations often had come from student movements associated with the Indian left and saw human rights education as a way to infuse preexisting ideas into a new framework with greater currency at state, national, and international levels. A state advisory committee member of the Institute of Human Rights Education in Orissa described the relationship as follows:

> The left movement originally initiated from the have-nots. These are the same people who suffer from atrocities. Just giving aid doesn't alleviate poverty; instead, poor people and peasants have to become aware of their rights. . . . So human rights education is necessary for students to understand the course of their life and the role of education. When I joined the Communist movement in my youth, we learned about dialectical materialism and historical materialism, and the process of development. Without understanding this, students might think—and their teacher might tell them—that if they are not doing well, it is because of their fate as someone from a Scheduled Caste (Dalit) group. They will say, "You are not meant to be educated." Human rights as a principle can inform them that there should be no social distinctions like between castes, or between Hindus, Muslims, and Christians. (Interview, July 2009)

The principles of egalitarianism drew many individuals with left-leaning politics to associate with human rights organizations in advisory capacities or as staff. Indeed, several IHRE staff members mentioned previous and current involvement in political parties and movements associated with the Indian left.

Even teachers who were active in their unions and in society often found human rights education to be a way to advance their political goals within a structure that allowed them to freely discuss their beliefs within a framework of human rights. For example, in Orissa, a retired teacher in her 60s still attended trainings and volunteered as a trainer because she found the program well-aligned with her political beliefs and commitment to social equality as a member of the Communist party. As mentioned earlier, active HRE teachers in Tamil Nadu convinced the state-wide teachers' federation to adopt human rights education as part of its platform in 2009. As such, for teachers already interested in left movements, HRE provided a way to fuse their larger political beliefs with a sanctioned curricular program that they were mandated to offer in their schools. Because human rights were by and large socially accepted at least at the discursive level, teachers might infuse their own ideas under its guise without any pushback, similar to what scholars Elsbach and Sutton (1992) found on how radical social movements utilized decoupling to gain legitimacy among their constituents in other parts of the globe.

Interestingly, in both West Bengal and Kerala, where HRE was offered on a limited scale, Communist governments were in power at the time of this research and did not express interest in adopting human rights education, despite advocacy efforts by IHRE. In the case of Kerala—where a unique blend of Communist social policy has resulted in near universal literacy rates—the state government was reluctant to adopt a program financed by foreign (Western) donors in its schools. The state government did, however, provide authorization for the HRE program to operate in government-aided schools that were jointly administered with religious (Hindu, Muslim, and Christian) organizations.

Despite the state's larger reticence for adopting HRE, teachers in the 226 schools in Kerala where the program was offered during the time of this research often were shaped by their involvement in unions and other political associations. As a result, their take on human rights was infused with advocacy and solidarity with oppressed peoples worldwide as related by two HRE teachers from Kerala:

> Education in Kerala is very good because the state has supported us to have [near universal] literacy. But HRE training has made us better teachers because we have stopped corporal punishment and we teach children about their rights. I feel very proud to be a HRE teacher. In Malappuram district, we are making a federation for HRE teachers and advocating for changes like making district-wide professional development opportunities for teachers, like counseling, career guidance, etc. In school, we also carry out many activities related to HRE with children. In 2006, when Israel attacked Lebanon, we had a march and the students prepared presentations about the situation in an assembly. We also had the children form a human rights parliament in the school. (Interview, December 2009)

While the content of the HRE textbooks primarily focused on basic rights and violations, such as discrimination, teachers' worldviews also shaped instruction beyond the classroom. The extent of continued education varied depending on teachers' interest. Some teachers from Kerala used additional school activities to discuss global events and link them to human rights. These practices are in some ways similar to the HRE for Global Citizenship approach discussed in Chapter Two. Global citizenship education as discussed earlier is generally offered in industrialized countries seeking to expand children's awareness about global inequalities. In the case of the Kerala teachers highlighted above, "global citizenship" was more solidarity based. Though these teachers and students still operated as members of the international community, they understood their role as one of raising one's voice against injustices. At another school in Kerala, students engaged in a peace march to mark Hiroshima Day in August, reflecting a distinct form of global solidarity aligned with marginalized groups worldwide. Whether driven by human rights or related to decoupled political practices, IHRE's large-scale experiment across 18 states played a significant role in the engagement by students with larger social and political issues.

FORMS OF RESISTANCE TO HUMAN RIGHTS EDUCATION

HRE was not always received with open arms. There were various sites of resistance—to human rights education and to the Institute of Human Rights Education's brand of HRE—within and outside of schools. Resistance often emerged from the debates highlighted in Chapter Three, namely that human rights are Western and incompatible with Asian realities, that duties or values education should take precedence over HRE, and that information on violations would harm children. Resistance from those committed to human rights education was manifested in arguments that HRE be integrated across all subjects rather than as a stand-alone topic in schools. There were also related debates about whether human rights content should be included on exams to offer this education greater legitimacy. Resistance took the forms of partial acceptance within the program, and externally, as refusal to adopt it.

Partial Acceptance and Internal Resistance

Many cases emerged where those charged with implementation of human rights education expressed initial or persistent reluctance to the program. One state advisory committee member involved in curriculum development of HRE from Tamil Nadu utilized the metaphor of matrimony—specifically, an arranged versus a "love" marriage—to describe how teachers first reacted to being told to teach human rights education:

> If you introduce a new thing, there's always resistance. It's a very natural phenomenon wherever you go. Another important aspect is who makes the decision. For some, you tell them, "The government says you must do this," and they simply accept. Having government sanction gives us an inherent advantage. But there is a difference between getting married and loving somebody. Sometimes you love someone and get married, other times you get married and later learn to love them. It works both ways. Once teachers try the new methodology and see the relevance, this kind of resistance will be slowly removed and they will accept it. There are a few cases where, out of their own prejudice, they were not able to accept it ever, but because of the government's orders, most of them still implement the program in some way. No matter how much external pressure you put, there are some who still may resist. (Interview, February 2009)

A few schools visited had distributed books to students, but for different reasons, were not offering instruction. In one case, the headmaster's resistance to the program was clear and this affected the allotment of periods for the teaching of HRE. One of the teachers in this school in Tamil Nadu asked me during our interview, "My headmaster says human rights education is a colossal waste of time. What do you think?" While the teacher himself stated his disagreement with this position, the students did not seem to be receiving regular instruction, as reflected in their limited ability to respond to questions about what human rights were. While I did not note outward verbal resistance by any teachers to HRE since authorization for the program came from high-level state and district officials, the distribution of textbooks with no corresponding instruction, as in the case of various schools, limited the benefits of human rights instruction.

Other schools were unable to offer human rights instruction due to the sheer lack of resources and systemic constraints, despite their own interest in the subject matter. In Orissa, regular teacher absenteeism (the state had a teacher absentee rate of 23.4 percent) meant that the teachers who did show up were often covering other classes or doubling up their classes so that students were not unsupervised (Kremer et al., 2005). In one such classroom I visited, I counted 144 students, with those in the back hardly able to see or hear their teacher. Needless to say, in such environments, I found teachers who were well-trained and interested in HRE, but had no time to teach students HRE.

Students did have the books and some had read them, but little impact was seen on these students in terms of internalizing and integrating information related to human rights.

External Resistance

Resistance to either IHRE's advocacy efforts or the general idea of human rights education was another part of policy discourse around the educational reform. In particular, HRE was resisted by certain officials in decision-making roles depending on their perceptions regarding content, the political orientation of advocates, and assumptions about the background knowledge of learners. Several policy actors resisted IHRE's efforts because of their association or conflation of the Institute and People's Watch, and the latter's record of legal and advocacy efforts around caste discrimination and police misconduct. Just as some teachers chose to adopt HRE because of the authority of the "messengers," or notable trainers, some policy actors decided *not* to adopt HRE because of the "messengers," namely: a vocal human rights organization.

Resistance to IHRE's brand of human rights instruction sometimes took the form of ignoring their work and expertise in this area. While selective permission was granted for the HRE program in certain schools and for certain populations, broad-based funding and access were not given in any of the 18 states in which the Institute operated. IHRE and its local partner sought to scale up their work in Karnataka state to 250 schools several years back. Authorities initially resisted granting permission, though later it was granted and the program expanded with donor funding. Operating since 2005, the state partner in Karnataka, SICHREM (The South India Cell for Human Rights Education and Monitoring), had held periodic human rights events where students were visible, speaking about what they had learned and actions they had taken. SICHREM had significant experience with human rights instruction and the development of human rights clubs at the secondary school level. In 2009, without formally consulting or appearing to review this fairly large-scale program, the state-level human rights commission issued a notice to all secondary schools instructing them to start human rights clubs. One staff member noted:

> One of our HRE teachers called me from one of the high schools and said that a letter came from the State Human Rights Commission (SHRC) via the Education Department Commissioner for Public Instruction, asking them to start human rights clubs in all high schools. All these teachers are calling me and asking me,

"We came to know that we need to start a human rights club. What are the guidelines? How do we constitute a club and what are the activities we need to do?"
(Interview, June 2009)

Whether the Karnataka State Human Rights Commission deliberately sought
to exclude or was truly unaware of their existence, many headmasters and
teachers who had previously attended trainings or events called upon IHRE's
state partner, SICHREM, one of the only sources of information on how to
establish human rights clubs. The government circular ordering the creation
of human rights clubs had not provided any additional guidance on how
schools could comply with this directive. While the introduction of human
rights clubs may have been influenced by SICHREM and IHRE's work, the
state's failure to include the organizations as knowledgeable experts was
notable.

Another form of resistance involved perceptions that HRE was too radical
and challenging for human rights to be made a separate subject of instruction. A senior educational policymaker that had been lobbied by IHRE to
introduce human rights education stated the following:

> Some people are just making propaganda. It's a good effort on their part, but it's
> too fragmented. Children need a holistic education. . . . All people should enjoy
> rights, not just through an activist approach for certain groups who are aggres-
> sively demanding their rights. All this time, if our mind is thinking only about
> legal provisions, then we become more mechanical and are not human beings.
> (Interview, April 2009)

That human rights education may challenge the unstated ideological prefer-
ences of at least some decision-makers is, while perhaps predictable, worth
thinking about and engaging further.

Other officials found HRE to be potentially harmful for students given its
focus on violations. Another national-level educational official raised objec-
tions to HRE, particularly IHRE's explicit focus on cases of abuse: "We have
to be cautious of the counter-productivity of teaching about discrimination.
This can, in fact, be planting the seeds of prejudice in children. Are we not
wrong by introducing these issues that make children afraid of this world?"
(Interview, April 2009). To this worldview, Dalit, Adivasi, and other children
are not aware of violations to their dignity. This official proceeded to quote a
1949 UN document that warned of teaching about the Holocaust for fear of
promoting prejudice like that which gave way to the genocide. As such, HRE
was resisted by certain officials in decision-making roles depending on their

perceptions regarding content, the political orientation of advocates, and assumptions about the background knowledge of learners. Still these officials had to engage with HRE because of inter/national (Vavrus 2005) pressure to enact and report back on India's progress in implementing these reforms. Of course policymakers had discretion and room in the ways they chose to implement HRE. While IHRE called for human rights to be incorporated into school curricula as a mandatory subject of education for all students, integrating the topic within existing subjects of instruction was another (and often, preferred) curricular policy position available to decision-makers.

Many individuals, particularly those in civil society, chose not to engage with HRE at all. Some utilized other terms entirely for their efforts, even those aligned with the reform. One retired high-ranking civil servant had started educational programs in the conflict-ridden state of Kashmir that sought to provide after-school education to youth on "social justice, democracy, human rights, and secularism." She felt that human rights had "become fashionable because there is money in it" and, instead, termed her work "peace action" or "cultural education" given the need for community acceptance in conflict areas. This work creatively drew on instances of cooperation from Sufi saints who fused Hindu and Muslim beliefs and sought to encourage coexistence, but deliberately rejected the term "human rights education," though state-violence and related human rights violations remained significant issues in the region. Other individuals preferred not to discuss issues in India in the framework of human rights, stating that international standards were not compatible with Indian realities, such as the need for poor children to work. Chapter Four highlighted the role of "sympathetic bureaucrats"; conversely, the reluctance of some officials and civil society partners to embrace human rights instruction also highlights the power of "unsympathetic" officials to subvert efforts to advance human rights.

CONCLUSION

Previous chapters explored some of the unintended consequences of human rights education, particularly backlash to the increased activism of marginalized youth, while this chapter examined unanticipated decoupling and resistance to these practices. If strategy as much as content and moral suasion determine how HRE expands "from below," perceptions of human rights education and the constituencies advocating for these reforms are also factors in the success and limitations of these initiatives. While global diffusion made human rights more attractive to some—and IHRE often catalyzed on this—other forms of decoupling and local debates about the irrelevance of human rights for the Indian context generated greater resistance for HRE efforts.

Decoupling or rearticulations of the premises of this form of education, not to mention outright resistance, force a reconsideration of the conditions of possibility for effective HRE in India. Initiatives to expand HRE require belief in its value; hence, further scholarly attention given to the diverse understandings and meanings of what human rights are can offer scholars and practitioners insights into the possibility of incorporating respect for human rights among different stakeholders in society. Certainly, government and international support, as well as the global diffusion of norms of universal human dignity can legitimize human rights education. Though in India, the omnipresence of larger Education for All (*Sarva Shiksha Abhiyan*) targets that subordinate other qualitative considerations to basic access to primary education requires reexamination in order to secure and deepen a substantial respect for human dignity through educational efforts.

Chapter Nine

Implications and Concluding Thoughts

"Education" is such a full development of human personality as to endow human beings with the power to resist the colonization of the mind by state, civil society, intergovernmental regimes and multinationals. . . . In this image, human rights education will be a distinctly autonomous, decolonizing, deglobalizing, heretical project in which the very act of learning will be simultaneously an act of insurrection aiming at the dissipation of imposed knowledges.

(Baxi 1997)

As human rights education (HRE) programs expand and deepen across the globe, greater empirical research—rather than repetitive claims of HRE's importance—would help deepen our understanding of the conditions of possibility for realizing these ideals as well as how various forms of human rights instruction interact with, challenge, and fuse with existing patterns of inequality, culture, and power. Previous studies of HRE have focused on age, constituency, national political context, and the generation of rights to situate discussions of how the educational project should be structured. This book has explored issues of ideology, strategy, and impact using a vertical case study approach that compared national policy, regional pedagogical development, and the postures of state officials, headmasters, teachers, and schoolchildren in one massive and deeply heterogeneous nation-state.

I have argued that ideological variation and strategy (namely, persuasive pragmatism) play a significant role in shaping the character of human rights education initiatives in national policy reform and non-governmental efforts. In-depth analyses of human rights education at the levels of international discourse, national policy, and local practice in India suggest that human rights initiatives can have a notable and widespread impact on the realization of basic values of human dignity in some of the most marginalized areas in India just as structural forces of discrimination and violence, as well as rearticulations of human rights concepts can impede the adoption, expansion, and implementation of HRE at all levels.

This book rests upon three primary arguments. First, not all HRE is the same. The ideology, content emphasis, and outcomes of HRE initiatives depend significantly on the implementing agency, teacher mediation of information, and constituency. In Chapter Two, I offered a schema for classifying human rights education, namely suggesting that HRE for Global Citizenship, Coexistence, and Transformative Action are broad categories in which to frame conceptual or rather ideological approaches to HRE within India and other nation-states. Chapter Three highlighted early nation-building efforts in India to create a secular state and the development of educational institutions to this end. The visions of independence leaders were juxtaposed with current indicators of social exclusion and uneven development in the country. Chapter Three also explored the landscape of HRE in India, focusing on national-level approaches that emphasize HRE for Global Citizenship. While the scope of these programs was broad, the intensity of impact of these approaches was limited. Conversely, Chapters Four through Seven examined an initiative with both broad scope and high intensity—the Institute of Human Rights Education.

Second, the book argues that strategy is as important as content and pedagogy in ensuring support for expanding HRE. The Institute of Human Rights Education used deeply contextual and relational approaches, what I call a strategy of persuasive pragmatism, to secure participation by a wide variety of interests and stakeholders nation-wide. This strategy ranged from identifying sympathetic bureaucrats who might support the expansion of an unprecedented NGO program in government schools to offering contextualized trainings and a variety of other incentives to headmasters and teachers. Global support for the diffusion of human rights norms helped to secure the interest of officials and participants, though there were notable instances of localized decoupling, or reinterpretations of HRE by participants resulting in HRE practice not quite matching up with a given program's intentions. Chapter Eight also mapped sites of resistance internally and externally based on rejection of human rights education or IHRE's curricular approach to these efforts.

Third, I assert that the impact of HRE, and the ability of various individuals to influence change in different moments, is heavily mediated by social location. In Chapter Five, marginalized youth's engagement with HRE offered them a framework in which to situate everyday realities and experiences. However, their actions were sometimes stifled by limited social status and the fear and reality of backlash. Such students were forced to approach their goals in a more strategic and relational fashion, for example by engaging in collective action or seeking support from teachers and textbooks. In Chapter Six, students with relative privilege in different situations, whether boys from marginalized communities or slightly more affluent students learning HRE, had significant success in addressing situations of abuse through actions grounded in solidarity and coalitional agency. For better and worse, social location had a notable role in shaping the types of human rights campaigns students develop.

Chapter Seven examined teachers' personal transformations, a factor often absent in discussions of HRE, as well as instructors' role as allies to students. Teachers' personal transformations were an integral part of the success of human rights initiatives. The role of educators and textbooks, underlined by the authority accorded to them in semiliterate settings, played an important part in addressing abuse in these communities. Textbooks within the classroom and as community resources offered HRE a life beyond the periods in school allotted to its study. Taken together, these three arguments, supported by data from across India, complicate our understandings of human rights education as a singular process with shared ideology and impact across the globe.

Broad efforts around educational reform in India have been primarily concerned with access to primary education, particularly the Education for All (*Sarva Shiksha Abhiyan*) mandates that have sought to remedy wide disparities in school attendance. SSA has achieved substantial increases in basic access to schooling, with some arguing that enrollment has been purely driven by India's nation-wide mid-day meal program rather than a belief in the benefit of education. In this context, questions of quality are the next step in assessing educational attainment. While Education for All is closer to being attained, larger questions of "education for *what?*" need to be considered, particularly, as this book suggests, when gains in enrollment are jeopardized by caste discrimination, insufficient facilities, widespread teacher absenteeism, and corporal punishment within schools. High dropout rates after primary school also complicate the fact of increased enrollments as many children reassess the value of poor quality schooling. The divergent character of instruction in Indian schools—from the world's finest elite schools in urban centers to dilapidated and neglected outposts in some rural areas—should concern scholars of development who equate simple access to schools with broader goals of social, political, and economic development.

What is the relationship of human rights education to development? The role of development efforts in tandem with human rights education in India can expand people's capabilities, as described by economists Amartya Sen and Jean Drèze. Sen argues that disparate social realities can impede inclusive growth and the exercise of freedom (Sen 1999). Sen and Drèze's capabilities approach relates directly to freedom and "the range of options a person has in deciding what kind of life to lead" (Drèze and Sen 1995, 10). Scholars, such as Nussbaum (1997, 2006), have advocated for education that expands freedom through critical thinking, global citizenship, and through the development of a narrative imagination. Nussbaum (2000) finds the concept of capabilities more expansive than rights, and educational scholars Walker and Unterhalter (2007) further note that "rights are features of persons, but they are also aspects of social arrangements whether or not this particular rights bearer is currently in a position to benefit from them" (242). Sen's capabilities approach has been taken up in educational research (e.g., Walker and Unterhalter 2007), particularly in discussions of system-wide reforms, but little educational scholarship has sought to examine experiments that seek to expand the space between lived reality and capabilities for marginalized groups through sustained intervention. Greater information on reforms, such as human rights education, that expand marginalized youth and coalitional agents' ability to work to dismantle barriers based on class, caste, gender, and/ or religion, can be seen as a mechanism by which to enhance one's opportunities and capabilities, though further scholarly attention is required to understand the "social arrangements" that may limit and/or enable action in distinct moments.

This book also draws attention to the critical role of power and social location in realizing a particular program's aims. While larger narratives exist in India about schooling as a transformative force, systemic social exclusion and constrained resources often limit the realization of ideals of equal educational opportunity espoused from India's immediate post-Independence period onwards. In their important work on young men and schooling in the northern Indian state of Uttar Pradesh, scholars Jeffrey, Jeffrey, and Jeffrey (2007) caution that despite the potential for education to lead to social mobility, "power and culture mediate people's access to the freedoms that education provides" (3). The authors highlight the challenges faced by members of marginalized groups in accessing the benefits of schooling due to social stratification in the labor market. Attention to the social context in which educational reform and innovation, such as HRE, operates is an essential component of understanding its role in youth's lives. Human rights education may provide yet another important way for youth to resist inequalities in their homes, schools, and communities.

IMPLICATIONS FOR GLOBAL HRE SCHOLARSHIP AND PRACTICE

Human rights education and training concerns all levels—preschool, primary, secondary and university—and all forms of education, training and learning, whether in a public or private, formal, informal or non-formal setting. It includes vocational training, particularly the training of trainers, continuing education, popular education, and public information and awareness activities.

Human rights education and training is an essential component of the right to education for all, as recognized in both the international and regional framework and the domestic law of different States. It is related to the full implementation of the right to education, particularly free compulsory primary education, and the widespread provision of basic education for all, including for illiterate persons, as well as to the development of secondary education, including technical and vocational education, and higher education.

(UN Declaration on Human Rights Education and Training, OHCHR 2011)

Education *about* and *for* human rights are internationally sanctioned goals as suggested by the United Nations Declaration on Human Rights Education and Training excerpted above. Given the historical role of education in mediating social and political conflict across the globe (Davies 2004), and views of schooling as a site of redemption, the field of human rights education has both proceeded with tremendous optimism and, at times, been content with implicit assumptions that simple prescription of content, pedagogy, and methods for implementation will achieve widespread transformation in social relations.

HRE is affiliated with different sectors in different societies (Tibbitts 2008). However, HRE also means different things to distinct individuals and entities promoting these initiatives. To some, HRE signals entry into the global community and membership benefits, as has been discussed, for example, in Turkey's national efforts to incorporate HRE in their accession bid to the

European Union (Hicks 2001). In the Gaza Strip, the United Nations Relief and Works Agency for Palestine Refugees in the Near East (UNRWA) runs a Human Rights Education Initiative to foster nonviolence, conflict resolution, and mutual understanding (UNRWA n.d.). In countries emerging from conflict, HRE embodies a reconciliation strategy often incorporated into government policy or peace accords as seen in nations as diverse as Guatemala, South Africa, and Rwanda, among others (Bernath, Holland, and Martin 1999; Freedman et al., 2008).

As discussed earlier, ideology, as much as location or other variables, shapes programmatic approaches to HRE. As historian Paul Zeleza (2002) has noted, "the challenge . . . is not to splinter 'The South' into more worlds— Third, Fourth, Fifth—but to dissolve the very duality of North and South, to conceptualize economic hierarchies and exploitation as much as in spatial and international terms as in social and intra-national terms" (74). Distance from power may be a more useful predictor of a program's ideological bent and strategy toward HRE than geographical location. For example, a human rights education program for low-income urban youth in New York City public schools, like the Human Rights Activist Project of the youth development organization Global Kids,[1] may be more closely aligned with the Institute of Human Rights Education in India's HRE for Transformative Action approach with regards to outlook, methodology, and practice than perhaps another Indian HRE program that espouses a HRE for Global Citizenship approach.

That different organizations with different social bases and worldview ground themselves in this discourse suggests the richness and possibility of HRE. The converse also holds that diverse agendas can get smuggled in under the guise of HRE as noted in Chapter Eight, sometimes working against the intentions of the project. By understanding better the role of power, inequality, and ideology in driving content, pedagogy, and the desired outcome of distinct programs and policies, scholars can develop a more nuanced picture of the conditions of possibility to deepen respect for human dignity through educational efforts. As HRE becomes more integrated into policy discussions at national and international levels, greater attention to what HRE is, does, and means will be needed to ensure that these practices are adapted to new human rights problems, learning contexts, and social reform initiatives. Many distinct proponents of HRE, however differently motivated, may serve to advance HRE efforts in a more comprehensive way. As such, empirical research and greater evaluation of the impact (both intended and unintended consequences) of human rights education initiatives can illuminate how local forces mediate instruction.

Recommendations

While most policies migrate or are transferred from the global "North" to the global "South" (Steiner-Khamsi 2004), Zeleza's caution on using these categories notwithstanding, one Indian NGO's adaptation and reinvention of HRE on an unprecedented scale offer insights on implementation, impact, equity, and quality for programs in other regions as well. IHRE's experience operating amidst larger debates about human rights and local concepts that selectively support, modify, or resist human rights education is instructive for others seeking to understand the limits and possibilities for HRE in other contexts. It suggests a set of lessons and recommendations for scholars and practitioners interested in educational equity and quality broadly, as well as those interested in experiences with human rights education specifically in other parts of the globe.

1. *Creative and diverse strategies should be employed that broaden support for HRE among a variety of stakeholders. These should include relational approaches and a consideration of multiple motivations for supporting and advancing HRE through a strategy of persuasive pragmatism.*

While human rights advocates, including human rights educators, often rely on moral imperatives about the inherent value of such claims, IHRE engages with the varied interests and motivations of stakeholders in India's regional school systems. The organization does this in ways that complicate some of the more narrowly ideological strategies suggested in much of the literature on and practice in human rights education, which tend to only secure the support of those already convinced about the need for HRE. Much human rights education literature, particularly that which is prescriptive in nature, assumes that teachers, learners, and parents agree with human rights principles and are willing to act upon them in the larger community. Despite the global diffusion and acceptance of "human rights" (Ramirez et al., 2007), it has been differentially defined and utilized, rendering the concept, in some respects, meaningless (Baxi 2006), but in other ways, malleable for recruiting a variety of constituents.

The discourse of human rights education at the global level certainly does not always translate into national practice, though grassroots efforts can utilize international support to expand support for initiatives. IHRE's experience with human rights curriculum offers an instructive case study of how international mandates and grassroots activism that seeks a wide coalition of

supporters together have given one educational reform significant momentum and arguably, influenced national-level initiatives and discussions.
Officials from IHRE were the only non-governmental representatives on a
high-level task force convened by Indian national agencies to develop HRE
materials. When the Indian government had to report to the United Nations
on progress in implementing HRE, the Institute was consulted as a leading
expert in HRE practice. The ability of a civil society group—through a comprehensive strategy and a large-scale experiment in government schools—to
shape debate around educational reform was predicated on a creative and
effective strategy going beyond mere moral exhortation.

2. *Human rights education efforts should consider social location when
   designing content, pedagogy, and action-oriented projects. Instruction
   should be developed with learners' backgrounds in mind.*

HRE programs should be designed to address the distinct realities of student
learners and the ways in which they may effectively take action. Giving students the tools to counter abuses may be counterproductive if students end
up frustrated and disillusioned by the disjuncture between these guarantees
and their realities; thus, HRE efforts should theorize social location, without extinguishing learners' nascent desire to act, in inspiring action. Students
should also be taught to analyze sociopolitical contexts and the potential for
political efficacy in the present and future. Collective action strategies that
enlist teachers, parents, textbooks, and other sources of authority may reduce
the potential for backlash and other constraints that frustrate attempts at
intervention. Coalitional agents should consider how their privileged status
(in a particular situation) amplifies their voice and examine how they might
work in tandem with victims to stop abuses and offer help that demonstrates
solidarity.

3. *Participants' own transformation and interest in human rights can benefit
   their households, schools, and communities in multiple ways, and should
   thus be central in reform efforts.*

Participants' transformation had important ripple effects. In particular,
teachers became allies to students through the process of learning about
human rights. These transformations worked to reverse common practices
of neglect and mistreatment and minimized the social distance between
teachers and pupils, allowing for increased democratization of the classroom and school. For privileged students, carrying HRE to their families

and communities also had spillover effects since their parents were in positions of influence or employers whose new learnings could affect others. Marginalized students were also given the room to reconsider age-old practices that cultivate resignation to internalized and externalized forms of oppression. As such, advocates of HRE should consider centering action around the role of students and teachers in the larger community in their calls for the greater prioritization of HRE in discussions of educational reform.

4. *Appropriate, contextualized, and engaging teacher training should be developed to incentivize participation and legitimize both the message and messengers of human rights.*

Teachers' transformation often flowed from their positive experiences with training programs carried out by IHRE. Such trainings differed from routine government-run trainings because they utilized participatory methods, took place in nice locations that teachers may not have previously visited, and provided examples and advice rooted in teachers' lived experience. IHRE also drew on noted experts. Teachers enjoyed interacting with these local luminaries since there were few settings where such crossing of social boundaries might occur. All of these dimensions taken together resulted in a great degree of teacher transformation. Coverage of the required material in HRE textbooks comprised a small part of teacher trainings; instead, teachers' support for human rights and integration of attitudes against corporal punishment, domestic violence, and other abusive practices was prioritized. This approach, as reflected in the data, proved useful in garnering interest and facilitating attitudinal and behavior changes among teachers. HRE trainings in other contexts might consider what components will attract teachers, facilitate their transformation, and secure their commitment to the principles of human rights prior to their deployment as messengers of these concepts in the classroom.

5. *Teachers and textbooks can provide legitimacy for human rights and be vital community resources for intervening in abuses; appropriate training and curricular development are thus critical in HRE.*

Teachers, who are respected authorities in many contexts, as well as textbooks, can provide greater legitimacy to human rights concepts, facilitating student action in visible and sometimes invisible ways. Even when teachers themselves do not take the lead in intervening in abuses, their elevated status, others' knowledge of their connections to human rights organizations, and their willingness to assist can be useful resources for students. The presence of a cohort of teachers in a community who are committed to human rights may prove to be a force for decreasing violations over time given their knowledge and vigilance. Investigating what critical mass is required for social dynamics to shift toward greater equity should concern scholars and practitioners of HRE.

While India's location in the global South, schooling structures, and patterns of human rights abuses may be unique, certain realities and processes resonate with those found internationally. Literature on HRE to date has emphasized the need for the creation of "human rights friendly" spaces (AI 2009).[2] Insights from research on grounded practice in HRE can certainly be analyzed vis-à-vis the many problems—from extreme competition in high stakes exams to school violence to dropping out due to child labor—that students face worldwide.

In India, HRE exists in national policy discussions, has appeared in some textbook reforms, and has been implemented by non-governmental organizations primarily in schools that serve students on the very margins of society. Most international discussions have focused on the factors that keep children out of school such as long distances to schools, the need to work, or school fees, exhorting governments and donors to address these issues. Practitioners and some scholars of education and development naively look to schools as a "panacea" for social ills (Vavrus 2003), ignoring the need for quality and equity within schools. Critical studies in the field of International and Comparative Education, however, reveal other factors at play in schools that deter students, such as discrimination, sexual abuse, limited quality, and teacher corruption (e.g., Mirembe and Davies 2001; Steiner-Khamsi 2005). This study offers a window into one reform that promoted in youth a willingness to confront abuses, engaging their peers and adults in demanding that their rights be respected.

Further studies of human rights education can illuminate the diverse ways that instruction has affected students, teachers, and families. While not all teachers continued teaching HRE and some students experienced it as a "time pass," many discussed the reform as a transformative experience with concrete changes in their behaviors, attitudes, and actions. An NGO program that operates in close to 4,000 schools and has influenced students and teachers deeply offers instructive lessons for scholars and practitioners worldwide engaging with themes of human rights and citizenship in education. As human rights education becomes an increasingly central part of larger human rights strategies and international educational policy discussions, the malleability and multiform nature of HRE needs to be examined more closely and openly without narrowly rigid presumptions about what constitutes valid HRE practice. Ultimately, vertical case studies (on HRE and other educational interventions) that examine policy, ideology, strategy, and experiences—such as the one presented here—can further illuminate the possibility and promise of schooling to impact, in some way, broader processes of social change.

Appendix A:

Operations of the Institute of Human Rights Education (IHRE)

State	State Partners	Schools	Children	Teachers
Tamil Nadu	Institute of Human Rights Education, Madurai	2268	150000	2634
Orissa	Institute of Human Rights Education, Bhubaneswar	618	34100	647
Kerala	South India Cell for Human Rights Education & Monitoring (SICHREM), Trivandrum	226	35000	250
Karnataka	South India Cell for Human Rights Education & Monitoring (SICHREM), Bangalore	153	10300	218
North Eastern States (Assam, Meghalaya, Arunachal Pradesh, Mizoram, Manipur, Nagaland)	North East Regional Co-ordination Council for HRE in schools, Guwahati	152	25118	182

State	State Partners	Schools	Children	Teachers
Andhra Pradesh	People's Action for Rural Awakening (PARA), Ravulapalem	81	6500	106
West Bengal	Loreto Day School, Sealdah, Kolkata	70	15000	71
Bihar	Asian Development Research Institute (ADRI), Patna	60	6000	70
Gujarat	PRASHANT—Centre for Human Rights, Justice and Peace, Ahmedabad	53	6000	90
Tripura	Tripura Govt. Law College, Agartala	50	6000	50
Maharashtra	SABRANG, Mumbai	50	6000	60
Chhattisgarh	Institute of Human Rights Education, Raipur	49	5776	57
Rajasthan	Sophia Girls College and Sameeksha, Ajmer	29	3200	40
Uttar Pradesh	People's Vigilance Committee on Human Rights (PVCHR), Varanasi	50	6000	50
	Total	**3909**	**314994**	**4525**

Appendix B:

Overview of Other NGO and School-Based HRE Initiatives

This project also surveyed a wide range of non-governmental organizations (NGO) and private initiatives aimed at imparting knowledge and values related to human rights. Some of the schools and NGOs discussed here work in tandem with the Institute of Human Rights Education (IHRE) profiled in Chapters Four through Seven of this book, while others advance human rights education independently and in distinct ways. School-based models included the following:

- The Loreto Sealdah School, Kolkata, West Bengal
- Navsarjan Trust Schools, Gujarat
- Riverside School, Ahmedabad, Gujarat
- Shanti Bhavan School, Tamil Nadu

Other supplemental programs also operated through after-school or during school programs led by NGOs. Such programs complemented school-based instruction. Some NGOs active in this include the following:

- KHOJ: Secular education for plural India, Mumbai, Maharashtra
- Centre for Social Justice, Education for Human Rights Program, Gujarat
- Indian Institute of Human Rights (higher education course on human rights), New Delhi

Many more programs and initiatives undoubtedly exist across India that were beyond the scope of this project to investigate.

As these models suggest, along with the Institute of Human Rights Education profiled in this book, HRE is not singular, and even in one nation-state, differing conceptions and manifestations exist. The diverse national, NGO, and school-based strategies reiterate a core tenet of this book that "human rights education" does not signal a common methodology or curriculum and that diverse approaches can serve distinct functions based on their constituency, context, and desired outcomes.

Notes

Chapter One: Introduction

1   Among the agencies most active in advocating for and supporting the integration of human rights education into national curricula are UNESCO, the Council of Europe, and the Office of the UN High Commissioner for Human Rights. The World Programme for Human Rights Education was established in 2005 to build on the considerable momentum toward HRE generated during the UN Decade for Human Rights Education (1995–2004).

2   Previous empirical research on human rights education in India has been limited with the exception of one noteworthy study carried out in 2004. As part of a multi-country initiative carried out by the Asia-Pacific Human Rights Information Center in Osaka, researchers surveyed over 2,000 secondary students from seven Indian states and one territory on their knowledge of human rights (Dev, Sharma, and Lahiry 2007). Students were not enrolled in human rights courses, but were queried about their knowledge of human rights through its integration into other subjects and extracurricular activities. Most students were familiar with the term "human rights," though understanding of what actually constituted human rights practice varied widely with correct answers ranging from 15 to 94 percent when asked about situations of abuse (Dev, Sharma, and Lahiry 2007). The report pointed to diverse levels of internalization and application of human rights information. The results of their study do, however, confirm the diffusion of human rights content in government school textbooks, as other scholars have found globally (Meyer, Bromley-Martin, and Ramirez 2010; Ramirez, Suarez, and Meyer 2007; Suarez 2007). The present book starts where the previous Indian study left off, seeking to understand the distinct types of HRE in India today, what impact (beyond familiarity and content-knowledge) one NGO-run program has had, and how the reform has gained popularity internally over the past 30 years.

Chapter Two: Human Rights Education: Definitions, History, Ideologies

1   Some scholars and activists have rejected the term "human rights education" in favor of "human rights learning," citing the latter's emphasis on an

inquiry-based perspective, more participatory pedagogy, and less informa-
tion-centered approach (Reardon 2010).

2   This diagram is originally from page 30 of the Council of Europe's *Compasito*
publication and is reprinted with permission (Flowers 2007).

*Chapter Three: Education and Human Rights in India: Policy,
Pedagogy, and Practice*

1   Leading independence leader Mohandas "Mahatma" Gandhi's ideas on education also shaped the early and continuing directions of rural schooling
(Gandhi 1932 as cited in Rajput 1998). Gandhi promoted an education system called "Basic Education," which focused on vocational education and the
use of local vernacular as the medium of instruction. He emphasized manual
labor and hands-on training in addition to intellectual pursuits to provide
holistic development as well as skills. According to him, education should be
provided for free and special attention should be paid to character building.
One of the main components of Basic Education was religious education (in
students' own religions), which, according to Gandhi, was synonymous with
the concepts of truth and nonviolence. He promoted education as a social
good, emphasizing social responsibility, rather than having students view
and use their educational qualifications solely for personal gains. Gandhi also
advocated for a program of "New Education," which emphasized through
practice the values of self-reliance, living within a community, and oneness
with nature (Prasad 1984).

2   Not all students in ADW schools are Dalits since rural children generally
attend the school closest to them. Additional incentives, however, are provided to Dalit children, such as free bicycles and school supplies to encourage
their enrollment.

3   I choose to use the term "Adivasi" for this group, despite the Indian government's use of the term "tribal" or "Scheduled Tribe," in accordance with what
scholar Gail Omvedt (2000) suggests in her article "Call us Adivasis, please."
For Omvedt, the term is one of greater respect and acknowledgment of the
ways that development projects have often disadvantaged these original
inhabitants of India. In certain instances, the word "tribal" is utilized syn-
onymously because of respondents' and officials' common use of the term.

4   "SC" refers to the government term for Dalit groups, "Scheduled Castes";
"ST" refers to the government term for Adivasi groups, "Scheduled Tribes."
Both terms refer to a government-compiled list or "schedule" that identifies
historically marginalized groups for demographic purposes and for providing targeted compensatory measures.

5   While multiple studies have noted high rates of teacher absenteeism in Indian
schools (e.g., Kingdon and Banerji 2009; Kremer et al., 2005), a 2008 study
conducted by an Indian teachers' association refuted the poor image of teachers presented, arguing that many absences were for official work or in-service

trainings. The All India Primary Teachers' Federation study concluded that, when sanctioned duties were taken into account, teacher absence for personal reasons was nearer to 10 percent in the three states (Orissa, Uttarakhand, and Tamil Nadu) under study (Eswaran and Singh 2008).

6   One answer for the discrepancy between transition rates and reading levels is that in states where more students stay in school, many weaker students are factored into the state average. Conversely, in states where more children (usually low-performing ones) drop out of primary school, those who persist tend to score higher on quality measures, such as reading tests.

7   Previous studies on HRE in India offer a window into local scholarship, tensions, and theorizing in this emerging field. The Indian Social Institute, a research and training organization supporting social movements in India, held a series of seminars on human rights education in the 1990s. These seminars were held largely in response to the moves by national bodies, such as the University Grants Commission (UGC), to implement human rights courses without any consultation with NGOs and social activists working in the field (Pal and Chakraborty 2000). The seminar and resulting book offer a window into a historical moment in which grassroots rights organizations were mediating the introduction of HRE from above as per the Indian government's obligations to the UN and wider international community. Seeking to influence the orientation of HRE, Saksena (2000) argues that abusive as well as rights-protective moments in Indian history should be taught at the university level to counter conventional understandings of the origins of human rights as purely Western. Participants also emphasized active pedagogy for human rights education (Ahmad 2000), the role of gender-based violence (Giri and Ruebel 2000), and the need to examine caste inequality and prospects for social equality (Pinto 2000) as central to an Indian HRE agenda.

8   The RTI Act was passed in 2005 and gives individuals the right to "to secure access to information under the control of public authorities, in order to promote transparency and accountability in the working of every public authority" (RTI 2005, 1). In practice, RTI has forced public agencies (including those administering education) to become more responsive and accountable to citizen demands due to penalties associated with failure to comply with RTI requests for information. Human rights activists and groups have been instrumental in seeking passage of RTI and in filing requests for information related to cases of mismanagement, corruption, and abuses (Mander and Joshi n.d.).

9   The University Grants Commission was established through an Act of Parliament in 1956 for "the coordination, determination and maintenance of standards of university education in India." The UGC also provides grants to universities and colleges and suggests improvements, reforms, and new directions in line with national and international priorities (UGC 2007b).

10   In the prefatory remarks to the *Recommendations of National Human Rights Commission on Human Rights Education at the University and College Levels*, the NHRC's joint secretary noted, "One of the key issues which has emerged in the analysis is that the human rights education programme could not make a dent in the education system largely owing to the programme being not marketable and, as such, hardly there is any taker of students/scholars who pursue human rights education" (NHRC 2007, preface).

11   The UGC's chairperson at the time of this research, Professor Sukhdeo Thorat, is a renowned scholar on issues of social exclusion and has authored numerous studies on untouchability, rural development, and economic empowerment for Dalits (UGC 2007a).

12   NCTE is primarily responsible for drafting the National Curriculum Framework for Teacher Education, but has worked closely with the National Council of Educational Research and Training (NCERT) for developing the content and approach. The 1988 Framework was spearheaded by NCERT and differences in foci, in addition to reflecting larger political and social issues of the respective period, may reflect differing visions held by individuals and institutions charged with drafting these documents. Tracing the genealogies of these policy documents, however, is beyond the scope of this book.

13   As noted in the previous chapter, India's government schooling system is comprised of a variety of types of schools, some of which are centrally administered; others (the majority) are overseen by state authorities. There also exists a continuum of purely government and completely private institutions on either ends of a spectrum, with some religiously run and government-aided schools in-between. Additionally, there are some ministries that run their own schools at the central and state levels, for specific populations like children who come from "Scheduled Tribe" and "Scheduled Caste" backgrounds.

14   According to one NCERT official interviewed, 14 states publish the NCERT textbooks wholesale without any modifications and other states utilize parts of the model textbooks, adapting content wherever necessary.

15   In 2000/2001, the ruling Bharatiya Janata Party (BJP), through NCERT, sought to "Indianize, nationalize and spiritualize" textbooks (Lall 2005, 5), removing references to the British and rewriting sections of history related to Muslim and Hindu contributions, favoring the latter. This move was termed the "saffronization" of education and was hotly debated, as well as addressed by the subsequent government and its appointees in NCERT (Lall 2005).

16   Kapur (2006, as cited in Pritchett 2009, 37) terms this phenomenon a "life cycle of innovations" wherein civil servants implement certain reforms, but are transferred before benefits are reaped and the next official seeks to advance his or her own agenda. The policy of frequent transfer and promotion for civil servants of the Indian government is discussed here as contributing to the limited sustainability of local-level reforms.

Chapter Four: Linking Laws, Liberties, and Learning:
The Institute of Human Rights Education

1   While I use similar terminology, "persuasive pragmatism" should not be confused with "pragmatic persuasion," which social psychologists and scholars
of communications utilize in their studies of how people are influenced to
change attitudes, tastes, and social beliefs (Wanke and Reutner 2009).

2   This can also be true of situations where human rights groups do not address
criminal violence and only focus on state-sponsored acts, limiting public
support given daily realities (Godoy 2005).

3   An Indian human rights organization, the South Asian Human Rights and
Documentation Center based in New Delhi, had already developed a univer-
sity-level textbook for human rights education, but did not have students to
pilot it with. The content was adapted for Tamil Nadu and the activities made
age-appropriate for the initial project launched by People's Watch in 1997.

4   Dr. Vasanthi Devi, Chairperson of IHRE at the time of this writing, was previously the Vice-Chancellor of the Manonmaniam Sundaranar University
(1992 to 1998) as well as the Chairperson of the Tamil Nadu State Commission
for Women from 2002 to 2005.

5   Staff members noted the intensity of the work involved with being a coordinator of IHRE. Oftentimes, a single staff member was responsible for the oversight
of more than 50 schools. Coordinators' pay was commensurate with salaries in
the NGO sector, but the working hours belied what some expected of an "NGO
job"—a sector known in India sometimes for a relaxed work environment and
limited hours. Other staff members, however, appreciated the opportunities for
professional development provided by IHRE. At the time of this research, 16
staff members of IHRE nationally were being fully funded by the organization for a two-year diploma course (that met for a few weekends each year in
Bangalore) on children's rights. Many staff members noted how such opportunities for professional development would positively impact their career trajec-
tories and how unique such investments in staff were since this, according to
respondents, was not common practice among other NGOs in India.

6   In the 17 states that IHRE has spread to since starting its work in Tamil Nadu,
the approach to staff selection and training varied depending on the local
partner, though all retained the model of frequent visits by staff members to
the schools in which the program was operating.

7   People's Watch and its Institute of Human Rights Education also inaugu-
rated a post-graduate course in human rights for students and community
members at its headquarters in Madurai, Tamil Nadu. The new strategy to
involve adult learners and those who voluntarily sign up for instruction is a
useful complement to mandatory instruction for students in those government schools that have adopted HRE.

8   Importantly, IHRE has never gotten official permission from the state
Ministers of Education for state-wide introduction of the HRE program.

Officials in other ministries that oversee schools have provided permission and these include the following, among others: in Tamil Nadu, the Adi Dravidar Welfare Department that runs schools for primarily Dalit children; in Orissa, the Tribal Welfare Ministry, which oversees schools for Adivasi or indigenous students; and in select districts where the Collectors have signed off on the program.

9   I thank Payal Shah for introducing me to Pritchett's (2009) work.

10   The Adi Dravidar Welfare Department in Tamil Nadu is a government agency charged with administering social service programs that address the socioeconomic hardships faced by Dalit and other low-caste populations. Among the programs overseen by this Department are provision of school education, scholarships, school supplies, boarding facilities as well as assistance in the fields of housing, agriculture, and small-scale industry.

11   Chennai has approximately 6 million residents and 286 government schools that fall under Chennai Corporation's jurisdiction.

12   A *lungi* is a fabric men commonly wear around the lower half of their body. It is typically worn as a nighttime dress to sleep in.

13   The three- to five-day duration of the training sometimes meant that it was easier for men teachers to attend than women given the latter's considerable responsibilities in the household. The organization tried to address this imbalance through different incentives for participation and encouraging female teachers to enlist support from household members, spouses, and neighbors to facilitate their absence for a few days.

Chapter Five: From "Time Pass" to Transformative Force: Human Rights Education for Marginalized Youth

1   While human rights concepts have been included in national- and state-level textbooks across disciplines, this study found that little was known about human rights when government school students (to whom no additional HRE course was given) were queried. At most, students referred to children's rights and UNICEF advertisements against child labor that they may have seen. Alternatively, when students of IHRE's program were asked to define and provide examples of human rights, most students had many examples and could identify specific lessons from their human rights education textbooks. The uniqueness of a stand-alone class in human rights, taught by trained teachers, and complemented by textbooks with stories, drawings, and participatory exercises seemed to account for this notable difference in retention.

2   The NCERT social science textbooks that were revised in recent years for standards six through eight contain numerous examples that could be classified as related to human rights and are inclusive of minoritized populations such as Dalits, Muslims, Adivasi communities, women, and the disabled. These textbooks are primarily textual and pictorial, with fill in the blank and multiple-choice questions at the end of units. Inquiry questions along

the side of the chapters encourage more participatory student reflection. However, history and social movements are generally presented as in the past and the questions included in the books seem to assume a middle-class learner who may not witness rights violations first hand. They are, nonetheless, a significant improvement upon previous iterations and offer a national model for states to consider adopting in their own languages for state-run government schools.

3   All student and most adult respondents have been assigned pseudonyms. The Institute of Human Rights Education is a unique and well-known nongovernmental organization, and it would be futile to attempt to protect its confidentiality by changing its name. In order to protect individual confidentiality, pseudonyms have been used for all staff members with the exception of senior-level administrators, since even the most rigorous attempts at confidentiality would not be able to conceal their distinct leadership roles and perspectives. As such, their permission was sought and granted to utilize their actual names in this study.

4   Many students' parents were involved in a government employment program targeted at the poorest of the poor in India. The 2005 Mahatma Gandhi National Rural Employment Guarantee Act (NREGA) "aims at enhancing the livelihood security of people in rural areas by guaranteeing hundred days of wage-employment in a financial year to a rural household whose adult members volunteer to do unskilled manual work" (MRD 2010).

5   Less-known internationally than independence leader Mahatma Gandhi, Dr. B. R. Ambedkar was a contemporary leader who drafted the Indian Constitution and was the Law Minister in India's first post-independence government. Ambedkar's first-hand experience of caste discrimination led him to be a leading advocate of human rights, women's equality, and particularly Dalit rights.

6   Students reported that when children are pulled out of school in this capacity, they earn approximately 150 rupees per week (less than US $4), but that even this amount could ensure their family's survival given the incidence of extreme poverty in the community.

Chapter Six: Building Solidarity and Coalitional Agency through Human Rights Education

1   This school was in a district where the Collector had granted permission for IHRE to operate in all the schools, including private ones, under his jurisdiction. This was an unusual case, but one that nonetheless resulted in more affluent students learning about human rights through the program.

2   Save the Children (2009) estimates that 20–40 percent of child labor is concentrated in domestic work in private homes. The organization further finds that two-thirds of child domestic workers face physical abuse.

3   Among many communities in Tamil Nadu, it was customary for young women to marry their maternal uncles. Historically, scholars have found this to be the case because of a desire to keep landholdings within the same family, though the issue of consanguineous marriage has come under scrutiny in terms of the genetic implications for future generations (Mukund 1999).

4   A UNICEF report (2003) found that less than 5 percent of children with disabilities were in school, as compared to an average gross enrollment ratio of over 90 percent in primary schools in India.

5   Direct violence includes any act that threatens one's physical security such as war, torture, rape, and domestic violence, among others. Widely known as the "father of Peace Studies," Johan Galtung (1969) defines structural violence as the ways in which groups of people are systematically limited from meeting their basic needs. Structural violence is rooted in social inequalities that limit access to resources and opportunities for individuals and groups.

Chapter Seven: Teachers and Textbooks as Legitimating Forces for Human Rights Education

1   While in most school districts, adolescent girls are not prohibited by law from continuing in school after getting married, headmasters often dissuade married adolescents from continuing their studies due to beliefs that married girls may share information that will "spoil" unmarried girls; the families into which women marry also often want their labor in agriculture or in the household.

2   A total of 118 teachers (n value) were interviewed for this study. Several teachers gave more than one type of response to the question asked about the impact of human rights education. As a result, adding the responses of each of the 5 categories in the figure presented calculates to an amount higher than 118 and closer to 155.

3   It is important to note that in India, for the most part, reporting abuses would result in an investigation where evidence would need to be presented for prosecution to take place. With a relatively vibrant and independent press—aside from severe limits on the freedom of press in conflict-ridden areas such as Kashmir (RWB 2010)—false accusations would rarely result in a penalty without a trial. India's 2005 "Right to Information Act" has also resulted in greater accountability of government entities given citizens' right to request official documents that pertain to public offices, programs, and services. This is not true of many other contexts, particularly where authoritarian regimes may render "reporting" of others' activities and behavior necessary and where false allegations may have serious consequences. Attention to context in examining human rights promoting practices is of course tremendously important and a theme worth discussing in its own right.

Chapter Eight: Divergence and Decoupling: Indian Human Rights Education in Focus

1 Well-known author and social activist, Arundhati Roy (2010), has written about the origins of the Naxalite movement and the Indian government's stance toward tribal or Adivasi communities in general: "The Indian Constitution, the moral underpinning of Indian democracy, was adopted by Parliament in 1950. It was a tragic day for tribal people. The Constitution ratified colonial policy and made the State custodian of tribal homelands. Overnight, it turned the entire tribal population into squatters on their own land. It denied them their traditional rights to forest produce, it criminalised a whole way of life. In exchange for the right to vote, it snatched away their right to livelihood and dignity. Having dispossessed them and pushed them into a downward spiral of indigence, in a cruel sleight of hand, the government began to use their own penury against them. Each time it needed to displace a large population—for dams, irrigation projects, mines—it talked of 'bringing tribals into the mainstream' or of giving them 'the fruits of modern development.' Of the tens of millions of internally displaced people (more than 30 million by big dams alone), refugees of India's 'progress,' the great majority are tribal people. When the government begins to talk of tribal welfare, it's time to worry."

Chapter Nine: Implications and Concluding Thoughts

1 Global Kids is a youth development organization based in New York City that runs during- and after-school programs to "educate and inspire urban youth to become successful students, global citizens and community leaders by engaging them in academically rigorous, socially dynamic, content-rich learning experiences." Launched in 1989, Global Kids reaches more than 15,000 youth per year through its workshops, online programs, and summer institute. The Human Rights Activist Project (HRAP) is one component of Global Kids' work and brings together urban high school students in New York City throughout the school year to learn about, develop campaigns, and raise public awareness on human rights issues. HRAP also has an international component where students travel overseas to learn about and take action related to critical human rights issues. (www.globalkids.org)

2 Amnesty International has published a report entitled "Guidelines for Human Rights Friendly Schools" that outlines how schools—through structure, pedagogies, and curriculum—can create atmospheres that respect children's rights (AI 2009).

Bibliography

Ahmad, Imtiaz. "Human Rights Education in India: Unresolved Problems of Perspective and Pedagogy." In *Human Rights Education in India*, edited by R. M. Pal and Somen Chakraborty, 43–9. New Delhi: Indian Social Institute, 2000.

Allport, Gordon. *The Nature of Prejudice*. Cambridge and Reading, MA: Addison Wesley, 1954.

Amnesty International. "Guidelines for Human Rights Friendly Schools." London: Amnesty International, 2009.

—. "Human Rights Education." Accessed December 30, 2010. http://www. amnesty.org/en/human-rights-education.

Appadurai, Arjun. "Deep Democracy: Urban Governmentality and the Horizon of Politics." *Environment and Urbanization* 13, no. 2 (2001): 23–43.

Appiah, Kwame Anthony. "Cosmopolitan Patriots." *Critical Inquiry* 23 (1997): 617–39.

Apple, Michael. "Reproduction and Contradiction in Education." In *Cultural and Economic Reproduction in Education*, edited by Michael Apple, 1–31. London: Routledge and Kegan Paul, 1982.

Aronowitz, Stanley and Henry Giroux. *Education Still Under Siege*. Westport: Greenwood Publishing Group, 1993.

ASER. "Annual Status of Education Report." New Delhi: Pratham, 2009.

Asia-Pacific Human Rights Network. "Right to Food: The Indian Experience." *Human Rights Features* (2002), http://www.hrdc.net/sahrdc/hrfeatures/ HRF58.htm

Babu, Rajendra. "National Conference on Human Rights Education at School Level." New Delhi: National Human Rights Commission, 2009.

Bajaj, Monisha. "Conjectures on Peace Education and Gandhian Studies: Method, Institutional Development and Globalization." *Journal of Peace Education* 7, no. 1 (2010): 47–63.

—. "'I Have Big Things Planned for My Future': The Limits and Possibilities of Transformative Agency in Zambian Schools." *Compare* 39, no. 4 (2009): 551–68.

Baxi, Upendra. "Human Rights and Human Rights Education: Arriving at the Truth." In *Human Rights Learning: A People's Report*, 117–36. New York: People's Movement for Human Rights Learning, 2006.

—. "Human Rights Education: The Promise of the Third Millenium?" In *Human Rights Education for the Twenty-First Century*, edited by George J. Andreopoulos and Richard Pierre Claude, 142–54. Philadelphia: University of Pennsylvania Press, 1997.

Becker, Gary. *Human Capital*. Chicago: University of Chicago Press, 1964.

Begum, Syed Mehertaj. "Human Rights Education in the Age of Globalisation: Role of UGC." In *Globalisation and the Changing Role of the States: Issues and Impacts*, edited by Rumki Basu, 221–30. New Delhi: New Dawn Press, 2008.

Bernath, Tania, Tracey Holland, and Paul Martin. "How Can Human Rights Education Contribute to International Peace-Building?" *Current Issues in Comparative Education* 14 (1999): 14–22.

Bhowmick, Nilanjana. "Why India's Teachers Do Not Spare the Rod." *Time*, May 02, 2009. Accessed April 24, 2011. http://www.time.com/time/world/article/0,8599,1895495,00.html

Biswas, Soutik. "Killing for 'Honour'." *BBC*, June 23, 2010. Accessed April 24, 2011. http://www.bbc.co.uk/blogs/thereporters/soutikbiswas/2010/06/you_can_get_killed_for.html

Boli, John, Francisco Ramirez, and John Meyer. "Explaining the Origins and Expansion of Mass Education." *Comparative Education Review* 29 (1985): 145–70.

Bray, Mark and Murray R. Thomas. "Levels of Comparison in Educational Studies: Different Insights from Different Literatures and the Value of Multilevel Analyses." *Harvard Educational Review* 65, no. 3 (1995): 472–90.

Bromley, Patricia. "Cosmopolitanism in Civic Education: Exploring Cross-National Trends, 1970–2008." *Current Issues in Comparative Education* 12, no. 1 (2009): 33–44.

Bunsha, Dionne. "Insecure Children: A Government Study States That Child Abuse Is Quite Common in India and That out-of-School Children Are Most at Risk." *Frontline*, May 4, 2007.

Cardenas, Sonia. "Constructing Rights? Human Rights Education and the State." *International Political Science Review* 26, no. 4 (2005): 363–79.

Chatterjee, Partha. *The Politics of the Governed*. New York: Columbia University Press, 2004.

Chavez, Karma and Cindy Griffin. "Power, Feminisms, and Coalitional Agency: Inviting and Enacting Difficult Dialogues." *Women's Studies in Communication* 32, no. 1 (2009): 1–11.

Clarke, Prema. "School Curriculum in the Periphery: The Case of South India." In *Quality Education for All: Community Oriented Approaches*, edited by H. Dean Nielsen and William K. Cummings, 123–38. New York and London: Garland Publishing, 1997.

Claude, Richard Pierre. "A Letter to My Colleagues, Students, and Readers of Human Rights Quarterly." *Human Rights Quarterly* 33 (2011): 578–85.

Council of Europe. "Education for Democratic Citizenship and Human Rights." Accessed December 31, 2010. http://www.coe.int/t/dg4/education/edc/default_en.asp

Das, Maitreyi, Gillette Hall, Soumya Kapoor, and Denis Nikitin. "India: The Scheduled Tribes." In *Indigenous Peoples, Poverty and Development*, edited by Gillette Hall and Harry Patrinos. Washington, D.C.: The World Bank, 2010.

Davies, Lynn. *Education and Conflict: Complexity and Chaos*. London: Routledge, 2004.

—. "Global Citizenship Education." In *Encyclopedia of Peace Education*, edited by Monisha Bajaj. Charlotte: Information Age Publishing, 2008.

Deccan Herald. "To Teach or Not to Teach." *Deccan Herald*, April 30, 2009. Accessed April 24, 2011. http://archive.deccanherald.com/Content/Apr302009/dheducation20090429133190.asp

Delpit, Lisa. *Other People's Children: Cultural Conflict in the Classroom*. New York: New Press, 2006.

Dembour, Marie-Bénédicte. "What Are Human Rights? Four Schools of Thought." *Human Rights Quarterly* 32, no. 1 (2010): 1–20.

Denzin, Norman K. and Yvonna S. Lincoln. *Handbook of Qualitative Research*. Second ed. Thousand Oaks: Sage Publications, 2000.

Dev, Arjun. "Human Rights: A Source Book." New Delhi: National Council of Educational Research and Training, 1996.

Dev, Arjun, Dinesh Sharma, and D. Lahiry. *Human Rights Education in Indian Schools*. Delhi, India: Academic Excellence Publishers, 2007.

DISE. "Elementary Education in India: State Report Cards." New Delhi: District Information System for Education Publications, 2009.

Drèze, Jean and Amartya Sen. *India: Economic Development and Social Opportunity*. Oxford: Oxford University Press, 1995.

Elsbach, Kimberly D. and Robert I. Sutton. "Acquiring Organizational Legitimacy through Illegitimate Actions: A Marriage of Institutional and Impression Management Theories." *Academy of Management Journal* 35 (1992): 699–738.

Eswaran, S. and Ajit Singh. *Teacher Absence in Primary Schools: A Study*. New Delhi, India: All India Primary Teachers' Federation, 2008.

Fagerlind, Ingemar and Lawrence J. Saha. *Education and National Development: A Comparative Perspective*. Oxford: Pergamon Press, 1989.

Flowers, Nancy, ed. *Compasito: Manual on Human Rights Education for Children*. Budapest: Council of Europe, 2007.

—. "How to Define Human Rights Education? A Complex Answer to a Simple Question." In *International Perspectives in Human Rights Education Vol 112*, edited by Viola B. Georgi and Michael Seberich, 105–27. Gütersloh: Bertelsmann Foundation Publishing, 2004.

—. "What Is Human Rights Education?" In *A Survey of Human Rights Education*. Hamburg: Bertelsmann Verlag, 2003.

Flowers, Nancy, Marcia Bernbaum, Kristi Rudelius-Palmer, and Joel Tolman. *The Human Rights Education Handbook: Effective Practices for Learning, Action, and Change.* Minneapolis: The Human Rights Resource Center and the Stanley Foundation, 2000.

Freedman, Sarah Warshauer, Harvey M. Weinstein, Karen Murphy, and Timothy Longman. "Teaching History after Identity-Based Conflicts: The Rwanda Experience." *Comparative Education Review* 52, no. 4 (2008): 663–90.

Freire, Paulo. *Pedagogy of the Oppressed.* New York: Continuum, 1970.

Fritzsche, Karl Peter. "Tolerance Education and Human Rights Education in Times of Fear." In *Educating Toward a Culture of Peace,* edited by Yaacov Iram and Hillel Wahrman. Charlotte, North Carolina: Information Age Publishing, 2006.

Fuller, Bruce and Richard Rubinson, eds. *The Political Construction of Education: The State, School Expansion, and Economic Change.* New York: Praeger Publishers, 1992.

Galtung, Johan. "Violence, Peace, and Peace Research." *Journal of Peace Research* 6, no. 3 (1969): 167–91.

Gayer, Laurent and Christophe Jaffrelot, eds. *Armed Militias of South Asia: Fundamentalists, Maoists, and Separatists.* New York: Columbia University Press, 2010.

Giri, D. K. and Iris Ruebel. "Tackling Dowry—A Human Rights Approach." In *Human Rights Education in India,* edited by R. M. Pal and Somen Chakraborty, 218–30. New Delhi: Indian Social Institute, 2000.

Giroux, Henry. *Schooling and the Struggle for Public Life: Critical Pedagogy in the Modern Age.* Minneapolis: University of Minnesota Press, 1988.

Godoy, Angelina Snodgrass. "La Muchacha Respondona: Reflections on the Razor's Edge Between Crime and Human Rights." *Human Rights Quarterly* 27, no. 2 (2005): 597–624.

Government of India (GOI). "Census of India 2001." Ministry of Home Affairs, Government of India, 2001. http://censusindia.gov.in/

—. "Census of India 2011." Ministry of Home Affairs, Government of India, 2011. http://censusindia.gov.in/

Halligan, John. "The Diffusion of Civil Service Reform." In *Civil Service Systems in Comparative Perspective,* edited by Hans A. G. M. Bekke, James L. Perry, and Theo A. J. Toonen, 288–317. Bloomington: Indiana University Press, 1996.

Hantzopoulos, Maria. "Encountering Peace: The Politics of Participation When Educating for Co-Existence." In *Critical Issues in Peace and Education,* edited by Peter Trifonas and Bryan Wright, 21–39. New York: Routledge, 2010.

Hicks, Neil. "Legislative Reform in Turkey and European Human Rights Mechanisms." *Human Rights Review* 3, no. 1 (2001): 78–85.

HRW. " 'Being Neutral Is Our Biggest Crime': Government, Vigilante, and Naxalite Abuses in India's Chhattisgarh State." New York: Human Rights Watch, 2008.

—. "Broken People: Caste Violence against India's 'Untouchables'." New York: Human Rights Watch, 1999.

—. "Hidden Apartheid: Caste Discrimination against India's 'Untouchables'." New York: Human Rights Watch, 2007a.

—. "India: Stop Hindu-Christian Violence in Orissa." New York: Human Rights Watch, 2007b.

—. "Sabotaged Schooling: Naxalite Attacks and Police Occupation of Schools in India's Bihar and Jharkhand States." New York: Human Rights Watch, 2009.

INEE. "Education for Life Skills: Peace, Human Rights and Citizenship." In *Guidebook for Planning Education in Emergencies and Reconstruction*, edited by Inter-Agency Network for Education in Emergencies. Paris: UNESCO, 2006.

INFHS. "Indian National Family and Health Survey—Domestic Violence." New Delhi: International Institute for Population Services, 2006.

IPC. "Literacy Rates for Scheduled Castes." (2006), www.planningcommission. gov.in/sectors/sj/Literacy%20of%20SCs_STs.doc

Iyengar, Radhika. "Different Implementation Approaches to a Common Goal: Education for All in the Indian Context." *Society of International Education Journal* 7 (2010).

Kapoor, Dip. "Popular Education and Social Movements in India: State Responses to Constructive Resistance for Social Justice." *Convergence* 37, no. 2 (2004): 55–63.

Keck, Margaret and Kathryn Sikkink. *Activists Beyond Borders*. Ithaca: Cornell University Press, 1998.

Kingdon, Geeta and Rukmini Banerji. *Addressing School Quality: Some Policy Pointers from Rural North India*. Cambridge, U.K.: Research Consortium on Educational Outcomes & Poverty, 2009.

Klees, Steven. "Reflections on Theory, Method, and Practice in Comparative and International Education." *Comparative Education Review* 52, no. 3 (2008): 301–28.

Kremer, Michael, Karthik Muralidharan, Nazmul Chaudhury, Jeffrey Hammer, and F. Halsey Rogers. "Teacher Absence in India: A Snapshot." *Journal of the European Economic Association* 3, nos 2–3 (2005): 658–67.

Kumaran, Muthusami. "Role of the Indian NGO Sector in the Public Policy Making Process." *South Asian Studies Association* (2008), http://www.slideshare.net/BrownBag/kumaran-on-ngos-in-india-presentation

Lall, Marie. "The Challenges for India's Education System." Chatham House. London: The Royal Institute of International Affairs, 2005.

Lincoln, Yvonna S. and Egon G. Guba. "Paradigmatic Controversies, Contradictions and Emerging Confluences." In *Handbook of Qualitative Research*, edited by Norman Denzin and Yvonna S. Lincoln, 163–88. Thousand Oaks: Sage Publications, 2000.

Lyn, Tan Ee. "High Prevalence of Child Marriage in India." *Reuters*, March 10, 2009. Accessed April 24, 2011. http://www.reuters.com/article/2009/03/10/us-marriage-child-odd-idUSTRE5295SA20090310

Magendzo, Abraham. "Problems in Planning Human Rights Education for Reemerging Latin American Democracies." In *Human Rights Education for the Twenty First Century*, edited by George Andreopoulos and Richard Pierre Claude, 469–83. Philadelphia: University of Pennsylvania Press, 1997.

—. "Pedagogy of Human Rights Education: A Latin American Perspective." *Intercultural Education* 16, no. 2 (2005): 137–43.

Mander, Harsh and Abha Joshi. "The Movement for Right to Information in India: People's Power for the Control of Corruption." *RTI Articles* (n.d.), http://www.humanrightsinitiative.org/index.php?option=com_content&view=article&catid=91%3Ashiva&id=669%3Arti-india-articles&Itemid=75.

Meintjes, Garth. "Human Rights Education as Empowerment: Reflections on Pedagogy." In *Human Rights Education for the Twenty First Century*, edited by George Andreopoulos and Richard Pierre Claude, 64–79. Philadelphia: University of Pennsylvania Press, 1997.

Meyer, John W. and Brian Rowan. "The Structure of Educational Organizations." In *Organizations and Environments*, edited by John W. Meyer, Brian Rowan, and W. Richard Scott. San Francisco: Jossey Bass, 1978.

Meyer, John W., Patricia Bromley-Martin, and Francisco O. Ramirez. "Human Rights in Social Science Textbooks: Cross-National Analyses, 1970–2008." *Sociology of Education* 83, no. 2 (2010): 111–34.

Meyer, John W., John Boli, George M. Thomas, and Francisco O. Ramirez. "World Society and the Nation-State." *American Journal of Sociology* 103 (1997): 144–81.

Mihr, Anja. "Minority Participation—a Challenge for Human Rights Education?" *Journal of Social Science Education* 1 (2006).

Mihr, Anjana and Hans Peter Schmitz. "Human Rights Education (HRE) and Transnational Activism." *Human Rights Quarterly* 29 (2007): 973–93.

Miller, Norman and Marilynn B. Brewer. *Groups in Contact: The Psychology of Desegregation*. Orlando, FL: Academic Press, 1984.

Ministry of Social Justice, Government of India. "Population Poverty Line, State-Wise." (2005). http://socialjustice.nic.in/socialg0405.php

Ministry of Tribal Affairs, Government of India. "Schemes." (2010). http://tribal.nic.in/index1.asp?linkid=325&langid=1

Mirembe, Robina and Lynn Davies. "Is Schooling a Risk? Gender, Power Relations, and School Culture in Uganda." *Gender and Education* 13, no. 4 (2001): 401–16.

MRD. "Mahatma Gandhi National Rural Employment Guarantee Act." Accessed July 31, 2010. http://nrega.nic.in/netnrega/home.aspx.

Mukul, Akshaya. "Sharp Decline In Out-of-School Children." *Times of India*, September 13, 2009. Accessed April 24, 2011. http://articles.timesofindia.

indiatimes.com/2009-09-13/india/28093766_1_girl-students-survey-age-group

Mukund, Kanakalatha. "Women's Property Rights in South India: A Review." *Economic and Political Weekly* 34, no. 22 (1999): 1352–8.

Müller, Lothar. "Human Rights Education in German Schools and Post-Secondary Institutions: Results of a Study." Boston: Human Rights Education Associates, Inc., 2009.

Murali, Kanta. "The IIT Story: Issues and Concerns." *Frontline* 20, no. 3 (2003). Accessed April 24, 2011. http://www.hindu.com/fline/fl2003/stories/20030214007506500.htm

Naik, C. D. *Thoughts and Philosophy of Doctor B.R. Ambedkar.* New Delhi: Sarup & Sons, 2003.

Nambissan, Geetha B. "Human Rights Education and Dalit Children." *PUCL Bulletin*, April 1995.

Nambissan, Geetha B. and Mona Sedwal. "Education for All: The Situation of Dalit Children in India." In *India Education Report*, edited by R. Govinda, 72–86. Oxford: Oxford University Press, 2002.

Navsarjan Trust and Robert F. Kennedy Center for Jusice and Human Rights. "Understanding Untouchability: A Comprehensive Study of Practices and Conditions in 1589 Villages." Washington D.C.: Robert F. Kennedy Center for Justice and Human Rights, 2010.

Nazzari, Vincenza, Paul McAdams, and Daniel Roy. "Using Transformative Learning as a Model for Human Rights Education: A Case Study of the Canadian Human Rights Foundation's International Human Rights Training Program." *Intercultural Education* 16, no. 2 (2005): 171–86.

NCDHR. "A Preliminary Study to Understand Caste Based Discrimination on Dalit Children in the Schooling Process." New Delhi: National Campaign on Dalit Human Rights, 2008.

NCERT. "National Curriculum Framework." New Delhi: National Council of Educational Research and Training, 2005.

NCPCR. "Minutes of the Meeting of the Committee, Constituted to Examine the Inquiry Report on the Corporal Punishment of Late Rouvanjit Rawla in La Martiniere for Boys, Kolkata . . . 6th July 2010." New Delhi: National Commission for the Protection of Child Rights, 2010. Accessed April 24, 2011. http://ncpcr.gov.in/corporal_punishment.htm

—. "Protection of Children against Corporal Punishment in Schools and Institutions." New Delhi: National Commission for the Protection of Child Rights, 2008.

NCTE. "Human Rights Education: Self-Learning Module for Teacher Educators." New Delhi: National Council for Teacher Education, 1996.

—. "NCTE at a Glance." New Delhi: National Council For Teacher Education. Accessed May 16, 2011. http://www.ncte-india.org/theintro.asp

NHRC. "Annual Report." National Human Rights Commission, 1996. Accessed April 24, 2011. http://nhrc.nic.in/ar95_96.htm

—. "Recommendations of National Human Rights Commission: Human Rights Education at the University and College Levels." New Delhi: National Human Rights Commission, 2007.

NHRC and KWIRC. "Human Rights Education for Beginners." New Delhi: National Human Rights Commission & Karnataka Women's Information and Resource Center, 2005.

Noddings, Nel. *Educating Citizens for Global Awareness*. New York: Teachers College Press, 2005.

Noguera, Pedro. *City Schools and the American Dream: Reclaiming the Promise of Public Education*. New York: Teachers College Press, 2003.

NPE. "National Policy on Education." Ministry of Human Resource Development Department of Education, 1986. http://www.education.nic.in/cd50years/g/z/7G/0Z7G0601.htm

Nussbaum, Martha. *Cultivating Humanity: A Classical Defence of Reform in Liberal Education*. Cambridge: Harvard University Press, 1997.

—. "Education and Democratic Citizenship: Capabilities and Quality Education." *Journal of Human Development* 7, no. 3 (2006): 385–98.

—. *Women and Human Development: The Capabilities Approach*. Cambridge: Cambridge University Press, 2000.

OECD. "Tackling Inequalities in Brazil, China, India and South Africa." Paris: Organisation of Economic Cooperation and Development, 2010.

OHCHR. "Open-Ended Working Group on the Draft United Nations Declaration on Human Rights Education and Training." Office of the United Nations High Commissioner for Human Rights, 2011. http://www2.ohchr.org/english/bodies/hrcouncil/education/1stsession.htm

Omvedt, Gail. "Call Us Adivasis, Please" (2000). Accessed April 24, 2011. http://hinduonnet.com/folio/fo0007/00070100.htm.

Osler, Audrey and Hugh Starkey. "Education for Democratic Citizenship: A Review of Research, Policy and Practice. 1995–2005." *Research Papers in Education* 21, no. 4 (2006): 433–66.

—. *Teacher Education and Human Rights*. London: David Fulton Publishers, 1996.

—. *Teachers and Human Rights Education*. Stoke on Trent: Trentham Books, 2010.

Oxfam. *Curriculum for Global Citizenship*. Oxford: Oxfam, 1997.

Pal, R. M. and Somen Chakraborty. *Human Rights Education in India*. New Delhi, India: Indian Social Institute, 2000.

Panda, Pranati. "Human Rights Education in Indian Schools: Curriculum Development." In *Human Rights Education in Asian Schools Volume IV*, 85–96. Osaka: Asia-Pacific Human Rights Information Center, 2001.

Pinto, Ambrose. "A Pedagogy for Human Rights Education." In *Human Rights Education in India*, edited by R. M. Pal and Somen Chakraborty, 50–62. New Delhi: Indian Social Institute, 2000.

Prasad, Devi. *Peace Education or Education for Peace.* New Delhi: Gandhi Peace Foundation, 1984.

Premi, Mahendra. "India's Literacy Panorama." *Seminar on Progress of Literacy in India* (2002), http://www.educationforallinindia.com/page172.html

Pritchett, Lant. "Is India a Flailing State? Detours on the Four Lane Highway to Modernization." *Harvard Kennedy School Faculty Research Working Paper Series* (2009). http://web.hks.harvard.edu/publications/workingpapers/citation.aspx?PubId=6599

"Protection of Human Rights Act." New Delhi, 1993.

PW. "Schooling for Justice and Human Rights." Madurai: People's Watch—Institute for Human Rights Education, 2008.

QCA. "Education for Citizenship and the Teaching of Democracy in Schools." London: Qualifications and Curriculum Authority, 1998. http://www.teachingcitizenship.org.uk/dnloads/crickreport1998.pdf.

Rajput, J. S. "Gandhi on Education." *National Council on Teacher Education.* (1998). http://www.ncte-india.org/pub/gandhi/gandhi_0.htm

Ramachandran, V. K. *Wage Labour and Unfreedom in Agriculture: An Indian Case Study.* Oxford: Oxford University Press, 1991.

Ramirez, Francisco O. and Christine Min Wotipka. "World Society and Human Rights: An Event History Analysis of the Convention on All Forms of Discrimination against Women." In *The Global Diffusion of Markets and Democracy,* edited by Frank Dobbin Beth Simmons, and Geoffrey Garrett, 303–43. Cambridge: Cambridge University Press, 2007.

Ramirez, Francisco, David Suárez, and John Meyer. "The Worldwide Rise of Human Rights Education." In *School Knowledge in Comparative and Historical Perspective,* edited by Aaron Benavot, Cecilia Braslavsky, and Nhung Truong, 35–52. Netherlands: Springer, 2007.

Reardon, Betty. "Aprendizaje En Derechos Humanos: Pedagogías Y Políticas De Paz / Human Rights Learning: Pedagogies and Politics of Peace." In *Conferencia Magistral Cátedra UNESCO de Educación para la Paz 2008–2009.* Universidad de Puerto Rico: Cátedra UNESCO de Educación para la Paz Universidad de Puerto Rico, 2010.

Roy, Arundhati. "Walking with the Comrades." *Outlook India,* March 29, 2010.

Roy, Rajeev Ranjan. "India's Teachers Get Training in Peace Education." *Indo-Asian News Service,* January 29, 2008. Accessed April 24, 2011. http://www.wichaar.com/news/152/ARTICLE/2390/2008-01-29.html.

RTI. "Right to Information Act." (2005), http://righttoinformation.gov.in/

RWB. "India." (2010), http://en.rsf.org/inde.html

Saksena, P. K. "India's Contribution to the Concept of Human Rights." In *Human Rights Education in India,* edited by R. M. Pal and Somen Chakraborty, 147–57. New Delhi: Indian Social Institute, 2000.

Save the Children. "Spotlight on Domestic Work in India." London: Save the Children, 2009.

Schugurensky, Daniel. "The Legacy of Paulo Freire: A Critical Review of His Contributions." *Convergence* 31, nos 1–2 (1998): 17–29.

Sen, Amartya. *Development as Freedom*. New York: Alfred A. Knopf, 1999.

Setalvad, Teesta. "Pluralism and Transformative Social Studies 'Us and Them': Challenges for the Indian Classroom." In *Peace Philosophy in Action*, edited by Candice C. Carter and Ravindra Kumar. New York: Palgrave Macmillan, 2010.

Soysal, Yasemin. *Limits of Citizenship*. Chicago: University of Chicago Press, 1994.

Stake, Robert E. *The Art of Case Study Research*. Thousand Oaks: Sage Publications, 1995.

Stanford, Jim. "Even with Kerala's Limited Economy, Its People Live Better." *Canadian Center for Policy Alternatives Monitor* (2010). Accessed April 24, 2011. http://findarticles.com/p/articles/mi_7497/is_201004/ai_n53507385/?tag=content;col1

Steiner-Khamsi, Gita, ed. *The Global Politics of Education Borrowing*. New York: Teachers College Press, 2004.

—. "Vouchers for Teacher Education (Non) Reform in Mongolia: Transitional, Postsocialist, or Antisocialist Explanations?" *Comparative Education Review* 49, no. 2 (2005): 148–72.

Steiner-Khamsi, Gita and Ines Stolpe. *Educational Import in Mongolia: Local Encounters with Global Forces*. New York: Palgrave Macmillan, 2006.

Strang, David and Chang Kil Lee. "The International Diffusion of Public-Sector Downsizing: Network Emulation and Theory Driven Learning." *International Organization* 60 (2006): 883–909.

Strauss, Anselm C. and Juliet M. Corbin. *Basics of Qualitative Research: Grounded Theory Procedures and Techniques*. London: Sage Publications, 1990.

Suárez, David. "Education Professionals and the Construction of Human Rights Education." *Comparative Education Review* 51, no. 1 (2007): 48–70.

Tarrow, Norma. "Human Rights Education: Alternative Conceptions." In *Human Rights, Education and Global Responsibilities*, edited by James Lynch, Celia Modgil, and Sohan Modgil, 21–50. London: Falmer Press, 1992.

Taylor, Aleesha. "Questioning Participation." In *Critical Approaches to Comparative Education*, edited by Frances Vavrus and Lesley Bartlett, 75–92. New York: Palgrave Macmillan, 2009.

Thornton, William H. and Songok Han Thornton. "The Price of Alignment: India in the New Asian Drama." *Journal of Developing Societies* 22, no. 4 (2006): 401–20.

Tibbitts, Felisa. "Human Rights Education." In *Encyclopedia of Peace Education*, edited by Monisha Bajaj, 99–108. Charlotte: Information Age Publishing, 2008.

—. "Transformative Learning and Human Rights Education: Taking a Closer Look." *Intercultural Education* 16, no. 2 (2005): 107–13.

—. "Understanding What We Do: Emerging Models for Human Rights Education." *International Review of Education* 48, nos 3–4 (2002): 159–71.

Tomaševski, Katarina. "Has the Right to Education a Future within the United Nations? A Behind-the-Scenes Account by the Special Rapporteur on the Right to Education 1998–2004." *Human Rights Law Review* 5, no. 2 (2005): 239–69.

Torney-Purta, Judith, John Schwille, and Jo-Ann Amadeo. "Civic Education Across Countries: Twenty-Four National Case Studies from the IEA Civic Education Project." Amsterdam: IEA Secretariat, 1999.

Tyack, David and Larry Cuban. *Tinkering Toward Utopia: A Century of Public School Reform.* Cambridge: Harvard University Press, 1997.

UGC. "Prof. Sukhadeo Thorat, Chairman." University Grants Commission, 2007a. http://www.ugc.ac.in/more/chairman_S.thorat.html.

—. "University Grants Commission Xth Plan." University Grants Commission, 2002. http://www.ugc.ac.in/financialsupport/tenthplan.html.

—. "University Grants Commission XIth Plan Guidelines." University Grants Commission, 2007b. http://www.ugc.ac.in/financialsupport/xiplan/guideline.html.

UN. "Human Development Index." New York: United Nations, 2010.

—. "Plan of Action: World Programme for Human Rights Education." New York: United Nations, 2006.

UNDP. "India Situation Analysis: Are the MDGs Attainable?" New Delhi: United Nations Development Programme, 2009.

UNESCO. "India Literacy Statistics." Montreal: UNESCO Institute of Statistics, 2006.

—. "Mapping Literacy in India: Who Are the Illiterates and Where Do We Find Them?" Paris: UNESCO, 2005.

—. "Para Teachers in India: A Review." Paris: UNESCO, 2004.

—. "Tens of Millions of Indian Children to Benefit from New Right to Education Act." http://www.unesco.org/new/en/education/themes/leading-the-international-agenda/right-to-education/single-view/news/tens_of_millions_of_indian_children_to_benefit_from_new_right_to_education_act/

UNICEF. "Examples of Inclusive Education." Kathmandu: United Nations Children's Fund, Regional Office for South Asia, 2003.

—. "India: Education." UNICEF, 2010. Accessed April 24, 2011. http://www.unicef.org/india/education.html

UNRWA. "Human Rights Education in Gaza." http://www.un.org/unrwa/publications/GazaFO/human_rights_education.pdf

van Woerkom, Marieke. "Seeds of Peace: Toward a Common Narrative." *New Directions for Youth Development* 102 (2004): 35–46.

Vandeyar, Saloshna and Heidi Esakov. "Color Coded: How Well Do Students of Different Race Groups Interact in South African Schools?" In *Addressing Ethnic Conflict Through Peace Education*, edited by Zvi Bekerman and Claire McGlynn, 63–76. New York: Palgrave Macmillan, 2007.

Vavrus, Frances. "Adjusting Inequality: Education and Structural Adjustment Policies in Tanzania." *Harvard Educational Review* 75, no. 2 (2005): 174–244.

—. *Desire and Decline: Schooling Amid Crisis in Tanzania*. New York: Peter Lang, 2003.

Vavrus, Frances and Lesley Bartlett. "Comparatively Knowing: Making a Case for the Vertical Case Study." *Current Issues in Comparative Education* 8, no. 2 (2006).

—. *Critical Approaches to Comparative Education: Vertical Case Studies from Africa, Europe, the Middle East, and the Americas*. New York: Palgrave Macmillan, 2009.

Viswanathan, S. "The Fall of a Wall." *Frontline*, 2008. Accessed April 24, 2011. http://www.frontlineonnet.com/fl2511/stories/20080606251112300.htm

Walker, Melanie and Elaine Unterhalter. *Amartya Sen's Capability Approach and Social Justice in Education*. New York: Palgrave Macmillan, 2007.

Wanke, Michaela and Leonie Reutner. "Pragmatic Persuasion or the Persuasion Paradox." Paper presented at the Annual Sydney Symposium on Social Psychology, Sydney, Australia, March 17–19, 2009.

Wax, Emily. "Can Love Conquer Caste? Indian Government Supports Mixed Unions, but Couples Who Defy System Face Violence." *Washington Post*, November 22, 2008. Accessed April 24, 2011. http://www.washingtonpost.com/wp-dyn/content/article/2008/11/21/AR2008112103971.html

World Bank. "India Economic Update." Washington, D.C. and New Delhi: World Bank, 2010.

—. "New Global Poverty Estimates—What It Means for India." World Bank, 2008. http://go.worldbank.org/51QB3OCFU0

Zeleza, Paul Tiyambe. "The Challenges of Writing African Economic History." In *Contested Terrains and Constructed Categories: Contemporary Africa in Focus*, edited by George Bond and Nigel Gibson, 59–84. Boulder: Westview Press, 2002.

Index

National Advisory Committee (NAC) 8,
60–2, 121 *see also* advisory boards
National Commission for Protection of
Child Rights (NCPCR) 31, 112, 122
National Council of Educational Research
and Training (NCERT) 47–9, 51
National Council for Teacher Education
(NCTE) 43–6
National Curriculum Framework
(NCF) 47, 48, 136
National Human Rights Commission
(NHRC) 49–51, 61, 65, 68, 135
National Knowledge Commission 51
National Policy on Education (NPE) 29
Nehru, Jawaharlal 28–9
non-governmental organizations (NGOs)
15, 17–19, 32, 37–9, 53–60, 140–5

Office of the United Nations High
Commissioner for Human Rights
(OHCHR) 3, 16–17, 155
Orissa 8, 32–7, 61, 68, 69, 70, 72, 91, 109,
110, 120, 126, 129, 138, 140, 142–3, 146
Osler, Audrey 20–1, 118–19
out-of-school children 30, 88, 105, 112,
126, 131

peace education 22, 25, 48–9, 133, 149
pedagogy 18, 22, 38, 44, 51, 54, 77, 78–9,
118, 131, 151, 158
People's Watch 2, 6, 9, 53–4, 57–8, 60, 61,
66, 70, 72–3, 100, 135, 147
persuasive pragmatism 54–60, 63, 65, 71,
95, 112, 117, 138, 151–2, 157
police 19, 51, 56, 57, 74, 81, 87, 106,
110–1, 127, 129–30, 142, 147
poverty 22, 23, 30, 35–6, 79, 80, 126, 127,
143
power relations 18, 21, 23–4, 26–7, 43, 92,
95, 96, 98, 112, 151, 154, 156

Ramirez, Francisco 3, 4, 15, 25, 45, 66,
134, 157
relational networks 61, 64, 68, 152
religion 42, 46, 58, 72, 78, 82, 94, 124, 136,
138, 154
Christianity 34, 100, 138–40, 143, 144

Hinduism 34, 38, 87, 136–40, 143, 144,
149
Islam 143, 144, 149
Right to Education Act (RTE) 5, 30, 31, 36,
39, 46, 104
right to food 29, 89, 103
Right to Information Act (RTI) 39, 50

Sarva Shiksha Abhiyan (SSA) 29, 105, 150,
153 *see also* Education for All
school meals 29, 31, 67, 78, 89, 91, 153
see also midday meals
secularism 44, 45, 149
self-help groups 81, 106
see also microfinance
skin color 58, 78, 136
social exclusion 9, 10, 23, 30, 33–5, 41, 52,
54, 87, 136, 152, 154
social justice 44, 47, 63, 121, 149
social location 3, 21, 76, 77, 90–5, 98–9,
114, 121, 153, 158
social movements 3, 15, 17, 18–19, 27, 56,
59, 79, 143, 144
solidarity 2, 9, 22–3, 26, 77, 83, 93, 94–115,
117, 153, 154, 158 *see also* coalitional
agency
Starkey, Hugh 20–1, 118–19
state violence 78
strategic agency 3, 26
structure of Indian education 31–2
summer camps 7, 8, 25–6, 59, 79, 83,
105–6, 140
superstition 141–2
'sympathetic bureaucrats' 63–6, 149, 152

Tamil Nadu 2, 8, 32, 34–6, 42, 56, 57–9,
61, 63–5, 68, 71, 73, 74, 78, 83, 86, 88,
90, 100, 101, 109–10, 113, 116, 117,
120, 123–4, 127, 129, 131, 138, 140,
144, 146
teacher educators 44–6
teacher training 29, 43, 45, 47, 51, 53, 62,
71, 79, 119–23, 137, 138, 159
interest 70–4
participatory format 16, 71, 121–2, 131
refresher course 71, 120
speakers 71, 121–2, 147–8